WILLOWS

the genus *Salix*

Willows

the genus *Salix*

Christopher Newsholme

Timber Press • Portland, Oregon

First published 1992
First paperback edition 2002

© Christopher Newsholme, 1992
All line drawings and colour
photographs are by Christopher
Newsholme

Typeset by Latimer Trend & Company
Ltd, Plymouth
Printed and bound in
Great Britain by
Butler & Tanner Ltd, Frome, Somerset

First published in the UK
by B T Batsford

Paperback edition published in
North America in 2003 by
Timber Press, Inc.
The Haseltine Building
133 S.W. Second Avenue, Suite 450
Portland, Oregon 97204, U.S.A.

ISBN 0-88192-565-9

A catalog record for this book is
available from the Library of Congress

Contents

Colour illustrations

Acknowledgements

I would like to commend the National Council for the Conservation of Plants and Gardens (N.C.C.P.G.) for the important part it is playing in encouraging national collections involving many plant genera.

Personally, I am indebted to Dr Kenneth Stott, recently retired as the Willow Officer, Long Ashton Research Station, Bristol, for his expert advice and generosity.

It has given me great pleasure to be acquainted with many other keen collectors of the genus *Salix* in the United Kingdom and overseas.

Also my thanks are due to The Rt. Hon. Michael R. D. Heseltine MP for his initial interest.

I am grateful to Mrs Lara Adams for her patience while typing the manuscript.

Finally, great praise is due to my wife for her unfailing support and forbearance throughout the preparation of this book.

"There is a willow grows aslant a brook,
That shows his hoar leaves in the glassy stream . . ."

The Queen of Denmark,
Hamlet,
William Shakespeare.

Preface

This book is dedicated wholeheartedly to the willow (genus *Salix*), to its role in industry and the environment over the ages, and, most of all, to its unfailing beauty throughout the year. Hitherto more publications have been concerned with methods of classification than with the ornamental qualities of this huge genus, with all its remarkable extremes of size, form, and colour.

It is my consuming obsession with the genus *Salix* that urges me to pass on to others the experience gained from the establishment of a national collection over a 12-year span, single-handed on rough terrain. My land is extremely precipitous, consisting of an elevated, exposed area, and descending steeply to a stream at the bottom. These extremes have enabled me to gain first-hand knowledge of willows, large and small, most suited to widely differing sites and greatly enhancing gardens of all sizes.

I am convinced that a comprehensive study of *Salix* species and hybrids for their ornamental value is long overdue. The selection of those of special merit for specific sites in gardens comprises the greater part of this book, which is intended to be of practical value to every keen gardener. It may well appeal to others who, like me, are past their prime and require quick results from their labour.

For consistency of definition, all Japanese, American and European common names commence with capital letters and inverted commas. Clones and cultivars are described as such in the text. Botanical synonyms are bracketed.

CHAPTER ONE

Introduction

Origin

Long before the advent of mankind, the willow (genus *Salix*) thrived throughout the world. Plants belonging to this genus are among the earliest recorded pre-Ice Age flowering plants. Geological research carried out on rock strata in Europe and Asia dating from the second and third glacial phases of the Ice Age during the Cretaceous period has revealed pollen grains and leaf fragments belonging to the botanical group known as Angiosperms, the earliest known flowering plants. These Angiosperm fossils, dating from 70 to 135 million years ago, provide the certain evidence that dwarf willows, notably *S. reticulata*, *S. herbacea*, and other Arctic willows comprised a large proportion of the flora at that time.

It is significant that perfect specimens of the honey bee (*apis mellifera*) have been found embedded in amber dating back 90 million years, well within the Cretaceous period. The pollination of willows, with a few exceptions, is still carried out by honey bees and, to a much lesser extent, by other insects.

In America most of the native *Salix* species are traceable to a pre-Ice Age origin. This is reflected in their present distributions, which would be impossible to explain without widespread disturbance resulting from the previous glaciation.

There is some botanical evidence supporting findings that the genus *Salix* originally arose in the warm temperate region or subtropics, then advanced insignificantly into the tropics, expanded mostly into the temperate regions, and later into the Arctic. The place of origin was probably somewhere in what are now the mountains of Eastern Asia. The most apparent links occur in this region between the small genus *Chosenia* with basic *Salix* characteristics, and some primitive members of the genus *Populus*, the poplars of pre-*Salix* origin, of the family *Salicaceae*, to which genus *Salix* belongs. Genus *Chosenia* is now generally included within genus *Salix* under the title *Urbanianae*.

An interesting table (*see* p. 12) gives support to the belief that the genus originated within the subtropics (ref: Robert D. Dorn. 'A synopsis of American Salix' 1976 Can. J. Bot 54).

As the temperature rose in the aftermath of the most recent ice period the vast glaciers linking the continents in the northern hemisphere melted. There followed a period of gradual inundation by the rising sea level, with the formation of great swamps and lakes trapped by huge terminal moraines. Vast rivers carried sediment from glaciers across the continents of Europe, Asia and North America. It is easy to understand that *Salix*, being one of the earliest

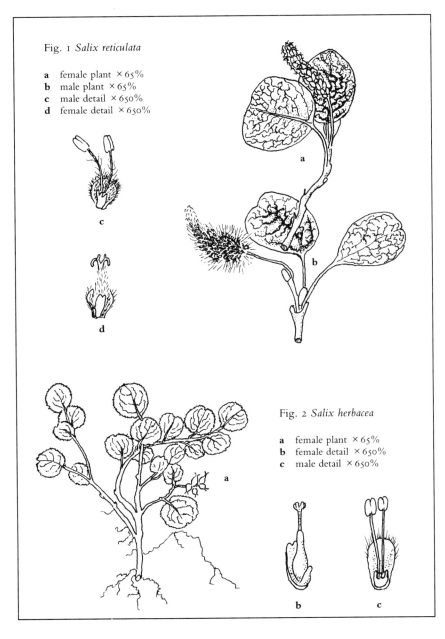

Fig. 1 *Salix reticulata*

a female plant × 65%
b male plant × 65%
c male detail × 650%
d female detail × 650%

c

d

a

b

Fig. 2 *Salix herbacea*

a female plant × 65%
b female detail × 650%
c male detail × 650%

a

b

c

colonizers of glacial sediment, thrived and spread over considerable distances during this period. Seed dispersal has always played a significant part in the distribution of *Salix* species, their seeds being extremely small and tufted, with fine hairs encouraging wind dispersal over wide areas. As conditions gradually adjusted, and the glaciers eventually receded towards their present limits, the *Salix* populations remained widely distributed, the heaviest concentrations being in moist situations throughout the temperate and Arctic regions of the northern hemisphere.

Some primitive and advanced characteristics in the genus _Salix_

Primitive	Advanced
Subtropical distribution	Temperate and boreal distribution
Trees	Shrubs
Diploids	Polyploids
Bud scales with free margins	Bud scales without free margins
Catkins at tips of branchlets of year	Catkins sessile on branchlets of last year
Catkins lax, loosely flowered	Catkins stiff, compactly flowered
Flower scales unpigmented, deciduous	Flower scales pigmented, persistent
Stamens more than 2	Stamens 1 or 2
Stipes long, styles short	Stipes short, styles long

Global distribution

Today, _Salix_ species are present in almost every part of the world. They are most numerous throughout the British Isles, Europe, Asia, Japan, China, North America, and Canada. They also exist as dwarf alpines in the Arctic. _S. humboldtiana_ is the main native species in South America. It is also present in central America as well as the West Indies. The ornamental orange-stemmed hybrid _S._ × _erythroflexuosa_ was originally discovered in the Argentine. Mexico has nine endemic species; only two other _Salix_ species are known to be native south of Mexico: _S. bonplandiana_ and _S. taxifolia_ in Guatemala. _S. taxifolia_ also exists in Puerto Rico. _Salix_ species are present in India, Egypt, and certain other parts of North Africa. In tropical Africa there are 12 named species or varieties, of which ten are endemic and extremely local, some being confined to a single river basin. In Australia large specimens of _S. alba_ and _S. fragilis_, as well as hybrids of these two species, and a number of other recently imported species grow on the banks of the main river systems. Some large _S. humboldtiana_ trees, _S. matsudana_, and a considerable number of recently imported species are thriving in New Zealand. _Salix_ are also found in a number of islands, many being native in Greenland, Newfoundland, and Iceland. A few species are present in the tropical islands of Ceylon, the Canary Islands, Madeira, the Philippines, and Madagascar. _Salix_ species have not been found in the Malay Peninsular.

Willow crafts

No study of factors affecting the international distribution of _Salix_ would be complete without emphasizing the influence of some of the most ancient crafts that have developed from the interchange of species and hybrids between

America, Europe, Asia, and the Far East over many centuries. These craft industries are steeped in history, and in Great Britain can be traced back to the Celts, who were experts in basket-making, passing on their skill to the Romans. Over the centuries osier willow-stems have been used in the construction of a great many items, ranging from hurdles, crab and lobster pots, eel traps, creels, coracles, log baskets and hampers, to the finest baskets.

Coracles

The coracle was one of the earliest forms of basketry applied to the construction of a very simple flat-bottomed boat. It made full use of the qualities of willow: flexibility, durability, and lightness. Animal hide or skin was stretched over broad interwoven willow slats cleft from stout poles and then tightly bound. Its lightness enabled it to be carried by one person over considerable distances between waterways, the coracle being strapped upside-down across their back.

The Ancient Britons used coracles several centuries before the arrival of the Romans. The coracle was utilized by fishermen on many major rivers, including the Teifi, Dee, Spay, Wye, and Severn. Its remarkably shallow draught rendered it ideal for the swamps of the Fens, where it was rowed by Queen Boadicea's followers, and, some ten centuries later, by supporters of Hereward the Wake during the Norman invasion. Coracles are still in service today on several Welsh rivers, a waterproof canvas skin replacing the animal hide.

Basketry: *Salix* osier clones

As basket-making has become more specialized over the centuries, in addition to the original British local osier strains, a large number of continental clones have been imported from France, Belgium, and Holland. Importation ceased with the Napoleonic Wars, and British willow-beds then came into full production. Willows were grown in osier beds in the Thames Valley, West Lancashire, the Trent Valley, Nottingham, and East Anglia. Peak production was reached in around 1900, declining thereafter as imports arrived from Eastern Europe and the Argentine. The disastrous east coast flooding of 1953 destroyed many willow beds, which have never been replanted. The greatest willow-growing area in Great Britain is now centred in the well-drained Somerset Levels in Taunton. Every year, during the winter and early spring, before the osier willows in these beds start breaking into leaf, they are cut to ground level (coppiced); the long, straight, leafless wands, known as rods, are then harvested for basket-making.

The three most important osiers specially grown for basketry are:

1 *S. triandra* (**Almond-Leaved Willow**) – yields good quality rods averaging 2 m (7 ft) long.
2 *S. purpurea* (**Purple Osier**) – produces very flexible, tough, thin, small rods approximately 1 m (3 ft) long, suitable for small, very fine baskets.
3 *S. viminalis* (**Common Osier**) – rods are pithy and thick, up to 4 m (12 ft) long, and are mainly used for coarse agricultural basketry and for hurdle construction.

Of these three species the one most favoured in basketry is *S. triandra*; a large number of its clones are in general use today, the most popular being *S. triandra* 'Black Maul'. In addition to the indigenous hybrids resulting from multiple crossbreeding between local strains of *S. triandra*, *S. viminalis* and *S. purpurea*, the survivors of clones introduced several centuries ago can still be found, many bearing attractive names indicative of origin, stem colour, or quality. A few examples are *S. triandra* 'Stone Rod', *S. triandra* 'Black German', *S. triandra* 'Grisette Noire', *S. triandra* 'Dark French', *S. triandra* 'Black Top', *S. triandra* 'Light Newkind', *S. mollissima* 'Black Spaniard', *S.* 'Whissenders', *S. purpurea* 'Dicky Meadows', *S. purpurea* 'Lancashire' strain, *S. purpurea* 'Leicestershire' strain, *S. purpurea* 'Welsh' and *S. purpurea* 'French' strains, *purpurea* 'Dark Dicks', 'Green Dicks', 'Brittany Dicks', and 'Franz Geel'.

The choice of rods obtained from male or female plants is an important factor in basketry. Rods from females are generally faster-growing and stronger than their male counterpart, whereas rods from male osiers are more delicate, and when tough are more suitable for finer baskets. Rods used in basketry are termed Brown Willows, Buff Willows, and White Willows. Brown Willows are dried rods with the bark remaining intact. Buff Willows are Brown Willows that have been boiled in tanks and then peeled. White Willows are rods peeled immediately before they sprout. The process of peeling the rods is carried out by drawing them manually, or by mechanical means, between two metal rods tightly sprung together, and called a Willow-Brake. Finally, the peeled rods are dried out, sorted into bundles, and distributed to the basket-makers.

In North America in particular there is now a craving among those basket-makers who have access to the countryside to use native *Salix* instead of imported cane. The ancient methods employed in medieval Britain of splitting saplings into annual rings, and subsequently cutting them into splints or skeins had also been independently practised by the North American Indians. Although laborious in

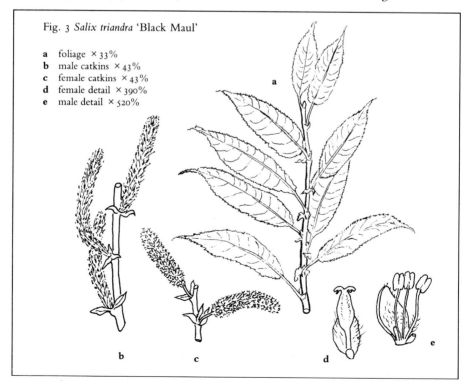

Fig. 3 *Salix triandra* 'Black Maul'

a   foliage × 33%
b   male catkins × 43%
c   female catkins × 43%
d   female detail × 390%
e   male detail × 520%

b   c   d   e

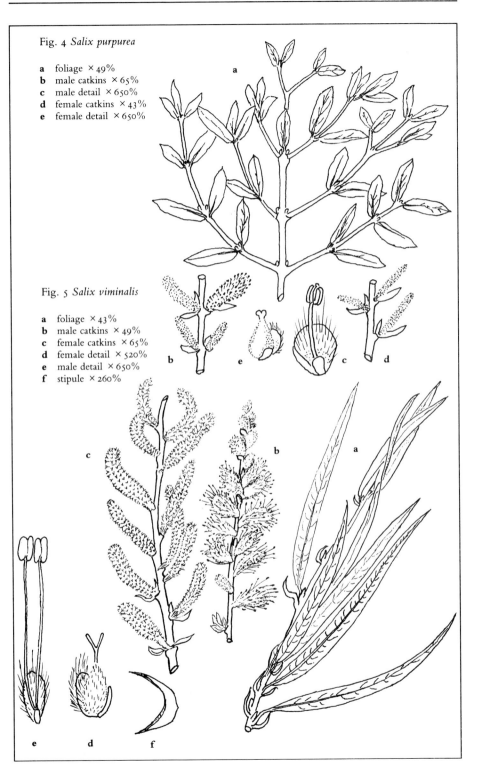

Fig. 4 *Salix purpurea*

a foliage × 49%
b male catkins × 65%
c male detail × 650%
d female catkins × 43%
e female detail × 650%

Fig. 5 *Salix viminalis*

a foliage × 43%
b male catkins × 49%
c female catkins × 65%
d female detail × 520%
e male detail × 650%
f stipule × 260%

preparation the results are still considered satisfactory by those following these methods today. Frame or ribbed baskets have been made from *Salix* and Ash, using Indian designs and imitating baskets introduced by settlers from Europe. Second to *S. scouleriana* in its wide distribution in North America, *S. eriocephala* is also common in many other regions. One of the most widely used basket willows is the ornamental male clone *S.* 'Americana', resulting from hybridization between *S. eriocephala* Michx. and *S. petiolaris* (*S. gracilis* Anderss.). Several North American native species of *S. rigida* (*S. eriocephala*) are grown for basketry, from New England to Virginia, and produce very tough, flexible rods. In America, the name *S. eriocephala* is generally preferred to the synonyms *S. rigida* Muhlenb. and *S. cordata* Muhlenb non Hook. *S. purpurea* (Purple Osier), particularly the two clones *S. purpurea* 'Dicky Meadows' and *S. purpurea* 'Red Buds', both with ground-hugging rods, provide excellent quality basket material. *S. pentandra* originated in Pennsylvania, and when coppiced it produces good osier-type rods named Lumley and Patent Lumley. *S. viminalis* was originally widely introduced into eastern North America from Europe for basketry and as an ornamental shrub, occasionally escaping in the eastern states and southern Canada. It has become very variable after many years of cultivation.

In Japan the native *S. kinuiyanagi* is widely cultivated for basketry and furniture. It is closely related to *S. viminalis* L. (Common Osier) and is mainly used for the coarser forms of basketry. *S. koriyanagi*, a native of Korea similar to the European *S. purpurea* L. (Purple Osier), is extensively grown in Japan. Coppiced regularly its fine rods are flexible and durable, rendering it ideal for the production of the finest quality baskets and specialized furniture. Rods obtained from the Japanese species *S. miyabeana* and *S. gilgiana* are sometimes used in basketry but are mainly grown for their ornamental qualities.

Cricket bat production

A specialized commercial use of the willow in Britain is the production of timber for the manufacture of cricket bats. The wood for this purpose is exclusively obtained from *S. alba* var. *coerulea*. Only female trees produce the uniformity and qualities required to enable standardization to be carried out. Very few male trees exist in Britain mainly because, as a result of the inferior and variable quality of the wood that they produce, only female cuttings are planted. *S. alba var. coerulea* produces timber possessing all the essential qualities that are needed, being tough, durable, light, springy, straight-grained, and white. Cricket was first played during the fourteenth century and exhibited none of the refinements of today's game. Bats were cut at random by the players from any variety of willow, producing very mixed results from a motley array of weapons.

Today the cricket bat industry is concentrated almost entirely in East Anglia, in the deep silt on the banks of the slow-flowing rivers in this area, allowing a minimum spacing of 9 m (30 ft) between each willow. *S. alba* var. *coerulea* is grown and marketed in Essex and Suffolk. When trees are ten or more years old, with a girth of approximately 1.5 m (5 ft), they are cut down into the standard lengths of a cricket-bat blade, three or four cylindrical sections of this length being produced from a single trunk. Each cylindrical section of trunk is then split into approximately eight segments radiating from the centre, each segment representing one bat blade after further processing. Hence the total yield from a single tree may be 24 or 32 cricket-bat blades, depending upon the number of trunk sections obtainable.

Diverse uses

Although too light for general furniture manufacture, two- or three-year-old rods of *S. viminalis* are used for basket furniture. Willow is also used in the production of charcoal, and is rendered into wood pulp for the paper industry.

The coppicing of willows every three to four years as a source of wood chips for fuel is an excellent way of producing renewable energy. Compared to oil and fossil fuels, wood is very economical as it produces heat rapidly, is clean-burning and leaves very little ash. The carbon emission during combustion is effectively neutral as the carbon dioxide released into the atmosphere is less than that absorbed by the willow while it is growing, an important factor in combating global warming.

The use of specially selected, quick growing, disease resistant clones for fast rotation coppicing is a useful alternative source of income for the farmer. Once established, a plantation can be regularly harvested for 25 years, or more, with minimal maintenance. In Sweden willow wood has largely replaced oil as a fuel for industrial and domestic use. In Denmark, where a carbon tax has been levied to reduce carbon-emission, willow and poplar coppicing to replace coal and oil is being widely encouraged. Apart from environmental considerations, this system of willow production significantly increases the local bird population.

Large tree species of *Salix* are vital in the economy of many villages situated in the dry inner valleys of Western Himalaya, where they are planted along irrigation channels. They are used for basketry, fuel, and building. The commonest species at lower levels is *S. acmophylla* Boiss. Other species include *S. alba* L. (White Willow), *S. excelsa*, *S. gmelin* (*S. fragilis auct.* non L.) (Crack Willow), and *S. babylonica* L. (Weeping Willow). *S. babylonica* is also cultivated in Nepal.

In Great Britain, at the Long Ashton Research Station, Bristol, the Willow Officer (1949–1989), Kenneth Scott pioneered research on many topics involving innumerable clones of willow, exploring all practical possibilities for their use. He provided advice and assistance to growers, scientists, and the general public, on basket and cricket-bat willows; willows for horticultural shelter and amenity planting; the amelioration of difficult environments; and, more recently, to farmers seeking diversification into wood production.

Soil consolidation

In various countries *Salix* species have been planted along the banks of big rivers that are subject to frequent flooding. Their spreading root system enmeshes the soil, effectively preventing the under-running and progressive erosion of the river banks. This method of controlling river erosion, using mainly Asian and European species, is proving successful in New Zealand. *S. purpurea* will grow in sandy conditions and, possessing a considerable tolerance for salt water, has been used for reclaiming land alongside estuaries. In North America, *S. interior* (Sandbar Willow) forms thickets in estuaries and swamps, and spreads rapidly with long surface roots producing numerous aerial suckers.

Windbreaks

Certain fast-growing strains of *S. viminalis*, especially when staggered with short growing *S. purpurea* clones create efficient and attractive windbreaks. *S. viminalis* 'Bowles' Hybrid' is exceptionally vigorous and can grow more than 4 m (12 ft) in one season following coppicing. *S. purpurea* ssp. *lambertiana* grows rapidly, and is also useful when incorporated in windbreaks. The triple hybrid *S.* × *hirtei* (Stratcher) is an extremely hardy, vigorous, upright shrub resulting from crossbreeding between *S. aurita*, *S. cinerea* and *S. viminalis*. Three distinct clones, *S.* × *hirtei* 'Delamere', *S.* × *hirtei* 'Reifenweide', and *S.* × *hirtei* 'Rosewarne', all make excellent fast-growing windbreaks, and thrive in poor soil. *S. cinerea* species (grey sallow) provide a high proportion of the vegetation comprising many mixed hedgerows throughout Great Britain; *S. cinerea* ssp. *oleifolia* (syns. *atrocinerea*) is outstandingly hardy and wind resistant, forming an excellent windbreak without any tendency to die back. Although relatively slow growing, it proves extremely durable in very exposed situations. *Salix* species provide rapid ground cover over wide areas devastated by hurricanes.

Fodder for livestock

Some *Salix* species provide good fodder for both ruminants and horses in various countries, particularly in Australia, where they are especially planted for this purpose. *S. purpurea* species are the exception in this respect, being extremely bitter and unpalatable, deterring not only farm animals but also rabbits. Where rabbits are troublesome, planting with a preponderance of *S. purpurea* species can limit the damage.

Medicinal

Some reference should be made to the medicinal properties of Salicin, a glucoside constituent of the bitter-tasting sap of young *Salix* stems, especially *S. purpurea*. For many years Salicin has been extracted and administered as a febrifuge and analgesic to patients exhibiting symptoms of fever. Its use has now been superseded by the synthetic production of aspirin containing salicylic acid.

Ecological

From an ecological point of view *Salix* plantations encourage a wide range of birds, including willow warblers, wrens, wagtails, and practically all members of the tit family. Insectivorous birds are attracted by the dense leaf canopy that harbours the caterpillars and aphids upon which they thrive. The genus also provides a rich source of nectar and pollen for bees very early in the year when supplies of these essential ingredients are in short supply. Commencing in January, the flowering periods of different *Salix* species overlap one another throughout the spring.

Most old pollarded *Salix* species, with trunks originally sawn 2–3 m (6–10 ft) above ground level, have remained unpruned for many years, their thick rods sprouting from the crown no longer being utilized for farm fencing. These trees have expanded into broad open crowns with central spaces and some cavitation, proving ideal as nesting sites for a number of bird species. In time, an increasing accumulation of leaves and organic debris becomes permanently entrapped within the area of the crown, eventually being rendered into a rich leaf mould. The process is assisted by the presence of normal harmless fungi and a mixed population including earthworms, woodlice, centipedes, weevils, and many varieties of beetle. Various mosses, lichens and ferns appear and a build-up of plant epiphytes occurs. This association is not detrimental to the trees, the epiphytes existing in an ideal environment as tenants until the host tree ultimately dies. These pollarded trees of *S. alba*, *S. fragilis* and their clonal hybrids can survive for 50 years or more. Throughout their lives they support a vast ecological cycle involving fungi, insects, worms, epiphytes, small rodents and a wide variety of birds, including predatory marsh harriers, hawks, and owls.

Ornamental and environmental

For their decorative effect in gardens of all sizes the members of genus *Salix* have enormous potential. Their speed of growth and natural vigour are unequalled. Their good qualities include the facility with which most of them can be propagated from a wide choice of species varying greatly in form and size, together with their remarkable powers of adaptability and survival, rendering them an ideal choice for practically any terrain. Attractive species can be specially selected to grow in the most inhospitable conditions. Small and large weeping forms are available and may be either planted with their own rootstock, or grafted. For the smallest gardens several species of *S. purpurea* are entirely suitable, either as very small weeping trees or small compact ornamental shrubs. Some sessile forms with long pendulous or trailing branches are best displayed in tall urns; alternatively they may be planted behind and overhanging a retaining wall or large boulder. A choice example for this situation is the Japanese *S. integra* 'Pendula'.

The Parks Departments in many big cities are already contributing much to the environment by the planting of large specimen *Salix* trees, *S. × chrysocoma* (= *S. alba* var. *vitellina* × *S. babylonica*) proving to be the most popular large weeping type. The artistic effect achieved by planting large parks with groups of weeping trees together, set apart from other groups of erect trees, is generally very successful. The arching and shrubby forms of *Salix* can also be grouped on their own. Several County Councils in Great Britain are planning extensive ornamental biomass collections. These will provide a valuable contribution to the environment, and will encourage the survival of some scarce species.

Salix species can be used successfully to hide unsightly buildings and factories: fast-growing large hybrid trees such as *S. × basfordiana* (*S. alba* var. *vitellina* × *S. fragilis*) and *S. × salamonii* (*S. fragilis* × *S. alba*) are suitable for this purpose. If smaller trees with a spreading crown are required *S. caprea* or *S. cinerea* may be preferred. In industrial areas accumulations of waste and slag heaps can be stabilized and effectively camouflaged by close planting with sets of *S. aurita*, *S. cinerea* ssp. *oleifolia*, and *S. repens*. Areas rendered desolate by open-cast mining and disused gravel pits, where top soil is virtually non-existent, can be revitalized by the introduction of hardy *Salix* species. Sand dunes on the margins of golf courses can be considerably enhanced by planting *S. repens* var. *argentea* and small shrub forms of *S. purpurea* species. Various species can be usefully placed in the vicinity of artificially constructed reservoirs, greatly softening and naturalizing the overall effect. *S. × elegantissima* (*S. fragilis* × *S. babylonica*) and *S. matsudana* 'Pendula', both large ornamental weeping trees, are ideal for this purpose. *S. alba* var. *aurea*, with bright golden foliage, and *S. alba* var. *sericea* (*argentea*), with silver sericeous leaves are also best observed beside water.

In North America *S. alba* and *S. fragilis* were introduced from Europe to Pennsylvania in colonial times. They were used ornamentally, providing shade, and also used for the production of gunpowder charcoal. *S. babylonica* was originally introduced into North America by settlers from Europe. It was used mainly in American cemeteries, where its voluminous weeping branchlets produced effects suited to the environment. *S. caprea* and *S. cinerea* ssp. *oleifolia* both reached North America in the same way, and provide the pussy willows of florists for Easter along with the native *S. discolor*. In eastern North America, particularly in Pennsylvania and Virginia, many gardens contain fine specimens of *Cornus florida*, the beautiful 'Flowering Dogwood', with its flower bracts ranging from pure white to deep rose-red in April and May. When combined with the graceful native shrub willows *S. petiolaris*, *S. sericea*, and *S.* × *subsericea*, with catkins also flowering in the late spring, the overall effect is greatly enhanced.

Very large specimens of *S.* × *sepulchralis* (*S. alba* var. *alba* × *S. babylonica*) provide shade for livestock on the banks of some of the main river systems of New South Wales and Victoria in Australia; along rivers in the southern states of North America, and, specially in South America, large *S. humboldtiana* trees also give shelter from the sun.

Certain species, notably *S. purpurea*, *S. caprea*, *S. cinerea*, *S. aurita* and *S. daphnoides* are extremely hardy, contributing considerable ornamental value and assisting in the filtration of cross-winds when planted along the sides of major trunk roads.

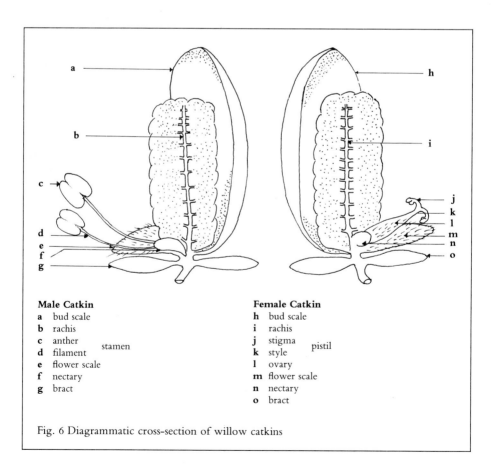

Male Catkin
a bud scale
b rachis
c anther   } stamen
d filament
e flower scale
f nectary
g bract

Female Catkin
h bud scale
i rachis
j stigma   }
k style   } pistil
l ovary   }
m flower scale
n nectary
o bract

Fig. 6 Diagrammatic cross-section of willow catkins

An excellent environmental diversion using basket willows is now well-established in Holland, Germany, and France. Along the margins of trunk roads in these countries, living 'willow-walls' form effective barriers, replacing many miles of monotonous concrete. These walls have a central earth core 3 or 4 m (10 or 12 ft) high with a wood-chip capping. They are wedge-shaped and broadly based in cross-section. Stout poles are driven into the ground on both sides of the wall at regular intervals, and osier rods woven in and out of the poles as in simple basketry. The poles are drawn firmly together towards both surfaces of the wall by connecting ropes passing through the earth core from one side to the other. The osier rods readily root when placed horizontally against the soil, and a perforated irrigation pipe, attached to a mains water supply and running throughout the length of the earth wall can be used during prolonged periods of low rainfall, and until a good root system is formed. The resulting living willow wall is an attractive feature considerably enhancing the environment; greatly absorbing noise; and trapping dust, exhaust fumes and litter. It provides a beautiful visual barrier against industrial installations and, unlike alternative materials, does not crack or warp and is difficult to vandalize. Maintenance is minimal. Initial results of experiments in Britain are very encouraging and, if generally adopted, will revitalize osier production. Large-scale planting of suitable clones for this purpose has already been undertaken in Suffolk and Kent.

Many species are ideal for their decorative effect in vases. If branchlets bearing immature buds are picked in midwinter and brought indoors, the colour changes that occur in the male anthers during the course of their development can be fully appreciated at a time when little alternative outdoor floral decoration is available. *S. sachalinensis* 'Sekka', a Japanese male clone, with its beautiful golden catkins and shiny mahogany-red fasciated stems is an ideal subject for floral arrangements.

With very few exceptions the genus *Salix* is dioecious, male catkins being produced by one plant and female catkins by another plant of the same species.

The fundamental difference between maturing male and female catkins is likely to influence one's choice in favour of the male sex from a purely ornamental viewpoint. While still immature, with the loss of the bud scale and the revelation of the silky or woolly hairs covering the flower scales in the early stages, there may appear to be little difference between the sexes. As development proceeds, however, the anthers surmounting the filaments of the stamens of the flowers in the male catkins eventually become fully exposed, revealing a remarkably vivid display of colours ranging from pale yellow, through gold and shades of red, to dark purple, according to species. This spectacular display is confined to the male of the species.

CHAPTER TWO

General Characteristics of Willows

Classification

Salix, Latin for 'willow', appropriately derives its definition from the Celtic word *sallis*: *sal* 'near', and *lis* 'water'.

Belonging to the plant family *Salicaceae*, of which poplars are also members, the genus *Salix* comprises some 400 species of willows and more than 200 listed hybrids, popularly known as willows, sallows, and osiers. It consists of mainly deciduous trees and shrubs bearing catkins (aments), which are usually stiff and upright, spreading, occasionally recurving or rarely drooping. Each catkin is composed of a number of tiny compact flowers, all subtended by a flower scale. The flower scales are entire, toothed, glabrous or hairy, and vary in colour with the species.

The genus consists of three main subgenera:

1 Subgenus *Salix* (*Amerina*), the true willows: typically upright, semi-pendulous or pendulous trees and large shrubs with narrow, acuminate, serrate leaves. Catkins arise from the tip of a shoot from an axillary bud produced from a stem of the preceding year. The flowering stem varies in length, having normal leaves without axillary growth buds. Catkins have uniformly coloured flower scales. Two or more nectaries are present in male flowers and either one or two in female flowers. *S. alba*, *S. babylonica*, *S. fragilis*, *S. nigra*, and *S. pentandra* are typical members of this subgenus.

2 Subgenus *Caprisalix* (*Vetrix*), the osiers and sallows: mostly shrubs and small trees with great variation in leaves, some narrow, acuminate, or oblong, obovate, or rounded, with entire or coarsely serrate or crenate margins. Catkins are frequently precocious and sessile arising from the previous year's leaf scars on bare stems. Both male and female have a single nectary. The tips of the flower scales are often dark brown, and ovaries are hairy in many species. Examples are *S. caprea*, *S. cinerea*, *S. aurita*, *S. myrsinifolia* (*nigricans*), *S. phylicifolia*, and *S. viminalis*.

3 Subgenus *Chamaetia*: dwarf, creeping, Arctic, or mountain shrubs with small rounded or blunt leaves. Catkins are produced terminally at the tip of ordinary growing stems bearing normal axillary buds. The flower scales are frequently tinged with pink, red or purple, and the nectaries are joined. Belonging to this subgenus are *S. reticulata*, *S. herbacea*, *S. retusa*, *S. myrsinites*, *S. tatrae*, *S. tarraconensis* and many other small species.

In addition to these three main subgenera the small genus *Chosenia* is now generally included as another subgenus. Formerly treated separately, *Chosenia* Nakai contains species with fundamental morphological characteristics typical of the genus *Salix*. The only significant differences are the presence of pendulous catkins and the absence of nectaries in *Chosenia arbutifolia* Skv. which is wind-pollinated like the poplars. *Turanga* (Bunge) Kimura, in common with genus *Salix*, possesses no terminal bud, but has unusual polymorphic leaves and is more closely allied to genus *Populus*.

Many attempts have been made by eminent botanists to produce an all embracing and fully comprehensive classification of all the species contained within the three main subgenera. To date, no single method, when used in isolation, has proved entirely satisfactory. There is no single distinguishing criterion that can be employed without making provision for a large number of exceptions caused by the remarkable diversification that exists within the genus. Genetic classification cannot be entirely relied upon, as chromosomal variations have been found to occur even between members of the same species of *Salix*. It is also important to realize that classification is still incomplete, especially in the case of some Arctic willows. It is uncertain whether several forms found in Alaska and the Yukon in recent years can be accorded specific, subspecific or varietal status. The evidence suggests that some of these cases may be transitional and are in the evolutionary process of becoming pure species.

Confusion and uncertainty exist in the taxonomy of this genus. Apart from numerous recorded synonyms for various species, botanists have differed in regard to their individual definitions of species, subspecies and varieties. Some names have been based upon inadequate specimens and imperfect evidence. Opinions as to the criteria determining subspecies and varietal status vary considerably. These differences can be trivial.

Although acknowledging that no method of classification below subgeneric level is entirely satisfactory, the following sub-division of genus *Salix* into groups and sections is intended as a taxonomic guide, indicating which species are generally considered to be closely related.

Subgenus *Salix*

GROUP 1
Trees or shrubs; stamens 3 to 10 (12); ovaries glabrous; 2 nectaries; flower scales glabrous and yellow.

Section Humboldtianae Pax. (Nigrae Schneid.)
Mainly large trees or shrubs; leaves linear–lanceolate; green above and beneath; catkins lax; stamens 3 to 12; nectaries in male flowers sometimes more than 2, and then connate at the base; flower scales deciduous; bud scales frequently adaxially free: *S. acmophylla*, *S. bonplandiana*, *S. caroliniana*, *S. falcata*, *S. gooddingii*, *S. humboldtiana*, *S. nigra*.

Section Floridanae Dorn
Large trees; leaves elliptic, lanceolate or ovate; catkins lax; stamens 2 (3 to 6); flower scales persistent; bud scales free overlapping margins: *S. floridana*.

Section Urbanianae Seem. (Chosenia Nakai)
Large trees; leaves oblong-elliptic, acuminate, glandular-serrate; catkins lax; stamens 5 to 9; 2 nectaries or none: *S. arbutifolia*, *S. urbaniana*.

Section Glandulosae Seem.

Medium trees or large shrubs; leaves narrowly oblong or elliptic; bilateral apical petiolar discoid glands; stamens 3 to 5; male flowers 2 nectaries; bud scales with free imbricate margins; style very short; ovaries glabrous: *S. chaenomeloides.*

Section Salicaster Dumort. (Pentandrae Borr.)

Medium trees or large shrubs; leaves lanceolate-elliptic to lanceolate, glossy, glandular-serrate; petioles and apex of flower scales usually glandular; stamens 3 to 8; nectaries in male flowers sometimes more than 2, and then connate forming a disc at the base: *S. ehrhartiana, S. lasiandra, S. longipes, S. lucida, S. meyeriana, S. paraplesia, S. pentandra, S. pseudopentandra, S. serissima.*

Section Amygdalinae Koch

Small trees or shrubs; leaves lanceolate; female flowers 1 nectary; stamens 3: *S. amygdaloides, S. medwedewii, S. triandra.*

GROUP 2

Erect or weeping trees and shrubs; catkins coetaneous or serotinous on leafy shoots; stamens 2, rarely 1; staminal filaments with basal hairs; female flowers 2 nectaries, flower scales pale yellow or brown-tinged, darker towards apex.

Section Fragiles Koch

Small to medium trees; leaves lanceolate, glabrous or glabrescent; female flowers 2 nectaries: *S. fragilis, S. matsudana.*

Section Salix (Subalbae Koidz.)

Medium to large trees; leaves lanceolate, variably pubescent; female flowers 1 nectary: *S. alba, S. babylonica, S. jessoensis, S. koreensis, S. oxica.*

Section Longifoliae Pax.

Large shrubs or occasionally small trees; leaves linear; roots producing suckers, thicket-forming: *S. exigua, S. fluviatilis, S. interior, S. melanopsis, S. sessilifolia, S. taxifolia.*

GROUP 3

Large shrubs or small trees; stamens 2; staminal filaments glabrous; flower scales persistent.

Section Magnificae Schneid.

Leaves entire, glabrous beneath; catkins 12–25 cm (5–10 in.) long: *S. heterochroma, S. magnifica, S. pella.*

Section Eriostachyae Schneid.

Leaves serrate, midrib pubescent beneath; catkins 5–15 cm (2–6 in.) long: *S. fargesii, S. himalayas, S. moupinensis, S. phanera.*

Subgenus *Caprisalix* (Dumort.) Nasar.

GROUP 4

Variable large or small shrubs or trees; catkins usually sessile or subsessile, precocious; male flowers – stamens always 2 totally distinct; female flowers only 1 nectary; flower scales persistent, darker towards apex.

Section Vetrix Dumort. (Capreae Koch)
Large shrubs or small trees; leaves variable, mostly large and broad; ovaries pubescent, style absent or short: *S. aegyptiaca, S. akame, S. ambigua, S. appenina, S. appendiculata, S. atrocinerea, S. aurita, S. bakko, S. balfourii, S. bebbiana, S. cantabrica, S. cinerea, S. coriacea, S. discolor, S. geyeriana, S. livida, S. multinervis, S. pedicellata, S. salviifolia, S. scouleriana, S. serissaefolia, S. silesiaca, S. starkeana, S. tatrorum, S. tetrapla, S. wallichiana, S. xerophila.*

Section Incubaceae Dumort.
Small shrubs rarely to 4 m (13 ft) high; leaves usually small; ovaries pubescent, style absent or short: *S. arenaria, S. gracilis, S. humilis, S. repens, S. rosmarinifolia, S. sericea, S. sub-opposita, S. subsericea, S. tristis.*

Section Villosae Anderss.
Large shrubs; leaves white pubescent or lanate beneath; ovaries pedicellate, style shorter than half the ovary: *S. alaxensis, S. candida, S. drummondiana.*

Section Cordatae Barr. ex Hook. (Hastatae Kern.)
Large and small shrubs or small trees; leaves glaucous or sericeously-pubescent beneath; ovaries pedicellate, glabrous, style shorter than half the ovary: *S. adenophylla, S. barclayi, S. canariensis, S. commutata, S. cordata, S. eriocephala, S. glaucophylloides, S. hastata, S. houghtonii, S. irrorata, S. japonica, S. mackenziana, S. missouriensis, S. monticola, S. myricoides, S. myrtillifolia, S. novae-angliae, S. pyrolifolia, S. rigida, S. syrticola.*

Section Arbuscella Ser. ex Duby (Phylicifoliae Dumort.)
Variable large and small shrubs or small trees; leaves mostly green beneath, glabrous or pubescent ovaries pedicellate, pubescent, style less than half the length of the ovary: *S. apoda, S. arbuscula, S. arbusculoides, S. bicolor, S. coactilis, S. foetida, S. glabra, S. hegetschweileri, S. hibernica, S. laggeri, S. mielichhoferi, S. nigricans, S. pellita, S. petiolaris, S. phylicifolia, S. planifolia, S. pulchra, S. reinii, S. waldsteiniana.*

Section Balsamiferae Schneid.
Tall shrub or small tree; leaves glandular-serrulate, base cordate; ovaries pedicellate, glabrous: *S. pyrifolia.*

Section Lanatae Fries. (Chrysantheae Koch)
Small shrubs or occasionally small trees; leaves pubescent or lanate; ovaries subsessile, glabrous (pubescent on *S. barrattiana*) and twice as long as style: *S. barrattiana, S. hookeriana, S. lanata, S. piperi, S. tweedii.*

Section Daphnoideae Dumort. (Pruinosae Koch)
Large shrubs or trees; branchlets with typically pruinose bloom; leaves lanceolate, glabrous; ovaries sessile, glabrous, twice as long as style: *S. acutifolia, S. daphnoides, S. kangensis, S. rorida.*

Section Viminales Bluff and Fingerh.
Shrubs or small trees; leaves mostly narrow, acuminate, sericeously-pubescent beneath; ovaries sessile, pubescent (glabrous on *S. hypoleuca, S. macroblasta,* and *S. rehderiana*), ovary twice as long as style: *S. cathayana, S. dasyclados, S. friesiana, S. helvetica, S. hypoleuca, S. kinuiyanagi, S. lapponum, S. macroblasta, S. rehderiana, S. sachalinensis, S. viminalis.*

Section Subviminales Seem. (Gracilistyla Schneid.)
Medium sized shrubs; leaves elliptic, narrowly oval to oblong; ovary pubescent; style longer than ovary; stamens 2, semi-connate or more: *S. gracilistyla, S. melanostachys.*

Section Canae Kern.
Medium sized or small shrubs; leaves linear, lanceolate or elliptic, sericeously pubescent beneath; catkins pedicellate; ovary glabrous, style absent or short, less than half as long as the ovary; stamens 2, filaments semi-connate or less: *S. elaeagnos, S. patula, S. reuteri, S. seringeana, S. subalpina.*

Section Purpurea Fries.
Small to large shrubs or small trees; leaves glabrous or pubescent beneath, ovary pubescent; style absent or short, less than half as long as the ovary; staminal filaments completely connate: *S. amplexicaulis, S. bockii, S. caesia, S. elbursensis, S. gilgiana, S. integra, S. kochiana, S. koriyanagi, S. microstachya, S. miyabeana, S. purpurea, S. wilhelmsiana.*

Section Sitchenses (Bebb) Schneid.
Large shrubs; leaves narrowly elliptic or obovate, persistently sericeously pubescent or lanate beneath; ovary pedicellate, pubescent; style distinct; stamens 1 or 2 per flower within one catkin: *S. sitchensis.*

Section Denticulatae Schneid.
Small to medium sized shrubs or occasionally small trees; leaves toothed, small, narrowly elliptic or elliptic-lanceolate; flower scales spathulate or truncate; stamens 2 with free filaments: *S. daltoniana, S. denticulata, S. hylematica, S. karelinii.*

Subgenus *Chamaetia* (Dumort.) Nasar.

GROUP 5
Dwarf or procumbent shrubs, less than 1 m (3 ft) high, leaves less than 10 cm (4 in.) long and not linear; catkins on leafy branchlets; flower scales persistent; stamens 2, occasionally 1.

Section Retusae Kern.
Small creeping shrubs; leaves glabrous; flower scales often greenish or yellowish; ovaries glabrous, female flowers 1 and rarely 2 nectaries: *S. alpina, S. brevipens, S. breviserrata, S. cashmeriana, S. chlorolepis, S. dodgeana, S. pauciflora, S. phlebophylla, S. polaris, S. retusa, S. retusoides, S. rotundifolia, S. serpyllifolia, S. setchelliana, S. stolonifera, S. uva-ursi.*

Section Chamaetia Dumort.
Small ground-hugging shrubs; leaves reticulate venation; ovaries pubescent, style short or absent; female flowers 2 nectaries: *S. cascadensis, S. cordifolia, S. neoreticulata, S. nivalis, S. reticulata, S. saximontana, S. vestita, S. yezo-alpina.*

Section Glaucae Pax.
Low shrubs; leaves usually pubescent beneath; ovaries pubescent, style distinct; staminal filaments pubescent; nectaries 1 or 2: *S. anglorum, S. arctica* Pall, *S. athabascensis, S. ausserdorferi, S. brachycarpa, S. glauca, S. glaucosericea, S. pyrenaica, S. reptans, S. sphenophylla, S. tarraconensis, S. tatrae.*

Section Myrtosalix Kern.
Prostrate, usually trailing shrubs; catkins and some branchlets arising at right angles to the stems; leaves glandular-serrate; ovaries pubescent; 1 nectary: *S. chamissonis, S. arctophila. S. fuscescens.*

Section Myrtilloides Borr.

Low shrubs with erect branches; leaves coriaceous, elliptic or narrowly elliptic; ovaries glabrous, pedicellate, style absent or short: *S. crataegifolia*, *S. myrtilloides*, *S. pedicellaris*.

Section Maccallianae Argus

Upright shrubs 1–2.5 m (3–8 ft) high; leaves coriaceous, concolorous on both sides; ovaries pubescent, styles long, subtended by tawny or yellow-green scales; stamens surrounded by cup-like nectary with 4 to 6 lobes: *S. maccalliana*.

Section Lindleyanae Schneid.

Small creeping mat-forming montane shrubs; leaves small, glabrous, lanceolate; catkins terminating leafy branchlets; ovaries glabrous: *S. lindleyana*.

Botanical characteristics

Catkins

Willows are dioecious, all male-flowered catkins being borne by one plant, and female-flowered by another. Exceptionally the flowers of one catkin may be bisexual, or catkins may produce both female and male flowers as sometimes occurs in *S. aegyptiaca*. There is considerable variation in the length and shape of catkins according to the species.

A specific feature is the relation between leaf and catkin production. When catkins are produced before the leaves, as in *S. gracilistyla*, *S. irrorata*, *S. acutifolia*, *S. daphnoides*, or *S. viminalis*, the descriptive term is precocious. When catkins and leaf production synchronize, the term coetaneous is used, as in *S. alba*, *S. babylonica*, *S. elaeagnos*, and *S. amygdaloides*. When catkins appear after the leaves have fully formed this is referred to as serotinous, as in *S. pentandra*, *S. lucida*, and *S. triandra*. *S. bockii* is exceptional, its catkin production being confined to late autumn, whereas *S. triandra* 'Semperflorens', as the name suggests, bears some catkins throughout spring and summer.

Glands

Minute nectaries or glands are situated between flowers, and in many species additional nectaries occur between flower and subtending scale, both groups of nectaries also sometimes becoming united. In some species glands may also exist at the apex of the petiole. The nectaries are thought to represent the perianth, there being no sepals or petals.

Female reproductive organs

Female flowers consist of a single ovary containing two parietal placentae to which the ovules are attached. The ovary is raised on a pedicel or stipe, or may be sessile. According to species the ovary varies in shape, and is glabrous, or sparsely, or densely hairy. The style is single, short, and sometimes forked above, or is not present in some species. There are two stigmas, usually retuse or divided into two lobes. When ripe the ovary constitutes a capsule which dehisces via two or four valves. The seeds are numerous, very small and bear a tuft of long hairs encouraging wind dispersal.

Male reproductive organs

In male flowers the number of stamens varies from one to twelve. Most species have two stamens, *S. triandra* has three, *S. pentandra* five to eight and *S. humboldtiana* has eight to twelve stamens. *S. purpurea* species and *S. sitchensis* have partially or completely connate filaments with a single stamen. The catkins of a few of the small Arctic creeping willows have a reduced number of flowers. *S. rotundifolia* generally has only three. Flowering shoots in some species, when present, are frequently short with a few small rudimentary leaves or bracts below the catkin. Winter buds are protected by a single non-resinous scale; terminal buds are present only in some dwarf species.

Leaves

The leaves, although generally deciduous, do remain skeletonized for varying periods in a few Arctic alpine willows, *S. phlebophylla* being a notable example. *S. myrsinites* regularly retains its dead leaves of the current year until the new young leaves appear in the following spring.

The leaves of willows exhibit a remarkable range of variation between species in size, texture, and shape. The range in size extends from the big leaves of *S. magnifica* (mature leaves 25 cm [10 in.] long by 12 cm [5 in.] wide), *S. fargesii*, and *S. moupinensis* at one extreme, to those of the tiny Arctic and alpine willows *S. polaris* and *S. serpyllifolia* (5 mm [$\frac{1}{5}$ in.] to 10 mm [$\frac{2}{5}$ in.] long).

Marked extremes in leaf texture and thickness occur between *S. appendiculata*, *S. coriacea* (*S. aurita* × *S. nigricans*), and varieties of *S. integra*. Leaves are simple with relatively short petioles and serrate, serrulate, or entire margins. Hairs are present above or below in some species, while the upper surface frequently is glabrous, and sometimes glossy in others. The under-surface of many species is glaucous, a bluish-grey colour. The youngest leaves, which are often tinted with pink, purple, or brown, are of very fine texture and frequently covered with very thin hairs (puberulent) that may disappear with maturity.

Leaf shape ranges from the long, lanceolate, tapering (acuminate) leaves of many of the large tree forms, to the orbicular, practically circular leaves of *S. tarraconensis* and several other alpine species. Leaf formations are generally alternate, but in *S. purpurea* and several *S. purpurea*-related species may be opposite. In certain species of *S. purpurea* some leaves may be alternate, some opposite, and some nearly opposite. The leaves are constantly subopposite in the exceptional Japanese willow *S. repens* var. *subopposita*.

Stipules

Stipules, small rudimentary leaflets, are found in most willows and are sessile, attached at the junction between petiole and stem. They are deciduous, or only present in young shoots, or are persistent, assisting identification of the species by their characteristics in size, shape, and margins.

Bark

Variations in colour and texture of the bark of different species occur. *S. chilensis* and *S. daphnoides* are smooth, whereas old specimens of pollarded *S. alba* and *S. rehderana* become deeply furrowed. *S. pentandra* has dark-brown bark, and in *S. amygdalina* the bark flakes off extensively towards the base of the trunk. *S. purpurea* species are typically yellow inside the bark.

Hybridization

Hybridization between *Salix* species is common, outnumbering those of any other genus. In addition to the naturally occurring hybrids in various parts of the world, a considerable number of others have been artificially induced by cross-pollination. Some are multiple hybrids that tend to produce mainly female progeny. Most hybrids are fertile and can cross with other hybrids or with pure species, often rendering identification very difficult. Many hybrids are very consistent in structure and appearance, and are frequently clones of only one sex. Most species of the subgenus *Salix* do not hybridize with species of the other two subgenera (*Caprisalix* and *Chamaetia*). Natural hybridization is affected by dioecism and is complicated by different flowering periods in various species.

Among the commonest British *Salix* hybrids are the various distinctive crosses between *S. alba* and *S. fragilis*, collectively referred to as *S. rubens*. Some of these hybrids were introduced originally as clones, and have been propagated from cuttings. A good example is *S. × rubens* var. *sanguinea*, of which only female specimens exist in Great Britain. *S. × basfordiana*, a hybrid of *S. fragilis* L. with *S. alba* L. var. *vitellina*, occurs naturally as a large tree with attractive orange/yellow branches, both sexes being represented in Great Britain.

Natural hybridization among wild populations of sallows occurs frequently in certain very localized areas with a high density of *S. caprea*, *S. cinerea*, *S. nigricans*, *S. phylicifolia*, and *S. aurita*. Within such areas various intermediate forms may be present. In Great Britain natural hybridization frequently occurs in moorland sites where *S. repens* and *S. aurita* occur together. In these areas, in addition to their true hybrid *S. ambigua*, a wide range of intermediate plants may exist that exhibit a preponderance of characteristics of either of the two parents.

Radical environmental changes predisposing to hybridization are caused by glaciers and flooding. High winds are also believed to facilitate the process. Most hybridization appears to take place in areas of major disturbance, particularly in those areas heavily settled by man. This probably explains why hybridization is stressed so much in Europe.

Although often causing complexities in identification, hybridization has its compensations in terms of hybrid vigour, as well as in the outstanding beauty of many of them.

Field identification

Great care is essential when gathering plant material from the wild for identification. Representative samples of both young and mature leaves, stipules, male and female catkins should all be obtained for a complete detailed examination. Many willows are not coetaneous, so several visits may be necessary to ascertain identity. It is important to mark or label the original plant from which earlier material has been obtained to avoid confusion on subsequent visits.

Young shoots frequently produce young developing leaves totally different in size and shape to mature leaves taken from the same plant. The leaves produced following coppicing tend to be larger than those on unpruned specimens. Young leaves also frequently exhibit indumentum, which is totally lost before they reach maturity.

The choice of site is important, dense shade causing abnormally big, glabrous or glossy leaves. Conversely, overexposure or drought conditions can give rise to abnormally small, hairy foliage. Isolated specimens often present less difficulty in identification than those within a dense mixed population, where the chance of meeting misleading variant forms is high.

Collecting a herbarium of dried and freshly pressed plant specimens is a useful exercise. Plant material from different sources and in different years can be compared, greatly assisting identification. It is essential when preparing a herbarium of *Salix* species to write a detailed description of each plant while it is still fresh. One should bear in mind that colour and glossiness will alter radically, small stipules will shrink, and the small hairs on stems and leaves are likely to disappear in the course of time.

Attractive features

A comprehensive study of the attractive qualities of *Salix* should include basic form and mode of growth, as well as the remarkably diverse features present in foliage, stems, and catkins. The prime virtue of the members of this genus, with few exceptions, is the remarkable vigour and speed of growth, the final form quickly becoming evident from rooted cuttings. The range of form includes erect types, weeping trees, semi-weeping (umbraculiform) trees, contorted trees, arching shrubs, bushy shrubs, and compact dwarfs, as well as ground-hugging and trailing dwarf species.

Foliage – type and colour

The colour range in leaves is extensive, with wide variations of green, from pale lime to very dark bottle-green. Leaves of many species are sericeous (silky-silver) due to a coating of fine adpressed hairs or an indumentum of minute hairs on one or both surfaces presenting a strongly overall luminous quality. Species possessing this feature include *S. alba* var. *argentea*, *S. cantabrica*, *S. seringeana*, *S. helvetica*, *S. glauco-sericea*, *S. lapponum*, *S. commutata*, *S. repens* var. *argentea* and *S. lanata*. In contrast, the mature leaves of *S. alba* var. *aurea*, especially when grown in full sun, are rich gold.

The youngest leaves in some species are translucent, with colours ranging from purple or red to subtle shades of brown or pink. Some of the most beautiful shades of colour can be seen in young terminal leaves of the *eriocephala* clones. *S. eriocephala* 'Russelliana' is an outstanding example, and in this clone the petioles and midrib of the leaf are pink or maroon. The colour range of the young unfolding leaves of *S. moupinensis* and *S. fargesii* is striking, in addition to the outstandingly attractive, polished, dark-red winter buds in both these species. Some clones of *S. purpurea* with linear leaves show a transition from pale orange to blue/green in their thin, smooth-textured young foliage, as seen in *S. purpurea* 'Riccartii' and in *S. purpurea* 'Nancy Saunders'. Young leaves produced at the tips of long trailing stems of *S. integra* 'Pendula' are a mixture of pale orange and pink.

The contrasting autumn tints of willow leaves are beautiful. *S. yezo-alpina* in particular changes dramatically from dark green to a vivid rich golden-yellow. Many other species develop attractive pale yellow autumnal hues, including *S. matsudana* 'Pendula', *S. humilis*, and *S. reinii*, while *S. foetida* becomes dark gold, slightly copper tinged. In some species the mature leaves are blue on both surfaces, markedly so in the case of *S. caesia* and *S. kochiana*. *S. alba* var. *coerulea* is strikingly blue on the under-surface, and *S. magnifica* leaves vary in colour, frequently exhibiting a blue tinge on their upper surface. In a large number of species the leaves are glaucous (bluish-grey) beneath, displayed to the best effect in weeping forms as their branches are blown aside in the wind. This effect is enhanced in waterside habitats. In numerous species the upper surface is glossy, particularly in *S. hibernica*, *S. glabra*, *S. pentandra*, *S. lucida*, *S. schraderiana* (bicolor), and *S. serissaefolia*.

Leaf variegation

Leaf colour variegation is restricted to mutations of a few varieties of well-known species that are usually selectively reproduced from cuttings. *S. integra* 'Alba Maculata' is a very beautiful small shrub. Many of its leaves are almost entirely white; others are dappled with light green. Young stems are coral pink and are very slender. The extreme variegation with consequent lack of chlorophyll in the leaves of this shrub reduces the chances of its survival, necessitating bold pruning to encourage new growth. There are two distinct clones of *S. cinerea* with variegated leaves. One, which could be described as *Salix cinerea* 'Variegata' is a strong-growing upright shrub with variable green-and-white variegation. The other clone, *S. cinerea* 'Tricolor' is a larger-leafed somewhat sprawling shrub with marbled pink, and cream-coloured variegation. Another interesting variegated leaved form is a clone of the Japanese *S. gracilistyla*.

Contrast in leaf form

Interesting effects in contrasting leaf shape can be obtained by planting thick-stemmed species bearing broad magnolia-type leaves characteristic of *S. magnifica*, and its hybrids in close proximity to *S. purpurea* 'Nicholsonii purpurescens'. The leaves of the latter, which arise from long slender rods, are long and linear, gently tapering to a fine point. Striking results can be obtained by taking advantage of the great difference in architectural form of the many species in addition to contrasting colour and leaf shapes. In addition to those species of *S. purpurea* with linear foliage, other species also typically possess narrow leaves. The section *Longifoliae* contains six shrub species with leaves that are long and narrow. The two most ornamental species within this section are *S. exigua*, which bears very beautiful silver foliage, and *S. fluviatilis*, with fine pale-green leaves. The Russian native *S. caspica* has narrow blue/green leaves, glaucous beneath. The European 'Hoary Willow' *Salix elaeagnos* (*incana*) is widely planted in European gardens for its ornamental long linear leaves, which are glabrous above and silky sericeous beneath.

Stems – colour and form

Stem colour is ornamental in many species, particularly during the autumn and winter seasons. Coinciding with leaf fall in the autumn, the yellow, orange, and red coloured stems gain in intensity as Xanthophyll pigment becomes restricted to the stems. Colours are most striking in the shining young stems arising from the branches pruned back in early spring. Notable examples are *S. alba* 'Cardinalis' with sealing-wax red stems, *S. alba* 'Chermesina' and *S. alba* 'Britzensis' varying from bright orange to scarlet; *S. alba* var. *vitellina* with rich yellow to orange stems, and *S. irrorata* with reddish-brown branchlets. Many *S. alba/fragilis* hybrids, including *S. basfordiana*, have attractive stems, from pale yellow to dark orange. Shoots of *S. glabra* and *S. mielichhoferi* are varnished dark reddish-brown. The young stems of *S. interior* are polished light brown, while those of *S. hibernica* are golden-green and very glossy. *S. elbursensis* and *S. petiolaris* both have distinctive shades of purple stem-colour.

In contrast with other winter species, *S. nigricans* (*myrsinifolia*), especially the straighter-stemmed female forms, has shining black stems. Various *triandra* clones also have attractive black stems. *S. triandra* 'Black German', used in basketry, being a good example.

The branchlets of some species are pruinose as a normal feature, bearing a variable amount of white bloom on their surface. This bloom may be diffuse or restricted to areas of stem or it can totally cover the young stems, which then appear to be encased in chalk. This feature is most marked in *S. canariensis*, *S. acutifolia*, *S. daphnoides*, *S. irrorata*, and *S. urbaniana*. Stems of the Himalayan dwarf carpeting species *S. hylematica* (*furcata*), *S. nepalensis* and *S. lindleyana* are dark red, or maroon, with very short internodes and tiny red buds.

Several *Salix* species have contorted stems and leaves, the most striking examples being *S. matsudana* 'Tortuosa', *S. matsudana* 'Caradoc', *S. alba* 'Snake', and *S.* × *erythroflexuosa*, which also has dark shining orange or copper-coloured branches. The foliage of *S. babylonica* 'Annularis' (*S. b.* 'Crispa') is unique, each leaf being spirally twisted into a rigid ring. *S. sachalinensis* 'Sekka' is very ornamental in form and habit, with highly polished mahogany stems typically exhibiting fasciation and curious scroll-like formations.

Many species are grafted onto straight stems to give them added height for ornamental purposes. In some cases this does display the grafted specimen to the best advantage, among the most suitable examples being a few weeping or trailing species that scarcely rise much above ground level if left ungrafted. These include the male *S. caprea* 'Pendula' (Kilmarnock Willow), the female *S. caprea* 'Pendula' (Weeping Sally), and *S. integra* 'Pendula'. However, many of the grafted species recently appearing in garden centres look ridiculously top heavy, do not thrive and totally rob the species of its normal growth habit and characteristics.

Catkins

Catkins are the crowning glory of the willow; their silver and gold colour wonderfully displayed when seen suspended above the dark leafless branches of the sallows *S. caprea* and *S. cinerea*, during the earliest days of spring. They are produced from buds arising in the axils of the leaves during the preceding summer. The time-scale of their subsequent development to maturity varies with the species and is also influenced to some extent by the prevailing climatic conditions during autumn and winter. In abnormally prolonged mild conditions catkins can mature prematurely, some even appearing in the early autumn before leaf fall.

When choosing *Salix* purely for catkin value it is best to select the male of the species. In the early stages of development catkins of both sexes in most species bear silky hairs presenting a silver-grey appearance that gives rise to the popular expression 'pussy willow'. This particularly refers, in Great Britain, to the female *S. caprea* and *S. cinerea* catkins, in which the silver hairs are more persistent. In eastern North America the term 'pussy' is similarly applied to the female catkins of *S. discolor*. Attractive colour changes restricted to male catkins occur during the process of maturation of the anthers. As the male flower scales are released, the unopened anthers are revealed. The darkest shades in the wide colour range of the male flower are seen at this stage, varying from dark purple, through a series of shades of red, to orange/yellow, depending upon the species. When the anthers open the pollen grains are revealed, causing a transition to yellow, rich shades in some species and very pale yellow in others. A close examination of a male catkin at this stage reveals that the numerous flowers compounded together in its formation do not usually open simultaneously. Anthers in those flowers near the base are often exposed initially, with anthers towards the apex gradually appearing over a period of a few hours or days. This variable delay maximizes the opportunity for insect pollination. This process also affects the overall colour combinations of male catkins at any one time.

The male catkin of *S. gracilistyla* var. *melanostachys*, is jet-black, after losing its brown bud scale, revealing the black flower scales beneath. As these are released, the bright red, unopened anthers are revealed, finally changing to very pale yellow as the anthers are fully exposed. *S. purpurea* species are among the most beautiful in the transition of colours involved in the maturation of the male catkin. A magnifying lens reveals these colour changes, which commence with dark purple, through crimson, orange and, finally to pale yellow. *S. purpurea* hybrids with *S. cinerea* (*S.* × *pontederana*) and with *S. caprea* (*S.* × *wimmeriana*) produce a spectacular display of bright orange-and-yellow male catkins. Male *S. humilis* catkins are brick red, turning yellow as the anthers become fully exposed. In some alpine dwarf species, including *S. myrsinites*, *S. myrtilloides*, and *S. brevipens*, male catkins are very striking, with purple anthers and staminal filaments pale maroon or pink. In other small alpine types the catkins are spherical and much reduced in size.

Beneath the outer protective bud scale of catkins of several *Salix* species there is a dense layer of white woolly hair. The anthers in these types are usually yellow without any visible colour transitions. Typical examples of species with woolly catkins are *S. hastata* 'Wehrhahnii', *S. hookeriana*, *S. lanata*, *S. candida*, and *S. smithiana*.

The scent of the flowering *Salix* is an important factor in attracting its chief pollinator, the honey bee, in the early spring. The catkins of *S. aegyptiaca* are among the earliest to mature, and are exceptionally fragrant.

Adaptability to environment

Under normal conditions the big species of *Salix* trees and shrubs grow in the fertile soil of river valleys, while dwarf creeping species are adapted to conditions of maximum exposure on mountains and in the Arctic regions. The intermediate members of the genus, including sallows and osiers, are located in mainly damp areas between these two extremes.

Salix, although thriving most in moist habitats, are outstanding as pioneer species, and are often present in the most unlikely places. They are among the first woody shrubs to colonize areas following natural upheavals caused by glaciation, earthquakes, and soil erosion associated with flooding. Most *Salix* species possess great powers of survival, tolerating long periods of drought. Their prolific seed production and highly effective adaptation to wind dispersal ensures their distribution over considerable distances. Rapid germination and outstandingly vigorous growth in the most unpropitious conditions render certain members of this genus particularly useful in land reclamation.

The sallows are especially suited to low-grade soils and will thrive on infertile, compacted, poorly drained land. The hardiest and most adaptable of the sallow species are *S. cinerea*, *S. aurita*, *S. caprea*, and their hybrids. They colonize denuded areas laid waste by man, spreading across land containing practically no humus or top soil. *S. cinerea* and *S. aurita* thrive on barren moorland and waste ground, even growing on old slag heaps in grossly polluted industrial regions. *S. caprea*, *S. cinerea*, *S. daphnoides*, and *S. purpurea* species all tolerate exposure to salt-laden air in seaside conditions, while several forms of *S. repens* are well adapted to growth in sand dunes. *S. purpurea* species are also very adaptable, surviving in extremely dry, sandy soils, and *S. daphnoides* is used in Europe for fixing sand dunes. In North America native *S. bebbiana* (Sarg) grows widely at high altitudes from Alaska and Canada to Idaho, Montana, along the Rocky Mountains to Colorado, New Jersey and Pennsylvania. It is frequently the first plant to cover burnt-out forest areas in all these regions.

Some mountain species, like *S. yezo-alpina* (*S. nakamurana*) of Japan, are well-adapted to exposure, moulding themselves tightly against rock surfaces and putting down claw-like roots into crevices at intervals from nodes along their procumbent stems, thereby ensuring stout anchorage against the elements. The habit of a plant can alter radically in response to environmental change. *S. repens*, which exhibits a relatively flattened spreading form of growth in exposed alpine conditions, becomes a small shrub with mainly ascending branches on many moorland sites. This adaptability is very obvious in the case of *S. purpurea* 'Procumbens'. This clone, normally with ground-hugging habit when space and light are available, develops ascending branches when overcrowded or grown in deep shade.

Most *Salix* species will adapt to a relatively impoverished hillside habitat. Even though large shrub and tree forms infinitely prefer fertile valleys they will, however, survive on steep slopes provided that young pot-grown plants with good root systems are used; each can be planted with its own carefully prepared miniature horizontal terrace cut out of the sloping ground. Scree can be removed and replaced by good, organically enriched soil. Trees grown under these conditions will start well and can establish themselves, retaining their basic characteristics in miniature. Occasional mulching is beneficial in replacing soil constituents reduced by leaching, and assists in moisture retention. Conversely, creeping mountain species can adapt to low-lying areas but do not survive indefinitely unless in well-drained soil, and must not be overhung by larger plants or trees.

Willows are great survivors and possess remarkable vitality and powers of regeneration. Total defoliation caused by the ravages of caterpillars and aphids early in the season is frequently followed by a second vigorous growth of new young leaves shortly afterwards. It is very exceptional that any permanent damage is caused by the numerous and varied assortment of aphids, caterpillars, willow beetles, and weevils that all participate actively in the ecology of the willow.

CHAPTER THREE

Management and Cultivation

Propagation

In the wild, propagation occurs sexually from seed and asexually from small twigs that take root after falling to the ground in gales. Asexual reproduction is restricted to the most brittle species, notably *S. fragilis* species (Crack Willow) and *S. fragilis* × *S. alba* L. hybrids under natural conditions. The propagation of *Salix* from cuttings is generally used in preference to the sowing of seed. There are three disadvantages to growing *Salix* plants from seed. The very small size of the seed restricts its food store, limiting the viability of the embryo and necessitating the sowing of very fresh fertile seed. When plants are raised successfully from viable seeds there is no certainty of their identity, or that they are a genetically pure species until detailed botanical tests are subsequently carried out. The third disadvantage in raising *Salix* artificially from seed is the delay in establishing a strong plant. Vegetative reproduction from cuttings ensures absolute uniformity and conformity to type, and enables the standardization of the many attractive willow hybrids as well as pure species.

Cuttings – basic considerations

The essential conditions for rooting cuttings are the presence of moisture, air, and a certain degree of warmth. The need for moisture is obvious, as the cutting, separated from its parent, will rapidly become desiccated. The formation of calluses, and the production of roots at the base of a cutting necessitates increased cambial activity, with consequent acceleration of respiration from the tissues. This indicates the vital need for good aeration around the base of the cutting, and is the reason for using sharp sand in striking cuttings. The sand allows air to enter freely without loss of contact. The air temperature should be lower than that of the medium in which the cuttings are inserted. This enables callus production and rooting to proceed while the development of buds and leaves is retarded. Practical experience has shown that, preferably, rooting should precede shoot growth. Hence bottom heating is often used for propagation, and is mainly confined to the rooting of soft, leafy, green cuttings. Hardwood cuttings, which comprise most of the propagating material used for *Salix*, usually require a considerable period for callusing and rooting. Heat may cause only the immediate growth of leaves and shoots without root production. This can occur when hardwood cuttings are planted outside in warm weather in spring. Their leaves and shoots, stimulated into rapid growth by the prevailing conditions, subsequently shrivel and die as the result of loss of moisture in the absence of roots.

Generally speaking *Salix* cuttings, with few exceptions, grow readily and provide the simplest and most rapid method of propagation. When carried out on a small scale the cuttings are best cultivated in pots, thereby encouraging a root ball with plenty of root hairs, which sustain minimal damage when eventually planted out. Cuttings can also be grown in a specially prepared bed but, in addition to lifting by frost, and damage caused by moles, their root system is frequently found to be confined to a single long tap root, which is liable to be damaged during removal.

Whether cuttings are grown in containers, cuttings beds, or in cold frames, the ideal medium is a mixture of coarse sand and peat. Sand stimulates root growth and prevents waterlogging, while peat retains moisture and prevents the sand from drying out. It is quite possible to root cuttings in pure sand provided that it is kept constantly damp.

Cuttings – practical techniques

The simplest way of achieving good results is to use a mixture containing one part of peat to two parts of coarse sand by volume. After thoroughly soaking a pot containing this mixture, cuttings are stripped of their leaves and immersed in a fungicidal solution. The base of each cutting is then dipped in rooting hormone solution, and the cutting inserted to at least half its length in the mixture, made firm, and labelled. Finally, to reduce the possibility of stem-rot occurring it is sound policy to cover the surface with a layer of fine pebbles or grit.

If only one cutting per container is required then the use of peat pots may be preferred. As these cuttings will root successfully even when placed very closely together, when multiple cuttings are required it is necessary to leave gaps of only about 5 cm (2 in.) between them in the same container. The ideal receptacle for this purpose is the standard plastic, square, liver container used by butchers (about 8 in. square and 8 in. deep). It is deeper than the average pot and the cuttings can be planted along all four sides as well as across the centre. Big holes should also be punched through the base to provide drainage.

When the cuttings are well rooted the container can be turned upside down and the contents gently removed in one mass. Each individual plant should be carefully separated, without shaking off all the sand/peat mixture. Single planting into pots is then carried out by using a mixture prepared from two buckets full of well-rooted light home-made compost (converted household scraps, vegetables, leaves, etc.), one bucket full of peat or leaf mould, and one generous handful of bonemeal. This combination should be very thoroughly mixed before potting is undertaken. The young plants grow rapidly in this organic mixture, which provides them with nourishment, moisture retention, and good drainage.

The foregoing procedure applies not only to woody cuttings taken between October and April, but also to green cuttings consisting of the current season's shoots taken from May onwards. The essential difference is that the woody cuttings will thrive at all stages in a sheltered position without being covered, whereas the green summer cuttings require cover to reduce moisture loss from transpiration, and to provide shade from sunshine. Mist propagation, involving the use of plastic tunnels, is generally used in commercial operations requiring the large scale production of plants from green cuttings. These requirements can also be provided by placing the summer cuttings in a cloche, or in a cold frame. If only a few containers are involved the plastic bag method has its advantages and is very simple. A recently watered container with its cuttings is placed within a suitably sized plastic bag, the mouth of which is tied off tightly after being inflated. Whatever method is used, summer cuttings should be kept well-shaded, out of direct sunshine. When the cuttings have developed and are well-rooted, gradual exposure should be practised until they are hardened off. They can then remain permanently in a shaded, sheltered position without artificial protection. Generally speaking, in the case of the slower growing dwarf *Salix* species, cuttings taken in the autumn become quickly established, ultimately producing a stronger root system than those taken in spring. Cuttings from large *Salix* species root most rapidly if planted in early spring when the sap is rising and the buds are swelling. This is also the best time for pruning or coppicing.

The catkin-bearing stems of *Salix* are often brought indoors and placed in water for decorative effect in the early days of spring. When these are removed after two or three weeks they will have come into leaf and be sprouting slender roots. Although it is tempting to pot these in light compost, most attempts end in failure, or, alternatively, one is left with a very unthrifty plant. When potting up is attempted, the trauma caused to stems that have produced root hairs in water has no seasonal significance. The transition is equally difficult whether attempted at any time throughout the spring or summer.

Sallow and osier cuttings

Sallows thrive in the poorest soils and, once established, the humus derived from dead leaves is adequate for their needs. Similarly, osiers (*S. viminalis* and *purpurea* species) do not require special treatment. If, however, they are being repeatedly cropped for the use of their rods in basketry and allied crafts, osier cuttings are planted in special osier beds during March or April, in clean fertile land. These cuttings, 45 cm (1½ ft) long, made from one-year-old rods, are pressed firmly into the soil, leaving one-third of their length above ground. Rows of cuttings are planted in this way, sometimes covering several acres, measurements between rows and between individual cuttings being exact, to allow space for the operation of mechanical cultivators. Throughout the first two years after planting the osier beds are kept clear of all weeds, and all shoots are cut back annually during the winter to encourage new growth. The first rods to be harvested for commercial use are cut during the winter of the third season, before the sap rises.

Spacing willows

If the area to be planted is extensive, and the soil is fertile, it is infinitely better to allow too much space initially than to overcrowd. The ideal spacing between trees and shrubs in the ornamental planting of salicta depends entirely upon their ultimate size and spread, varying with the nature of the soil, and with the prevailing climatic conditions in any given locality. However, an approximate idea of the minimum requirements can be calculated. If the largest spreading specimen trees are planted in adjacent positions they should be spaced at least 9–12 m (30–40 ft) apart. Medium-sized trees or large shrubs should be at least 6–7.5 m (20–25 ft) apart. The planting distance between small trees and shrubs can vary from 1.5 m to 3 m (5 ft to 10 ft) according to spread and ultimate size. Dwarf willows can be planted approximately 1–1.5 m (3–5 ft) apart, preferably in an open, rocky setting set apart from the larger species.

Soil and preparation for planting

Salix will grow in practically any soil, a neutral or slightly alkaline pH (not less than 6.5) being most favoured by the big timber producing types like *Salix alba* var. *coerulea*. Many of the dwarf species flourish in more acid soils. All species dislike lime-rich soils, which require neutralizing with manure, compost, or peat. Under ideal conditions members of the subgenus *Salix*, the tree forms and large shrubs, respond best to planting in deep, rich soils comprised of mixtures of silt and clay. Adequate drainage is essential to prevent waterlogging.

Before commencing to plant standings of *Salix* in a salictum for their ornamental value, very careful consideration should be given to their anticipated ultimate height and spread. The temptation to crowd plantings by filling all available gaps in the early stages is liable to produce an inpenetrable jungle. Planting too closely causes the most vigorous species to rapidly outgrow and overshadow others, resulting in tremendous variations in overall form, and causing diminution in size of the majority. Excessively close planting is also very conducive to the spread of Honey Fungus (*armillaria*) between the roots of adjacent trees and shrubs.

In sites where mixed *Salix* plantings are contemplated it is advisable to plant the largest-spreading specimen trees first, allowing maximum space between these and the remaining species. By obeying this basic rule the natural form and beauty of each planting will be accentuated. When water is available weeping forms can be used to the best advantage. They provide much-needed charm and character for artificially created lakes and reservoirs, their reflected beauty greatly enhancing and naturalizing the overall effect. The speed of growth of *Salix* species carefully planted in good, well drained soil is remarkable. Within three or four years a substantial growth of shrubs and trees up to and exceeding 20 feet in height can be achieved.

Open planting – unrooted cuttings

Cuttings can be inserted into their permanent positions from the outset, or, alternatively, can be transferred from containers in which they have produced a good root system.

In deciding whether to plant unrooted cuttings in their permanent positions the determining factor should be the quality of the soil. If it is deep and fertile, a freshly cut and defoliated section of a two- or three-year-old stem 1 m (3 ft) in length can be planted to approximately half its length in the soil, at any time between October and April.

The best results are obtained from these large-diameter cuttings if both ends are cut across at an angle of 45 degrees or less. This assists in firmly embedding the cuttings, with less chance of leaving an air pocket below. The angled top of the cutting sheds rain-water, maintaining a healthy crown. A metal probe or crowbar can be inserted first to facilitate planting. A little coarse sand dropped into the hole before firmly embedding the cutting will assist in stimulating root production. Finally, the adjacent soil must be firmly compressed against the cutting, checking at later intervals, especially after strong gales and frosts, firming the soil again if necessary. Cuttings can be grown successfully in the open at any season, but between May and October severe drought conditions can adversely affect their progress.

Open planting – rooted cuttings

If the soil is poor, necessitating some form of organic enrichment, it is undoubtedly best to plant well-rooted container-grown plants instead of unrooted cuttings. This will enable soil improvement and planting to be synchronized. An area at least 1.5 m (5 ft) in diameter for trees or large shrubs, or at least 1 m (3 ft) across for smaller shrubs should be thoroughly dug two spits deep. The excavated soil should be heaped to one side and freed of old roots and perennial weeds, especially couch grass and docks. The subsoil should be left *in situ*, loosened and aerated by forking, before applying a layer of well-rotted manure or compost across the bottom of the hole. The manure or compost can then be covered by about 3 cm (1–2 in.) of the excavated top soil, to which bonemeal has been added.

The plant can next be removed from its container, after being thoroughly soaked, taking particular care not to damage the roots. Planting can then be carefully carried out, spreading out the roots and filling in with the remainder of the excavated soil enriched with more bonemeal. After firming with one's hands the plant should stand at the same depth as it occupied in its container. The great advantage of using container-grown plants is that planting can be carried out at any season, provided that water requirements are monitored in the early stages. Mushroom compost can be used if neither garden compost nor manure are available. Alternatively leaf-mould and peat enriched with bonemeal, or with fish, blood, and bonemeal are a good substitute.

To achieve the best results when planting in grass, it pays to keep the newly planted site clear of deep-rooted perennial weeds like docks and couch grass for the first three years. If a site is liable to dry out on the surface, a mulch of compost, peat, or leafmould applied in early spring helps to retain moisture round newly planted willows. The application of mulches of compost or manure periodically, and the spreading of wood-ash and a little bonemeal between plantings every two years is also very beneficial. Well-rotted manure applied in the autumn is particularly valuable in the early stages, enriching the soil and conserving moisture, preceding the natural build-up in leafmould.

Planting dwarf alpine willows

Dwarf alpine willows require different conditions to those needed by other species. The ideal site consists of a bed raised higher than the surrounding land, totally exposed, and not overhung by shrubs or trees, thereby simulating natural conditions experienced in the wild. The soil must be both moisture-retentive and well drained. If these conditions do not already exist and the soil is heavy or lime-rich the systematic preparation of a satisfactory alpine bed for growing the small mountain willows is well worth the labour involved. The existing soil should be removed from the site to a depth of approximately 30 cm (1 ft). The excavated bed is then filled in with a thoroughly mixed combination of equal parts of loam, peat, and grit. A small amount of bonemeal and wood-ash included in the mixture will provide essential minerals and trace elements. After firming down the bed, rocks are seated into position in the same plane for natural effect. Their upper surface should slope slightly back towards the plants placed behind them, providing an extra catchment area for rainwater. The alpine bed is completed with a fine layer up to 5 cm (2 in.) deep of quarter-inch natural shingle. Dwarf alpine *Salix* species will flourish among the rocks in this situation. The best results are obtained by planting out well-rooted container-grown specimens.

Pruning

The traditional phrase that 'growth follows the knife' is very true in practice, particularly when applied to coppicing in the production of osier rods. The coppicing of osier willows is usually commenced at the end of their first growing season, during the winter or the early spring, when they are cut down to ground level. The result is dramatic, a mass of shoots sprout from the severed base and grow into straight stems or rods, increasing annually in height and thickness. The harvesting of these rods occurs regularly, every year in some cases, according to the size required, and the 'stool' or 'crown' can go on producing for 30 or 40 years.

Pruning, apart from its specialized use in coppicing, is of vital importance in the radical removal of all dead or diseased wood. Branches sometimes cross one another, causing deep wounds that render them prone to invasion by fungi. Judicious pruning in the early stages will overcome such problems. Some *Salix* are more susceptible to 'die-back', particularly associated with prolonged wet weather and fungal infection. Wherever this occurs the affected stems should be pruned back to reveal healthy tissues and the resultant dead material should be collected and burnt. Similar pruning of the tips of young branches shrivelled by late frosts in the spring stimulates the production of fresh shoots.

There is no doubt that many of the shrub *Salix* species benefit from hard pruning every three or four years, preventing them from becoming prematurely woody and prolonging their life span. This procedure is very applicable in the management of windbreaks. The staggered planting of mixed osiers and sallows in at least two rows, forming windbreaks, provides the opportunity for beneficial pruning to be carried out. Alternate trees can be pruned to ground level during successive years, thereby radically thickening the windbreak during the early years of its formation. It will also inhibit trunk formation and any tendency to produce a broad spreading top. Windbreaks treated in this way withstand the most powerful gales and, although deciduous, their twigs provide a very effective wind filter and shelter belt in the winter months.

Pruning is very productive in displaying the brilliant stem colours of many species; annual coppicing achieving the best results. Some species that are ornamentally attractive as unpruned trees also exhibit beautiful young shoots when pruned. In such cases it is worthwhile retaining a representative specimen tree intact in addition to a coppiced form of the same species. *S. daphnoides*, a beautiful tree form if left unpruned, provides a good example, also producing an abundance of very attractive pruinose purple rods when coppiced.

Dramatic results can often be achieved by severe pruning of unthrifty or overextended shrub willows, which respond with vigorous new shoots from below. Pruning for no good reason can, however, become an obsession. It should not be carried out in ornamental collections of specimen trees possessing characteristic architectural form. The only exception arises in the removal of diseased, dead or crossing branches. *S. eriocephala* 'Rouge d'Orleans' presents a good illustration. When left untouched it produces a very elegant and balanced arching form, only to be replaced by a mass of dead-straight rods if pruned. It is obviously sound practice to provide such species with plenty of space from the outset, in order to eliminate the need for pruning.

Dwarf species also respond to pruning. Old gnarled specimens that have become excessively woody can often be rejuvenated by cutting them back in the early spring. Those *Salix* with procumbent trailing habit, as well as carpeting forms that are overgrowing others in alpine beds or rockeries, can always be propagated to meet the popular demand for these small species.

Pollarding constitutes the most drastic form of tree pruning and, although rarely carried out today, used to be standard practice in riverside plantings on many farms. The trunks of young trees of *S. alba*, *S. fragilis* and their clonal hybrids were sawn off 2 to 3 m (6 to 10ft) from ground level. Numerous shoots subsequently sprouted from the flat tops, out of reach of cattle. These shoots were allowed to grow for 12 or more years and were then cut for farm fencing. A succession of crops of poles were taken in this way over many years.

Pollarding has been carried out in many countries, especially in Holland and Britain. In North America some big specimens of *S. alba* and *S. fragilis* derived from those originally introduced from Europe in colonial times have been similarly treated.

General maintenance

When overcrowding has occurred in collections of *Salix* the soil rapidly becomes depleted of nutrients and moisture, resulting in obvious general growth retardation. The large lowland species of *Salix* require regular organic mulching to achieve maximum growth. Well-rotted farmyard manure, or good friable compost spread widely between trees every two years is ideal. This should be applied during the autumn to allow the organic constituents to be absorbed into the soil before new growth commences in the spring. Mulches applied in the spring often dry out rapidly with the advent of warm, dry conditions. As *Salix* have comparatively shallow, widely spreading root systems, it is inadvisable to dig in the mulches. The application of bonemeal, or of blood, fish, and bone mixture, although beneficial and easily carried out, does not produce the same physical effect on soil condition as the liberal autumn mulching with manure or compost taken down by earthworms. If species are coppiced annually to reveal their stem colour, unless the soil is exceptionally fertile, an annual mulching is necessary if the maximum production of vigorous young shoots is to be maintained.

Most dwarf and creeping *Salix* species have a relatively slow growth rate, and do not drain nutrients from the soil to the same degree as the large lowland species. The application of a light, friable compost, containing a little bonemeal, every two or three years is beneficial for these small species. It not only provides nourishment, but also retains moisture.

Apart from food and moisture an equally important factor is the provision of adequate light. The judicious pruning of branches overshadowing smaller species is vital, especially when shrubs have been placed too closely together.

Damage to young trees by rabbits, hares, or squirrels can be prevented by using distensible plastic sleeves. Moles can be a menace, severing the roots of dwarf *Salix* species. They also frequently undermine and uproot small cuttings. The only effective remedy is trapping. The ravages of caterpillars and other insect pests, including larvae of various weevils and willow beetles rarely prove fatal and do not warrant the use of insecticidal sprays.

The application of a fungicidal spray to dwarf species can be very effective in combating rust and fungal die-back. The best results are obtained by prompt treatment during the early stages of the infection.

Plants grown in association

The planting of young trees and shrubs with ample spacing to allow for their unrestricted future growth may result in the whole area appearing rather bare initially. To remedy this, the planting of shallow-rooting, attractive, perennial ground cover will greatly enhance the site. *Lamium galeobdolon* 'Variegatum' rapidly forms dense ground cover 15 to 30 cm (6 in. to 1 ft) in depth beneath trees, as well as in exposed places in practically any soil. It is the variegated form of the Wild Archangel, and the leaves, with their most attractive patterned silver variegation, are retained throughout the winter. It is stoloniferous, shallow-rooting and easily removed from the immediate vicinity of planted willows. Apart from the beauty of the leaves they shield the soil, conserving moisture and inhibiting weeds. It produces whorls of yellow flowers in June and July. Various forms of *Lamium maculatum*, especially 'Beacon Silver', 'White Nancy', and 'Aureum' have attractive leaves and flowers. The range of good ground cover suited to moist shady situations below willows is very extensive and includes *Pulmonaria*, *Omphelodes verna* 'Alba' and *O. cappadocica*, *Tiarella*, *Mummularia aurea*, *Epimedium*, *Symphytum grandiflorum*, *Waldsteinia*, *Tellima grandiflora*, *Brunnera macrophylla* 'Variegata', and several variegated *Ajuga*. Certain species of *Euphorbia* form strikingly attractive ground cover for use under big trees. Among the most vigorous is *Euphorbia griffithii* 'Fireglow', which, in good soil, produces a very dense barrier inhibiting weeds. *Euphorbia sikkimensis* is also useful, although not so vigorous. Both species are too big to use among small willows and their aerial stems die down during winter.

Valerianaphu 'Aurea' produces a display of bright yellow foliage throughout the winter, thriving in damp soil and dense shade.

Many attractive fern species grow well in moist shady situations beneath trees. *Osmunda regalis* (the royal fern) is spectacular and will also grow in full sunshine. Marshy areas provide ideal conditions for two species of the arum-like *Lysichiton*, the yellow-flowering *Lysichiton americanus* and the white-flowering Japanese *Lysichiton camtschatcensis*. After early spring flowering they produce massive broad leaves from ground level.

Bulbs and corms flourish in the accumulating leaf-mould under trees and greatly contribute to the overall effect. The corms of *Colchicum autumnale* (the autumn crocus or meadow saffron) are ideal for brightening up dark areas between willows during the autumn. Once planted they will survive and increase for many years, producing clumps of lilac, pink, or white blooms from September to November. *Fritilleria* species, *Eranthis* (winter aconite) and *Anemone nemorosa* (wood anemones) are among the most beautiful early-flowering types. *Cyclamen hederifolium* and *C. coum* (including white-flowering forms) produce extremely attractive cordate leaves marbled with silver. Apart from exotic plantings, our wild indigenous species of snowdrops, primroses, bluebells, wood anemones, and wild daffodils provide a wonderful backcloth of colour for ornamental willows throughout the spring months.

Lathraea clandestina is an interesting plant, well worth introducing into collections of *Salix* species. It will grow rapidly from seeds applied to the exposed roots of willows, especially in permanently moist situations. It develops as a commensal (a non-parasitic relationship), forming clumps on willow roots, has attractive perfumed flowers in shades of mauve, pink, and occasionally white, and is completely harmless.

The selection of willows for specific sites

The choice of species should be related not only to the total area of land available, but also to the soil fertility. If fertility and climatic conditions are good, the growth of shrubs and trees will be correspondingly greater. Conversely, in conditions of extreme exposure with very poor soil, the growth rate and ultimate size of willows, regardless of species, will be retarded. As an additional complication, an individual tree or shrub may thrive abnormally, beyond its anticipated limits. Bearing in mind these basic considerations it will be appreciated that some latitude is required in the choice of species for specific sites. The final spread of the largest species can be voluminous, ideal for specimen trees in parks and large estates.

In an estate or garden of several acres all types of willow can be arranged in groups according to size and habit. Weeping trees are most effectively placed in waterside habitats.

Obviously, it is unwise to attempt to grow the largest tree species, with roots which can spread far and wide, in a small garden, thus robbing the garden of all moisture and light, and constituting a menace to foundations and drainage systems. Trees in this category include *S. babylonica* and *S. fragilis*.

Small shrub willows in large areas tend to become eclipsed by big trees unless they are placed in a site specially reserved for them.

Dwarf *Salix* species are ideally suited to an alpine bed, whether in the smallest garden, or in a bed set apart within a parkland area. The smaller the garden the more specialized is the range of willows required to achieve the best results. Smaller gardens do, however, provide wonderful opportunities for specialization in creeping alpine willows for rockeries, and scope for small shrub willows, including the smallest weeping types.

CHAPTER FOUR

Ornamental Trees and Shrubs for Large Gardens, Parks and Estates

If a substantial acreage is available for the establishment of a representative biomass collection of willows, full use can be made of a sector with the poorest soil for the planting of indigenous sallows together with a selection of their clonal hybrids. The most fertile areas can then be left for the planting of species and hybrids of the subgenus *Salix* (*amerina*) in addition to other willows of subgenus *Caprisalix*, excluding the sallows.

Hereafter a representative selection of species and hybrids of the genus *Salix* is described alphabetically, concentrating particularly upon those with ornamental value. Brief coverage is also given to those of lesser merit.

Salix acmophylla Boiss.   A large shrub or large tree belonging to the section *humboltianae*; leaves are dimorphic, in common with other tropical African *Salix* species, with very small entire deciduous spring leaves, followed by much larger serrulate summer leaves; summer leaves lanceolate-elliptic or elongate-lanceolate; bud scales with free overlapping margins; catkins long, cylindric, slender and pendulous; flower scales deciduous; stamens three to nine; ovaries pedicellate, stigmas subsessile.

A tropical or subtropical species, native of Iran, extending west to Palestine and south-east Turkey. *S. acmophylla* is not hardy in cold temperate conditions and is not ornamentally significant.

Salix acutifolia Willd. S. daphnoides Vill. var. acutifolia (Willd.) Doell   A shrub or small tree 4 m (12 ft) to 6 m (20 ft) with spreading crown of slender reddish purple branches, markedly pruinose and glabrous; leaves 5–12 cm long, their length exceeding five times their width, linear-lanceolate, sharply acuminate, serrulate; lamina glabrous on both surfaces, dark green above, greyish-green below, base cuneate, young leaves with sparse indumentum; stipules lanceolate, serrate, acuminate; catkins appearing before the leaves, flower-scales ovate covered with long silky-silver hairs, a conspicuous feature for four or five months from late autumn throughout the winter before flowering; peduncles short; two stamens sometimes partly connate with golden anthers.

Native of Poland and Russia, extending to east Asia. An extremely attractive willow the gleaming silvery sericeous catkins on very dark slender branchlets forming a spectacular display in the winter landscape.

Salix acutifolia 'Pendulifolia'   A small tree up to 6 m (20 ft) with slender pruinose branches generally deeper red and less purple than *S. acutifolia*. Very pendulous leaves up to 16 cm long; catkins similar to *S. acutifolia*. Extremely ornamental.

Salix acutifolia 'Blue Streak'   An attractive male clone with dark-violet pruinose stems. Up to 9 m (30 ft) high.

Salix acutifolia 'Lady Aldenham'   A very good male clone with catkins larger than the type and with dark violet or almost black trunk and branches. Rarely exceeds 4 m (12 ft) in height.

Salix adenophylla Hook. (*S. cordata* Michx.) 'Furry' or 'Heart-leaved willow'   A loosely-branched shrub 2 m (6 ft) to 4 m (12 ft) high. Branchlets thick and densely pubescent; leaves 6–12 cm long ovate-lanceolate to broadly ovate, abruptly acuminate, glandular-dentate-serrate, cordate or rounded base, lamina lannate on both surfaces; large cordate-ovate stipules; catkins appearing with the leaves; female catkins 3–6 cm long; only female shrubs in cultivation.

A relatively slow-growing species of north-eastern North America. The overall whitish appearance of this shrub contrasts effectively with other darker leaved background willows.

Salix × 'Aegma Brno'. (*S. aegyptiaca* L. × *S. magnifica* Hemsl.)   A wide, spreading, small tree 3 m (10 ft) to 6 m (20 ft) high, with a smooth grey trunk and thick, stiff dark-brown branchlets, leaves dark green, glabrous above, glaucous below, up to 15 cm long and to 8 cm wide, obovate or elliptic, apex cuspidate or acute, base obtuse; leaf margins coarsely and irregularly serrate. A female clone with stiff erect catkins up to 10 cm (4 in.) long.

A handsome tree, with an unusually rigid form, well worth inclusion in a large garden.

Salix aegyptiaca L. (*S. medemii* Boiss.)   A shapely small tree up to 4.5 m (15 ft) high, with thick branches; branchlets and petioles purple and pubescent; the youngest leaves brown tinted and pubescent on both sides; mature leaves 5–15 cm long, glabrous above, glaucous and pubescent below, oblong, obovate, or narrowly elliptic, apex acute, base obtuse; leaf margins serrate-undulate and revolute; small serrate stipules.

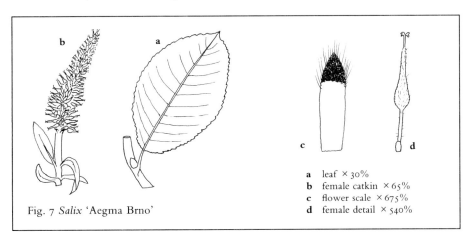

a	leaf × 30%
b	female catkin × 65%
c	flower scale × 675%
d	female detail × 540%

Fig. 7 *Salix* 'Aegma Brno'

Although occasional trees are bisexual, most are dioecious. The strikingly attractive, sweet-smelling, sessile male catkins, with stamens up to 3 cm long, appear in February or early March before the leaves. A native of Iran, Armenia, and the mountains of Asia.

An excellent large-leafed ornamental tree, ideal for any large garden.

***Salix alba* L. 'White Willow'**   A large, fast-growing, elegant tree, with deeply furrowed bark, up to 25 m (80 ft) high; a many-branched somewhat conical crown, the branchlets being compactly arranged and drooping at their tips; leaves lanceolate, silky-hairy on both surfaces when young, becoming dull glabrous green above and glaucous silky below when mature, serrulate and elongate-acuminate at apex and base; catkins sub-erect, narrowly cylindrical-elongate, appear with the leaves on short leafy stalks in late April or early May; male flowers with two stamens, yellow anthers and two nectaries; female flowers with ovaries conical, sessile, and glabrous, a single nectary and two-cleft stigma. The silky hairs on the under-surface of the mature leaves ruffled in the wind present a distinctive silvery/white appearance when the tree is viewed from a distance. Widely distributed throughout the lowlands and fertile valleys of the British Isles and Europe. *S. alba* was introduced to North America in colonial times and is also present in North Africa, north and west Asia.

Imposing trees, only suitable for large parks and extensive estates.

***Salix alba* L. var. *argentea* Wimm. (*S. a.* var. *sericea* Gaud.; *S. alba* var. *splendens* Schneid.) 'Silver Willow'**   A small tree 8 m (25 ft) to 12 m (40 ft) high; one of the most intensely silver-leaved willows, the sericeous hairs remaining on both sides of the mature leaves. Leaves remain on the tree until late November or early December; mostly cultivated from one or two clones, although a few dwarf forms have been found in the wild.

Outstandingly effective foliage colour contrasts result from siting *S. alba* var. *argentea* and *S. alba* var. *aurea* together.

***Salix alba* L. var. *aurea* 'Gold Leaf Willow'**   One of the most beautiful ornamental trees, 6 m (20 ft) to 10 m (35 ft) high, regularly branched, broadly pyramidal and

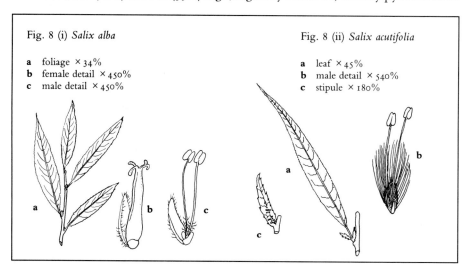

Fig. 8 (i) *Salix alba*

a foliage × 34%
b female detail × 450%
c male detail × 450%

Fig. 8 (ii) *Salix acutifolia*

a leaf × 45%
b male detail × 540%
c stipule × 180%

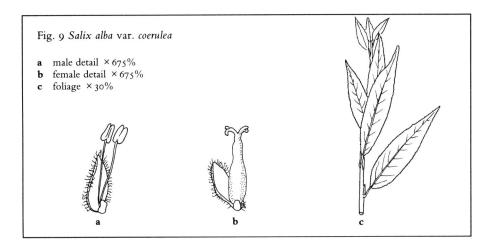

Fig. 9 *Salix alba* var. *coerulea*

a male detail × 675%
b female detail × 675%
c foliage × 30%

a   b   c

compact in habit; branchlets glabrous pale greenish or golden-yellow; young leaves silky-hairy becoming glabrous on both surfaces later. Leaf colour is lime green at first, changing to bright gold when mature, especially when trees are not overcrowded and receive plenty of light. The foliage tends to become increasingly more brilliant during the summer months, eventually turning paler in the autumn. *S. alba* var. *aurea* is not found in the wild and is relatively uncommon in cultivation. Both *S. alba* var. *argentea* and *S. alba* var. *aurea* are slower-growing types than pure *S. alba* L. They should be treated as specimen trees and are best left unpruned. Hitherto their ornamental value has been generally ignored by horticulturalists. *S. alba* 'Vitellina', specializing in stem colour and found in most garden centres, is no substitute in respect of foliage and form.

***Salix alba* L. 'Britzensis'** A normally conical small tree up to 6 m (20 ft) high. Usually coppiced to encourage the growth of the young stems, which are a very rich deep-red colour, similar to *S. alba* 'Cardinalis'. Originally raised from seed at Britz in Germany, it is represented in cultivation by a male clone.

***Salix alba* L. var. *coerulea* (Sm.) Koch, (*S.* 'Caerulea' *S. a. calva* G. F. W. Meyer) 'Cricket Bat Willow' or 'Blue Willow'** A magnificent large tree up to 30 m (100 ft) high and 4.5 m (15 ft) to 6 m (20 ft) in girth, of pyramidal habit with branches more erect than the 'White Willow' arising at an angle of approximately 60 degrees and lacking a central main stem; branchlets coloured reddish-brown at their tips; leaves lanceolate, finely acuminate and cuneate, glossy green above, silky pubescent below, becoming glabrous and glaucous-blue later. Only female clones are under cultivation.

Ideally sited in deep alluvial silt beside water in large estates. Allowing a spacing of 9 m (30 ft) to 12 m (40 ft) between this and any other large tree encourages optimal growth. A mature specimen of *S. alba* var. *coerulea* presents a very imposing spectacle, enhanced by the glaucous-blue colouration of the under surface of its leaves.

***Salix alba* L. 'Cardinalis'** A small tree narrowly conical, 4.5 m (15 ft) to 6 m (20 ft) high. The habit and stem colour very similar to *S. alba* 'Britzensis'. The leaves of *S. alba* 'Cardinalis' are narrower and it also differs by being a female clone.

Salix alba L. **'Chermesina'**   A small tree up to 7 m (25 ft) high with attractive carmine-red winter branchlets. Although it also originated in Germany this clone is not synonymous with 'Britzensis'.

Salix alba L. **'Chrysostela'**   A small erect poplar-like tree 6 m (20 ft) to 9 m (30 ft) high, with a narrowly conical crown and golden branchlets with dark orange/red at their tips. Coppicing in early spring produces numerous bright orange/red rods.

Salix alba L. × *Salix babylonica* L.:   (see *S.* × *salamonii*)

Salix alba L. × *Salix fragilis* L.:   (see *S. rubens*)

Salix alba L. **'Liempde'**   A tree with a well-defined leading trunk and stem; branches erect, forming a narrowly ovoid crown; young stems red-tipped. A male clone, very popular in Holland.

Salix alba L. var. *vitellina* × *Salix babylonica*
Salix alba L. **'Vitellina Pendula'**   } (see *S.* × *chrysocoma* Dode.)
Salix alba L. **'Vitellina Tristis'**

Salix alba L. var. *vitellina* L. Stokes (*S. a.* ssp. *vitellina* L. **'Golden Willow'**)   Not known in the wild, clones with orange/yellow young stems in the autumn and winter have been cultivated in Britain ever since the Roman occupation. Being tough and flexible the rods were originally used for tying and bundling. It is now replaced in basketry by other clones of finer quality. *Salix alba* var. *vitellina* is commonly planted in gardens of all sizes. Annual pruning encourages the production of its attractive young rich yolk-coloured stems and greatly enhances the winter scene. *S.* 'Alba Tristis', *S.* 'Alba Vitellina Tristis', and *S.* 'Vitellina Tristis' are names used in many garden centres to describe a clone with a straight vertical trunk, semipendulous branchlets and entirely vitelline throughout.

Salix alba **'Snake'.** *S. a.* var. *argentea* **Wimm.** × *S. matsudana* **'Tortuosa'**   A small pyramidal, contorted tree up to 4 m (12 ft) high with spirally twisted branches; branchlets undulating, sinuously contorted and finely pubescent; axillary buds pubescent reddish-brown; young leaves sericeous with fine hairs covering both surfaces; mature leaves curled, lanceolate, serrate, apex elongate and narrowly acuminate, base acute, lamina glossy dark-green above, sericeous-pubescent beneath; petioles pale pink 0.25 cm to 0.5 cm long; catkins appearing with the leaves on leafy lateral shoots; male catkins many-flowered, two stamens with golden anthers.

A curiously contorted ornamental willow with a silvery-white aura created by the conspicuously sericeous young leaves.

Many ornamental clones of *S. alba* are widely grown in Europe for parks and large gardens, particularly in Holland and Germany. Clones of special merit are *S. alba* 'Barlo', 'Belders', 'Bredevoort', 'Drakensburg', 'Hetgoor', 'Lichtenvoorde', 'Malorntelelo' (Hungary), 'Lievelde', 'Raesfeld' (Germany), 'Rockange', and 'Vries'.

Salix × *alopecuroides* **Tausch.** *S. speciosa* **Host.** (*S. fragilis* L. × *S. triandra* L.)   A large shrub or tree with pale glabrous, glossy, brown branchlets; leaves lanceolate or oblanceolate, acuminate, 6–15 cm long, coarsely serrate, dark green above and glaucous beneath; stipules prominent, semi-lunar, acute and serrate; catkins, produced in leafy lateral shoots, are narrowly cylindrical, 5–10 cm long with pale-yellow pubescent flower scales; ovary is distinctly pedicellate.

Present in Austria and Romania. Two male clones in cultivation.

Salix 'Americana'. (S. eriocephala Michx. × S. petiolaris Sm.), (S. rigida Muhlenb. × S. petiolaris Sm.); or, (S. cordata Muhlenb. non Michx. × S. petiolaris Sm.) A loosely spreading shrub up to 3 m (10 ft) high with arching young stems; branches pubescent; yellowish-green at first, becoming glabrous, glossy, reddish-brown later; the youngest terminal leaves are typically deflected to one side, translucent, thin, coloured in pale shades of brown, orange, and pink, sparsely pubescent on the upper surface and on the mid-rib beneath; mature leaves thin, lanceolate, serrate, acuminate, cuneate, glabrous green above and below; stipules large, persistent and reniform; petioles pink 1–1.5 cm long; catkins 2–3 cm long, cylindrical or slightly conical, staminal filaments half connate, unopened anthers dark orange, golden-yellow when mature. Only the male clone in cultivation.

Introduced to Britain and Europe from North America where it is extensively grown for basketry. Very hardy, tolerating poor soil.

An ornamental male clone with attractive catkins and beautiful young leaves.

Salix amplexicaulis (Bory. and Chaub.) Schneid. A small, many-branched erect shrub 2 m (6 ft) to 3 m (10 ft); branches purple to brown, glabrous; branches and branchlets very straight, paired and opposite; branchlets green, glabrous; leaves opposite, sessile, oblong or obovate, entire or slightly serrulate towards apex, apex acute or slightly rounded, base rounded or cordate; lamina dark green and glabrous above, glaucous and glabrous beneath; catkins appearing before the leaves in April or early May are cylindrical, opposite and sessile; stamens connate.

Native of the Balkans, it is found in Bulgaria, Yugoslavia, Albania and Greece.

An ornamental shrub with distinctive characteristics, closely related to *S. purpurea* L., very hardy and tolerating dry soil.

Salix amygdalina L.: (see *S. triandra*)

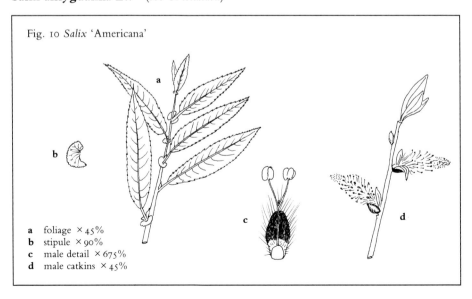

Fig. 10 *Salix* 'Americana'

a foliage × 45%
b stipule × 90%
c male detail × 675%
d male catkins × 45%

***Salix amygdaloides* Anderss. 'Peach Leaf Willow'**   A tall shrub or small tree 10 m (30 ft) or more high, frequently with one to three leaning fissured trunks, dark brown or reddish-brown and ascending grey-brown branches; branchlets drooping, flexible, glabrous, glossy yellow to reddish-brown with yellowish, glossy buds; leaves 6–15 cm long, 1.5–3 cm wide, lanceolate to ovate-lanceolate, acuminate, caudate, finely serrate, base rounded or obtuse, glabrous yellowish-green above, glabrous and glaucous below; stipules absent; petioles glabrous, yellowish, often twisted, 6–20 mm long; male catkins up to 5 cm long with four to seven stamens; female catkins up to 10 cm long on leafy shoots; catkins coetaneous, linear and lax, flower scales lanceolate or ovate glabrous outside, yellow, villous within and deciduous.

     A North American native, thriving in alluvial soils near rivers, from north-east of New York state and adjacent Quebec to south-east British Columbia to Kentucky, Texas, and Arizona.

     An attractive ornamental tree with handsome foliage. Needs rich soil, ideally situated beside water.

***Salix andersoniana* Sm.:**   (see *S. myrsinifolia* [*S. nigricans*])

***Salix angustifolia* Willd. non Wulf.:**   (see *S. wilhelmsiana)*

***Salix appendiculata* Vill.**   A small slow-growing tree 3 m (10 ft) to 6 m (20 ft) with a short, smooth trunk and short, thick, stiff branches spreading to form a flattish crown; branchlets greyish-green, pubescent, glabrescent, exhibiting longitudinal striae when peeled; young leaves pubescent, coloured brown towards their base; mature leaves glabrescent, thick, coriaceous, dark green, rugose, with deeply impressed venation above; lower surface of mature leaves dense raised reticulate venation and persistent pubescence; leaf shape variable, mostly widest above the middle, oblanceolate or obovate, acute, cuneate, with coarsely and irregularly serrate to entire margins; stipules persistent, semi-cordate, serrate; petiole 1 cm long; buds dark brown; male catkins numerous, concentrated towards the ends of the branchlets, ovoid or nearly spherical when in full bloom, staminal filaments 1 cm long with long basal hairs, anthers pale yellow; female catkins – pedicel as long as, or longer than the grey-pubescent ovary.

Fig. 11 *Salix amygdaloides*

     a   foliage × 30%
     b   male detail and portion of rachis × 360%
     c   female detail × 540%
     d   male catkins × 45%

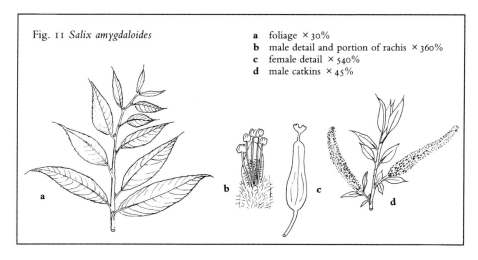

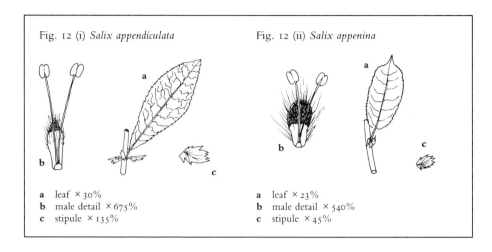

Fig. 12 (i) *Salix appendiculata*

Fig. 12 (ii) *Salix appenina*

a leaf × 30%
b male detail × 675%
c stipule × 135%

a leaf × 23%
b male detail × 540%
c stipule × 45%

Native of the Alps in central Europe, the Apennine Mountains and in the north-west Balkan peninsula.

An excellent, extremely hardy, trouble-free willow, particularly suited to well-drained hillside habitats. The male trees have a good show of conspicuous pale-yellow catkins.

Salix appenina Skv. An attractive strong-growing large shrub or small tree 5 m (15 ft) to 9 m (30 ft) high with many flexible ascending and spreading branches; branchlets sparsely pubescent becoming glabrous later; young leaves puberulent and faintly brown-tinged; mature leaves variable, elliptic, obovate or oblong, leaf base rounded and unequal, apex cuspidate, lamina vivid light green and glabrous above, glabrous and glaucous beneath; leaf margins undulate and coarsely serrate; stipules persistent, serrate; catkins mainly confined to the tips of the branchlets and very numerous, male catkins broadly ovoid with staminal filaments 1 cm or more long, anthers golden-yellow.

Distribution restricted to the Apennine Mountains in Italy. The vigour, bright leaf-colour and display of male catkins combine to form a very desirable willow.

Salix 'Aquatica Gigantea'. *S. dasyclados* Skv., not × *dasyclados* Wimm. A large shrub or more often an elegant tree, with a curved trunk and thick arching branches; branchlets and petioles grey-green pubescent; leaves elongate-lanceolate or elliptic, entire, slightly revolute, dark green glabrous above, light green glabrous beneath showing prominent venation, mature leaves 18–20 cm long and 3–4 cm wide; stipules persistent, lanceolate, up to 1 cm long; catkins precocious, large and floriferous, staminal filaments 1.5 cm with pale yellow anthers.

Salix 'Aquatica Gigantea Korso' A male clone, displays elegant habit and has unusually large erect catkins with long silky-hairy flower scales. A good tree particularly suited to waterside habitat.

Salix arbutifolia Pall. *Chosenia arbutifolia* (Pall.) Skv.; *C. bracteosa* (Turcz.) Nak.; *S. bracteosa* Turcz.; *C. macrolepis* (Turcz.) Komar.; *S. macrolepis* Turcz., in part; *C. eucalyptoides* (Schneid) Nak.; *S. eucalyptoides* Mey. ex Schneid.

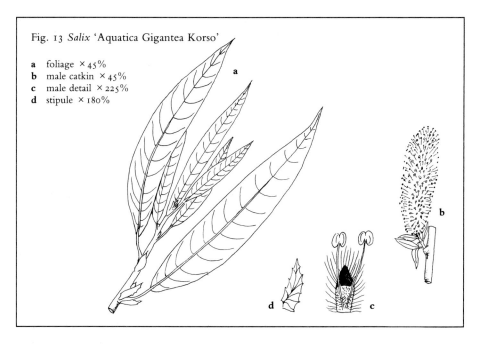

Fig. 13 *Salix* 'Aquatica Gigantea Korso'

a   foliage × 45%
b   male catkin × 45%
c   male detail × 225%
d   stipule × 180%

Originally included in genus *Chosenia*; a large tree up to 30 m (100 ft) high in its natural habitat; bark of young trees covered with a white bloom, becoming scaly with age; branchlets glabrous, often glaucous; leaves lanceolate or oblong-lanceolate 5–10 cm long, apex acuminate, base cuneate, glabrous, entire or indistinctly serrulate; petioles up to 6 mm long. Catkins coetaneous, pendulous, suspended from short leafy lateral shoots. Male catkins slender, 1.5–2.5 cm long; flower scales broad-ovate, obtuse. Five stamens, joined to the flower scale. Female catkins 5 cm long in fruit; flower scales as in male catkins, deciduous. Ovary glabrous, short-stalked; style divided to the base, each arm with two linear stigmatic lobes, deciduous in fruit. No nectaries, unlike other species (except some dwarf *Salix*) and is wind-pollinated.

Native of north-east Asia, including Japan. It has been introduced to Europe but does not thrive.

***Salix atrocinerea* Brot.:**   (see *S. cinerea* ssp. *oleifolia*)

***Salix aurita* L. 'Eared Willow'**   An extremely twiggy, many branched shrub usually under 2 m (6 ft) high. Twigs slender, dark brown, pubescent, rapidly becoming glabrous; wood of twigs with many prominent striae; leaves obovate or oblong, dark green rugose above, ashen grey below and pubescent, with prominent venation, apex rounded or shortly acute, often with a twisted tip; leaf base cuneate tapering to a short petiole 2–5 mm long; margins undulate-serrate, prominent persistent auricular stipules with undulate-serrate margins. Catkins precocious in April and May, sessile, erect, cylindrical, 1–2 cm long, 0.5–1 cm wide; short silver-haired bracts; flower scales oblong, fuscous and hairy. Male catkins with two free stamens, filaments glabrous with oblong yellow anthers; single oblong nectary truncate at apex. Female catkins longer than male, ovary narrowly flask shaped and grey-tomentose, pedicel distinct; style very short or lacking; stigmas shortly oblong, usually entire.

S. aurita is commonly present on acid heaths and moorland in the British Isles, and is widespread in central and northern Europe including Russia. It is a very hardy species, thriving in the most adverse exposed conditions. The male catkins, although small, are numerous and attractive when mature. In other respects *S. aurita* is not very ornamental but is extremely useful for populating dry, barren sites.

Salix babylonica L.   A voluminous weeping tree not usually exceeding 10 m (40 ft) high but reaching 20 m (80 ft) in optimum conditions. The furrowed trunk divides low down, producing a wide spreading flattened head of branches, from which the long slender branchlets carrying the leaves hang perpendicularly in a dense curtain. Branchlets green or brown, glabrous except at the nodes; leaves lanceolate or very narrowly elliptic, narrowly acuminate and cuneate, serrulate, 5–10 cm long, 1–1.5 cm wide, sericeous when young, becoming glabrous and light green above, glaucous beneath; stipules caducous lanceolate or ovate; catkins: only female forms under cultivation, narrow 2.5–5 cm long, appear with the leaves in April or early May; flower scales persistent, lanceolate, hairy and pale yellow; a single short nectary; ovary with very short pedicel, ovoid and glabrous, style short and thick; stigmas bilobed, spreading.

A very spectacular weeping tree. This female clone, in cultivation in Europe, west Asia and north-east Africa, is believed to have originated from northern China 300 years ago. Male clones exist in Tibet and northern India. *S. babylonica* is common in east Asia, large specimens growing along the Yangtze river. It is also present in Manchuria and Turkestan, and more recently widely cultivated in Japan. In the colder regions of Europe it is becoming rare, being susceptible to frost damage, and is now mainly superseded by *S.* × *chrysocoma* (*S. babylonica* L. × *S. alba* var. *vitellina*).

Salix babylonica 'Annularis' S. b. 'Crispa'   A small, slow-growing, stiffly erect small tree; branchlets densely covered in leaves spirally twisted with upturned margins forming rigid rings. Interesting purely as a somewhat grotesque curiosity, this willow is best placed with other contorted forms. It neither blends nor contrasts with normal species. Its exact origin is unknown.

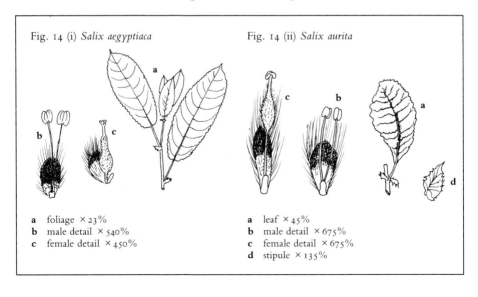

Fig. 14 (i) *Salix aegyptiaca*   Fig. 14 (ii) *Salix aurita*

a   foliage × 23%
b   male detail × 540%
c   female detail × 450%

a   leaf × 45%
b   male detail × 675%
c   female detail × 675%
d   stipule × 135%

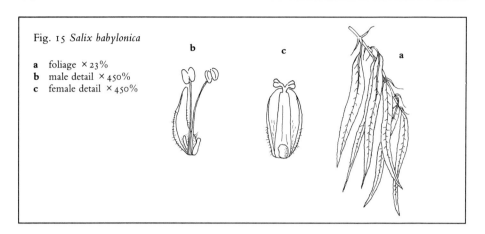

Fig. 15 *Salix babylonica*

a foliage × 23%
b male detail × 450%
c female detail × 450%

b

c

a

Salix × ***balfourii*** **Lint. (*S. caprea* L.** × ***S. lanata* L.)**   A wide, spreading, flat-topped bush 1 m (4 ft) to 3 m (10 ft) high and up to 6 m (20 ft) wide, exhibiting the characteristics of both parents. Branches and branchlets stout and rigid; branchlets and axillary buds pubescent; young leaves densely lanate; mature leaves coriaceous, ovate or elliptic, apex acute, base obtuse, sparsely pubescent becoming glabrous, reticulate and dark green above, glaucous and pubescent beneath. Catkins appear before the leaves in April. Male catkins similar to *S. caprea* with long staminal filaments and golden anthers. Originated in Scotland.
    A very fine ornamental shrub requiring plenty of space and light.

Salix bakko **Kim.**   A small tree 6 m (20 ft) to 10 m (35 ft) similar to *S. caprea*. Branches greyish-brown, pubescent, showing sapwood with longitudinal striae; petioles 1–2 cm; leaves oblong or elliptic, 5–12 cm long, 3–5 cm wide, acute, undulate-serrate, base rounded, bright green above, glaucous and densely pubescent beneath; male catkins up to 5 cm long, broad, short pedunculate, densely flowered, two stamens with free filaments with basal hairs; female catkins up to 10 cm long in fruit; ovary villous, style and stigmas short, glabrous.
    Native of Hokkaido and Honshu, Japan. The Japanese equivalent of the European *S. caprea*. *S. bakko* has larger catkins; the male form is very attractive in full bloom.

Salix × ***basfordiana*** **Scaling ex Salter (*S. alba* L. var. *vitellina*** × ***S. fragilis* L.; *S.*** × ***rubens* (Schrank.) *basfordiana* (Scaling.) Meikle.)**   A vigorous, fast-growing erect tree 10 m (35 ft) to 15 m (50 ft) high, with a relatively short trunk and spreading branches; branchlets glabrous, glossy orange-yellow, buds elongate, flattened, pale yellow; leaves pubescent at first, glabrous later, narrowly lanceolate, acuminate, 10–15 cm long, under 2 cm wide, glossy green above, glaucous below, base cuneate, margins unevenly serrate. Stipules narrow, caudate-acuminate, glandular-serrate and caducous. Catkins appear with the leaves in April and May on short leafy lateral shoots; rachis and peduncle densely pubescent. Male catkins spreading or pendulous, narrowly cylindrical, up to 10 cm long; usually two stamens, sometimes up to four; filaments free, glabrous above with basal pubescence, 3–4 mm long; anthers golden-yellow. Female catkins up to 12 cm long and pendulous; two oblong nectaries; ovary subsessile, flask-shaped tapering to narrow apex, glabrous.

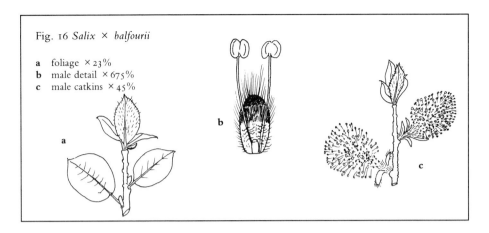

Fig. 16 *Salix × balfourii*

a foliage ×23%
b male detail ×675%
c male catkins ×45%

Originally discovered by William Scaling in 1870 in his nursery. It has become widely distributed in England, is rare in Scotland and unrecorded in Ireland.

One of the best *Salix* trees, the orange-yellow twigs giving strong colour to the whole tree during the winter. The pendulous catkins and lustrous leaves also provide beauty in the spring.

Salix bebbiana Sarg. *S. rostrata* Rich. 'Beak Willow' A shrub to 4 m (13 ft) or sometimes a tree to 9 m (30 ft) high, with short, divaricate, brown branches; branchlets pubescent becoming glabrous; leaves narrowly elliptic to oblong-lanceolate 3–10 cm long, 1.5–3 cm wide, apex acute or acuminate, base cuneate, sparsely serrate or entire, dull green above, glaucous with prominent reticulate venation beneath; young leaves pubescent on both surfaces becoming glabrous at maturity; petioles 4–12 mm long; stipules semi-cordate, deciduous; catkins subprecocious and subsessile, April to June, female catkins up to 6 cm long and 1–2 cm wide, very lax on bracted peduncles 5–20 mm long; flower scales thinly hairy, narrowly oblong, acute 1–2 mm long, pale yellow and pink-tipped;

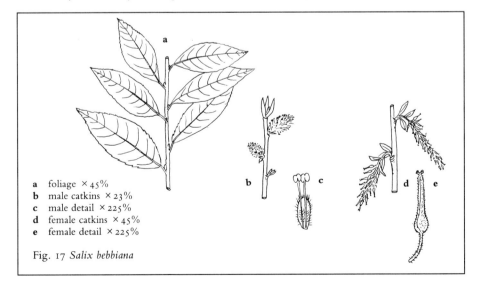

a foliage ×45%
b male catkins ×23%
c male detail ×225%
d female catkins ×45%
e female detail ×225%

Fig. 17 *Salix bebbiana*

male catkins up to 3 cm long, two stamens; filaments 1 cm long, free, with basal hairs; capsules lanceolate-rostrate (long-beaked) 6–10 mm long, pubescent; pedicels slender 3–6 mm long, finely pubescent; styles 0.1–0.2 mm long; stigmas 0.1–0.3 mm long, entire to divided.

Widespread in North America from Newfoundland to Alaska, south to New Jersey, South Dakota and in the west to New Mexico and California. It is also found across the Bering Straits to far eastern Russia and Siberia.

Salix bebbiana **Sarg. var. *perrostrata*** **(Rydb.) Schneid.**   Branchlets glabrescent; leaves glabrescent, smaller and thinner. Distributed from Nebraska to Colorado, New Mexico and Utah.

Salix bebbiana **Sarg. var. *capreifolia*** **Fern.**   Branchlets stout, densely and persistently grey-tomentose; leaves ovate or obovate, grey pubescent beneath.

Native of Newfoundland, Nova Scotia and adjacent Quebec.

Salix bebbiana **Sarg. var. *luxurians*** **Fern.**   A tree up to 6 m (20 ft) high; leaves up to 10 cm long, less rugose to plane; capsules to 10–12 mm long; pedicels 6–9 mm long.

Restricted to the Gaspé Peninsula, Quebec.

Salix bicolor **Hort:**   (see *S. schraderiana* Willd.)

Salix × ***blanda*** **Anderss. (*S. babylonica* L.** × ***S. fragilis* L.) 'Wisconsin Weeping Willow' or 'Niobe Willow'**   A weeping umbraculiform tree up to 12 m (40 ft) high, with a wide, open crown and short pendulous or semi-pendulous brown branches; branchlets dull green and brittle; leaves lanceolate 6–15 cm long, 1.5–2.5 cm wide, long acuminate, serrate, cuneate, very dark glossy green above, glabrous glaucous blue beneath; petiole pink 5–15 mm long; stipules ovate-acuminate, caducous; catkins slender 2–3 cm long; two stamens, with glabrous filaments pubescent at their base; ovaries short-stalked, style short, stigma emarginate.

A good ornamental tree, requiring adequate space. Very hardy, with no tendency to die-back. It is totally different from *S.* × *elegantissima*, another excellent weeping tree which is also a clone of the same parentage.

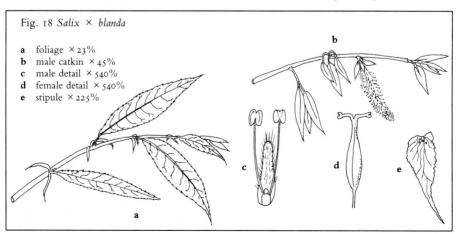

Fig. 18 *Salix* × *blanda*

a   foliage × 23%
b   male catkin × 45%
c   male detail × 540%
d   female detail × 540%
e   stipule × 225%

Salix bonplandiana Schneid.   A large subtropical tree related to *S. humboldtiana*; bud scales with free overlapping margins; leaves mostly lance-linear or lanceolate to lance-ovate, stomata absent on the upper surface; catkins elongate, cylindrical and pendulous; stamens usually three to eight, sometimes up to 12; flower scales deciduous in fruit.

A native of South America and southern North America; it is not hardy in cold temperate regions.

Salix 'Bowles' hybrid' (*S. viminalis* hybrid)   A tall, very fast-growing, vertically ascending shrub or small tree up to 12 m (40 ft) high. When coppiced in fertile soil will produce 5 m (15 ft) rods in one year's growth. If left unpruned, the main stems tend to remain unbranched forming a narrow, very flexible, vertical tree. Leaves longer than pure *S. viminalis* L.; mature leaves up to 24 cm long and 2–3.5 cm wide, lanceolate, apex attenuate-acuminate, base obtuse or cuneate, glabrous, glossy dark green above, sericeous and densely pubescent beneath, leaf margins undulate and irregularly crenate.

A strikingly erect tree if left unpruned, occupying very little ground space. Useful in windbreaks.

Salix buergeriana Miq.   A small tree up to 6 m (20 ft) high, branchlets white-pubescent becoming glabrous; leaves oblong, obovate or widely elliptic, apex acute, base acute or obtuse, margins undulate-serrate, white or brown villous becoming glabrous above, glaucous beneath; slender male catkins 5–8 cm long, short-pedunculate, staminal filaments with basal hairs; female catkins 3–4 cm long (up to 10 cm long in fruit); ovary pubescent, style elongate, stigma cleft.

An ornamental native of Kyushu, Japan.

Salix × calliantha Kern. (*S. purpurea* L. × *S. daphnoides* Vill.)   An erect small tree or loose-limbed tall shrub up to 6 m (20 ft) high; branches glabrous light green, very tough and flexible, yellow beneath the bark; conspicuous large yellow buds; leaves lanceolate or oblanceolate, apex acute, base cuneate, 5–10 cm long, crenate, pubescent becoming glabrous when mature, glossy dark green above, glaucous blue-green beneath; stipules small and caducous, petioles 1 cm long; catkins precocious, 2–4 cm long, flower scales obovate, pubescent, apex black; two stamens, with filaments connate at the base; ovary pubescent and subsessile.

An extremely hardy hybrid of more interest to the collector than for its ornamental value. Hereditary influences from both parents are well-defined, but without the pruinose bloom of *S. daphnoides*.

Salix × calodendron Wimm. (*S. cinerea* L. ssp. *oleifolia* Macreight × *S. caprea* L. × *S. viminalis* L.)   An erect tall shrub or tree, occasionally up to 12 m (40 ft), although usually about 6 m (20 ft) high, resembling *S. viminalis* L. in habit, with erect branching and a narrow crown. Branchlets densely and persistently tomentose, becoming dark brown in their second year, sapwood exhibiting prominent longitudinal striae; buds prominently ovoid, densely pubescent, dark brown; leaves oblong-elliptic, acute or shortly acuminate, base rounded, approximately 15 cm long, 3–5 cm wide, sometimes larger, dull green and sparsely pubescent above, densely pubescent ash-grey with prominent venation beneath, leaf margins narrowly recurved; stipules conspicuous, auricular, acuminate, glandular and denticulate; catkins appear in March or early April before the leaves, crowded towards the ends of the branchlets as in *S. viminalis* L., cylindric, elongate and subsessile, 4–8 cm long; leafy bracts silky pubescent; style long, stigma thick and shorter than the style. Only the female is known. It occurs in the wild sporadically throughout Britain and is widely cultivated in Europe and Scandinavia.

This hybrid, represented by a single clone exhibiting characteristics of all three parents, is an interesting and ornamental large-leafed shrub.

Salix canariensis Ch. Sm. A shrub with stiffly ascending and spreading branches up to 4 m (13 ft) high; branchlets thick, purple, glabrous and markedly pruinose; leaves 5–10 cm long, up to 1 cm wide, narrowly lanceolate or narrow-elliptic, remotely serrate, acuminate, base rounded or cuneate, glabrous, glossy and dark green above, glabrous and glaucous blue beneath; stipules small or absent; petioles green 0.5–1 cm long; catkin bud scales glossy, bright red; catkins erect, cylindrical and thick, up to 4 cm long and 1 cm thick, spaced out along the branchlets; male catkins – staminal filaments glabrous, anthers dark orange becoming yellow.

S. canariensis is closely related to the North American *S. irrorata*, which is a looser, more bushy shrub with more slender branchlets, slightly broader, thinner leaves, and with smaller catkins concentrated towards the ends of the branchlets.

Native of the Canary Islands and Madeira, it is frost-hardy in spite of its origin. A very attractive species throughout the year with its dark-purple branchlets and pruinose white bloom.

Most often a medium-sized shrub suitable for all but the smallest garden.

Salix cantabrica Rech. A many-branched, widely arching shrub 3–5 m (10–15 ft) high; branchlets covered with dense shining pubescence, becoming glabrous later, peeled wood revealing striae; leaves broadly lanceolate or lanceolate-elliptic, apex acute, base rounded or acute, leaf margins entire or partially serrate, lamina with an indumentum of silky appressed hairs on both surfaces, denser beneath, midrib and venation prominent beneath; petiole short; stipules persistent, lanceolate and acute; catkins – only female flowers are known. Ovary silky-tomentose; pedicel shorter than bract.

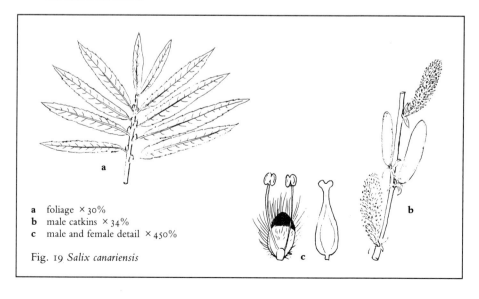

a   foliage × 30%
b   male catkins × 34%
c   male and female detail × 450%

Fig. 19 *Salix canariensis*

Found along the Cordilleran mountain rivers of Sierra Cantabrica in northern Spain.

An extremely ornamental, widely spreading shrub with a very beautiful silver/ white luminous quality.

Salix capensis Thunb.   A medium sized tree 6–15 m (20–50 ft) high with long pendulous branches and branchlets; leaves, in common with other South African *Salix* species, are dimorphic, two types being produced at different seasons. The earliest (spring) leaves, which are very small and entire, similar to the leaf bracts below catkins on flowering branchlets, also occur on the vegetative shoots. The spring leaves are caducous, falling off as the larger, mostly serrate or serrulate summer leaves develop. The summer leaves of *S. capensis* Thunb. are oblong-linear, 6–10 cm long, 2–4 mm wide, apex acuminate, base cuneate, regularly serrate or serrulate dark green, glabrous and glossy above, paler glabrous green beneath; catkins develop on leafy lateral branches, male anthers golden-yellow.

Distributed throughout the Orange River basin in the Cape, South Africa, and extends northwards to the headwaters of the Vaal River in the Transvaal.

A very fine tree with ornamental habit and foliage. Not hardy in cold western temperate conditions.

Salix capensis Thunb. var. gariepina Anderss., p.p. (S. gariepina 'Burch' in Herb.)   A very similar tree to *S. capensis* Thunb., with long pendulous branchlets, differing in the leaves which are shorter and wider, 5–8 cm long, 4–6 mm wide, elliptic-lanceolate.

This variety is mainly found concentrated in the Vaal River basin, South Africa.

Salix caprea L. 'Goat Willow' or 'Great Sallow'   A small tree with grey fissured trunk, average 6 m (20 ft), exceptionally to 9 m (30 ft) high, with spreading branches forming a wide head; branchlets thick, pubescent, becoming glabrous reddish-brown or yellow/green within the first year; wood of peeled branchlets devoid of striae. Buds ovoid, rounded, the bud scale becoming glossy chestnut-brown. Catkin buds prominent and often red-tinged. The leaves are the biggest of all British sallows, broadly elliptic or obovate, length one-and-a-half times the width, similar to those of apple trees, puberulent dull green above, and greyish tomentose with prominent reticulate venation beneath; leaf base rounded or cordate, apex shortly acute; leaf margins undulate glandular-serrate; petioles 1–3 cm long; stipules auricular, acute, with undulate-serrate margins, usually deciduous; catkins precocious, on bare stems in March, ovoid, erect, up to 3 cm long and 2 cm wide; flower scales ovate, acute, black-tipped with a thick covering of sericeous hairs; female flowers with a silvery sericeous tapering ovary supported by a prominent pedicel; male flowers with two long stamens, glabrous filaments to 1 cm long and golden anthers; a single oblong nectary.

Hybridization between *S. caprea* and *S. cinerea* species is very common. *S. caprea* is generally easily distinguished from the numerous intermediate stages that can occur when these are found growing together in the wild; the colour of its year-old branchlets, which are relatively thicker, are characteristic features of the 'Goat Willow'.

S. caprea tolerates dry soils, often growing on the outskirts of woods and hedgerows throughout the British Isles, and in the lowlands of Europe and central Asia. Closely related species (*S. bakko* and *S. akame*) are natives of Japan and China. Several male clones are cultivated in Europe. Two good examples are

S. *caprea* 'Atlas', very floriferous with a wide spreading head and smooth silver/grey trunk, and S. *caprea* 'Silberglans', also floriferous with a narrower crown.

A group of S. *caprea* trees provides a magnificent display of gold and silver catkins in the very early spring, when all else is dark and leafless.

Salix caprea L. var. sphacelata (Sm) Wahlenb. S. coaetanea Hartm. A small shrub, or occasionally a small tree up to 9 m (30 ft) high; twigs pubescent, becoming glabrous and dull brown; buds darker red than S. *caprea* var. *caprea* and more puberulent; leaves variable, tending to be narrowly obovate-elliptic, sometimes broad, densely sericeous on both surfaces at first, becoming glabrous above, remaining sericeous below later; leaf base cuneate, apex acute, margins entire or nearly so; exstipulate or stipules soon lost; coetaneous, catkins with the leaves in May and June; female catkins pedunculate with a densely pubescent peduncle and prominent bracts, but otherwise similar to S. *caprea* var. *caprea*; male catkins usually smaller and more scattered than those of a typical 'Goat Willow'. A distinct variety with its sericeous, entire, exstipulate leaves.

Variety *sphacelata* generally replaces S. *caprea* pure species at high altitudes in the Scottish Highlands, Scandinavia, Russia and the European Alps.

Salix × capreola Kern. (S. caprea L. × S. aurita L.) A small tree 3–6 m (10–20 ft) high, with thick, somewhat gnarled dark-grey branchlets. Leaves 6–8 cm long, 3–4 cm wide, ovate, obovate or elliptic, coarsely undulate-serrate, coriaceous, with impressed venation and prominent persistent auricular stipules.

An extremely hardy sallow hybrid of no particular ornamental value.

Salix caroliniana Michx. 'Carolina Willow' or 'Ward's Willow' A large shrub or tree to 12 m (40 ft) high or more; branchlets, bud scales and short petioles yellowish to dark brown, densely white-pubescent at first; stipules 6–12 mm long, broadly reniform, acute, serrulate, glaucous. Leaves linear-lanceolate to

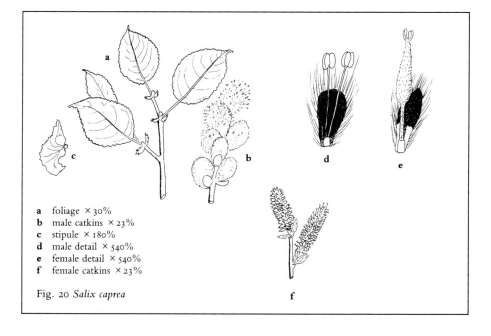

a foliage × 30%
b male catkins × 23%
c stipule × 180%
d male detail × 540%
e female detail × 540%
f female catkins × 23%

Fig. 20 *Salix caprea*

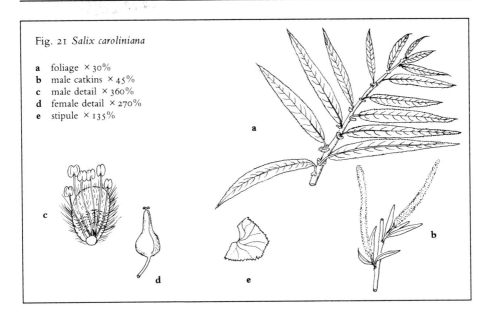

Fig. 21 *Salix caroliniana*

a foliage × 30%
b male catkins × 45%
c male detail × 360%
d female detail × 270%
e stipule × 135%

lanceolate 8–15 cm long, 1–3 cm wide, attenuate-acuminate, closely shallowly serrulate, base rounded, dark green above, densely glaucous and often slightly pubescent beneath, especially on the midrib; catkins coetaneous in April and May, 3–10 cm long, 8–15 mm wide, lax, on leafy penduncles; flower scales obovate, yellowish, villous, deciduous; four to eight stamens; filaments free, pubescent at base. Ovaries 3–5 mm long, narrowly ovoid-lanceolate, glabrous; pedicels 1.5–4 mm long; styles 0.1–0.2 mm long, entire; stigmas minute.

A North American species found in rocky soil along the Potomac and Ohio River valleys to Pittsburgh, and south to Indiana, Montana, north-east to Kansas and south to the Gulf and south-west Texas; also in Cuba.

A handsome tree with foliage strongly glaucous blue beneath and long pendulous catkins.

Salix caspica Pall.   A large shrub or small tree with grey, smooth branches and long tapering grey or light-brown branchlets becoming pale yellowish-white, glabrous and glossy. Leaves 5–12 cm long, 0.5–0.75 cm wide, narrowly linear-lanceolate, acuminate, strict, margins entire, glabrous and blue/green above and glaucous beneath when mature; venation prominent beneath; stipules small or absent; petioles 2–5 mm pale green; catkins 2.5 cm long; ovary sericeous becoming glabrous, subsessile or shortly pedicellate.

A native of Russia in Georgia, and Kazakh north and east of the Caspian Sea, and in west and central Asia. Present in a few British collections.

A very ornamental willow with beautiful linear blue/green foliage, ideal for a waterside situation.

Salix chaenomeloides Kimura, Salix glandulosa (Seem.), Akame-Yanagi
A large, vigorous arching shrub or tree with long smooth green branches spreading laterally over a wide area from the base, and some ascending vertically. Branchlets finely hairy, becoming glabrous brown or yellowish, slender; leaves narrowly elliptic, oblong or obovate 5–12 cm long, 1.5–5 cm wide, apex short-

acuminate or acute, base acute, margins serrate with sharp incurved teeth, young leaves reddish-brown above and sericeous with very fine hairs on both surfaces, mature leaves becoming glabrous dark bluish-green above, remaining finely sericeous beneath; lateral nerves numerous (18–22 pairs) and prominent on both surfaces; stipules lanceolate, acute and persistent; petioles pubescent pink 5–12 mm long with a small discoid gland near the apex in each side; catkin buds prominent, covered by a purplish-pink bud scale; male catkins 2.5–6 cm long, silky-hairy, silver tinged with pink at first, loosely flowered with glabrous staminal filaments, anthers dark orange becoming yellow; female catkins 2.5–4 cm long, up to 10 cm long in fruit; flower scales 1.5 mm long, pubescent; styles very short; stigma bifid; capsules 3–5 mm long, ovoid and glabrous.

A Japanese native growing in Honshu, Shikoku and Kyushu; also present in Korea and China.

An exceedingly ornamental willow, requiring considerable space; allow at least a 5 m (15 ft) radius from its base when planted in fertile soil.

The vigorous habit, attractive foliage, colourful catkin buds, and attractive catkins all contribute towards making this one of the most desirable large shrubs.

Salix cathayana Diels.   A shrub to 4 m (13 ft) high, with pubescent branchlets; leaves oblong or narrow-elliptic, obtuse or acute, entire or minutely glandular-serrulate, glaucous and slightly pubescent on the midrib beneath, or overall silky; scales hairy, style short, distinct.

A native of western China, related to *S. hypoleuca*.

Salix chilensis Molina.   A very erect, slender, flexible, smooth-barked, medium-sized tree, up to 12 m (40 ft) or more high, with a narrow crown of very slender ascending pale-yellow branchlets. When in leaf the crown becomes pendulous. Leaves 5–10 cm long, 1–1.5 cm wide, lanceolate, narrowly acuminate, cuneate, margins regularly serrulate, both laminal surfaces covered with minute silver sericeous hairs, pale green above, glaucous below; stipules absent or small and early caducous.

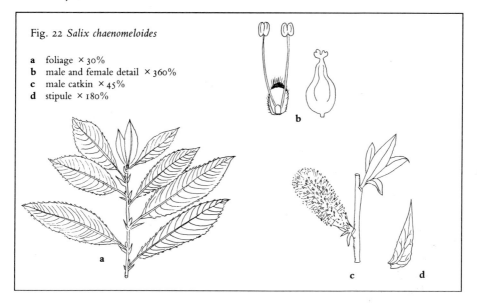

Fig. 22 *Salix chaenomeloides*

a foliage × 30%
b male and female detail × 360%
c male catkin × 45%
d stipule × 180%

This species may possibly be related to *S. humboldtiana* (although this is doubted by Schneider and R. D. Dorn). It is possibly a *S. humboldtiana* hybrid with *S. alba*, with a preponderence of *S. alba* characteristics. *S. alba* was imported from Europe to the Argentine early in this century. The leaves of *S. chilensis* are very similar to those of *S. alba*.

A graceful silvery-leaved tree bearing few lower branches, permitting planting reasonably close to other shrubs.

Salix × chrysocoma Dode (*S. alba* L. var. *vitellina* × *S. babylonica* L.) *alba* var. *vitellina pendula* (Spath.) Rehd.; *S.* × *sepulcralis* Simonkai var. *chrysocoma* (Dode) Meikle; *alba tristis*; Hort. 'Golden Weeping Willow'
A large tree with thick main branches rising at an angle of 45–50 degrees, bearing long pendulous tapering branchlets, often sweeping the soil below; branchlets golden/yellow and silky pubescent, turning greyish and glabrous during their second year; leaves narrow-lanceolate to narrow-elliptic, apex attenuate-acuminate, 8–11 cm long, 1–1.5 cm wide, serrulate and finely silky on both sides at first, becoming glabrous above, glaucous and sparsely pubescent beneath; petioles up to 9 mm long, pubescent; catkins coetaneous in early spring 3.5–5 cm long, slender, on leafy stems; both sexes occur on the same, separate branchlets, or are androgynous with the female flowers at the apex of the catkin; bisexual flowers may also occur. Flower scales lanceolate, hairy towards their base, hairs on scales and rachis longer in male flowers. Ovaries glabrous; style short.

The commonest weeping willow in many parks and large gardens. A very graceful tree, at its best beside water. It thrives particularly well during long, hot, dry summers. Although its young shoots can suffer some damage from late spring frosts it is not nearly so susceptible as *S. babylonica*, which is rapidly being replaced by *S.* × *chrysocoma* throughout the colder regions of Europe.

Salix cinerea L. ssp. *cinerea* 'Grey Sallow'   A branching shrub 3–6 m (10–20 ft) high or occasionally more; branchlets densely pubescent often for the first two years; wood with prominent striae; leaves obovate or oblong with undulate-

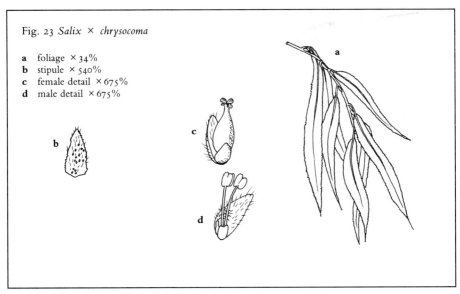

Fig. 23 *Salix × chrysocoma*

a   foliage × 34%
b   stipule × 540%
c   female detail × 675%
d   male detail × 675%

serrate margins; lamina drab green and shortly pubescent above, densely pubescent below, becoming less pubescent and grey later; stipules broadly auricular, big and persistent. Catkins precocious, appearing in March and April, erect, sessile becoming shortly pedunculate, narrowly ovoid 2–3 cm long, 0.5–1 cm wide; bracts short and pubescent; flower scales dark brown, oblong, acute and densely hairy. Male catkins with two free stamens, filaments glabrous 5–8 mm long, anthers oblong and yellow; nectary oblong. Female catkins smaller; ovary flask-shaped, pubescent; pedicel usually longer than the nectary; stigmas oblong, erect or spreading, sub-entire or double cleft.

The distribution in Great Britain is localized mainly to the fens and marshes in Norfolk, Suffolk, and Lincolnshire. Moving further to the west of England it tends to hybridize with, or to be replaced by *S. cinerea* ssp. *oleifolia*. The subspecies *cinerea* occurs widely in Europe, extending as far east as Siberia.

Salix cinerea L. ssp. *oleifolia* Macreight. (*S. atrocinerea* Brot.) 'Rusty Sallow'

A taller shrub than *S. cinerea* L. ssp. *cinerea*, and often forms a small tree 6–9 m (20–30 ft) high, with a fissured trunk. Branchlets become glabrous, dark reddish-brown; wood exhibits only faint striae; leaves oblong or oblanceolate, often entire and slightly undulate-serrate; lamina shining dark green above, brownish-grey below, with an indumentum of rusty hair and tiny black glands; the rusty colouration is most noticeable in shoots during the early autumn; stipules small and caducous; catkins identical to ssp. *cinerea*.

S. cinerea ssp. *oleifolia* is by far the most common willow in hedgerows and marshes throughout the British Isles, except in East Anglia and Norfolk, where ssp. *cinerea* tends to predominate.

Salix cinerea 'Tricolour'
Salix cinerea 'Variegata' } (see p. 31)

Salix coactilis Fern.

A large shrub up to 6 m (20 ft) high, with arching branches; branchlets puberulent and yellow tinged at first, becoming glabrous and grey; leaves narrow to broadly elliptic-lanceolate, or occasionally ovate-lanceolate or oblanceolate, 5–14 cm long, 2–4 cm wide, acuminate, serrate to dentate, base acute or rounded, dark green and glabrous above, glaucescent and densely sericeous beneath; stipules semi-ovate 6–12 mm long, acuminate; petioles slender 6–20 mm long, puberulent; catkins coetaneous in May, up to 5 cm long and 7–8 mm wide on leafy stalks up to 15 mm long; flower scales obovate, obtuse, hairy and blackish; two stamens, with glabrous, free filaments. Capsules lanceolate and blunt 5 mm long, pubescent; pedicels up to 1.5 mm long, pubescent; styles entire 0.3–0.6 mm long, stigmas entire or divided; nectary short.

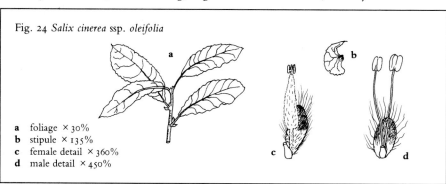

Fig. 24 *Salix cinerea* ssp. *oleifolia*

a   foliage × 30%
b   stipule × 135%
c   female detail × 360%
d   male detail × 450%

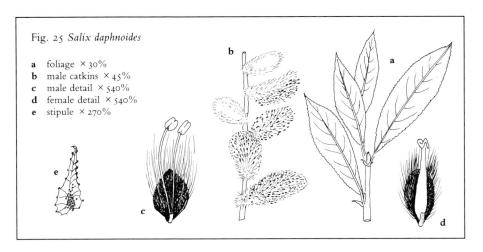

Fig. 25 *Salix daphnoides*

a foliage × 30%
b male catkins × 45%
c male detail × 540%
d female detail × 540%
e stipule × 270%

Native of swamps and river banks in north-eastern North America, and closely related to *S. sericea*.

An elegant shrub with attractive arching form. Requires ample space, thriving in damp silt.

***Salix coaetanea* Hartm.:**   (see *S. caprea* var. *sphacelata*)

***Salix* 'Coriacea' (*S. myrsinifolia* Sal. × *S. aurita* L.)**   A small slow-growing, somewhat gnarled, sallow hybrid with thick, dark, coriaceous leaves, exhibiting characteristics of both parents.

Of botanical interest for inclusion in a group of sallows in a Salictum.

***Salix daltoniana* Anderss.**   A shrub up to 3 m (10 ft), or sometimes a small erect tree to 5 m (16 ft) high; branchlets dark brown and glabrous; young leaves densely silky-pubescent beneath, mature leaves large, 7–10 cm long oblong to narrow-elliptic, glabrous or sparsely hairy above, densely brown-hairy beneath, leaf margins finely dentate; catkins precocious or coetaneous in May or June, male catkins slender, 3.5–6 cm long, brownish-green; scales spathulate, lanate; staminal filaments hairy; female catkins axillary, up to 12 cm in fruit.

A native of central Nepal extending to Arunachal Pradesh, most concentrated on stream banks and open slopes in the lower alpine zone.

***Salix daphnoides* Vill. 'Violet Willow'**   A tall erect tree varying in height from 9 m (30 ft) to 18 m (60 ft). Male trees tend to form a broad spreading crown, the females being usually columnar and taller. The trunk is generally smooth outside and yellow inside. Main branches arise at a fairly acute angle; branchlets are erect or outspread, slightly downy when young, becoming glabrous and dark shining purple with a bluish-white pruinose bloom; leaves thick-textured 5–10 cm long, three to four times as long as wide, oblong-lanceolate, or oblong-ovate, acute or acuminate, glandular-serrulate, soon glabrous, dark, shining green above, glaucous beneath; lateral veins 8–12 pairs; stipules large, semi-cordate; petiole 2–4 mm; catkins 3–4 cm long, precocious, flowering very early, subsessile, erect, cylindrical, densely silky-hairy, flower scales blackish at apex, obovate; two stamens, filaments glabrous, anthers golden-yellow; ovary ovoid-conical, glabrous, subsessile; style long and slender.

S. daphnoides cannot be considered to be indigenous in Great Britain, although scattered specimens exist in isolated areas in northern England. Originally a native of Norway and Sweden, it has been widely planted particularly in central and eastern Europe and in central Asia. It occurs in the Pyrenees, Alps, Apennines, Yugoslavia and Poland, extending east to the Urals. In spite of its distribution, it has rarely become naturalized.

It is undoubtedly one of the finest, most hardy and least demanding of all ornamental *Salix* species.

Salix daphnoides Vill. 'Aglaia' (*S.d.* 'Latifolia') An extremely attractive male clone; vigorous, many branched with red, glossy, less pruinose branchlets; leaves wider, glabrous and non-glaucous beneath; petioles 0.5–1.5 cm long; stipules ovate, serrate 2–3 mm long.

Salix daphnoides Vill. 'Continental Purple' An outstandingly ornamental male clone with widely spreading branches and a tendency for the main limbs to leave the trunk near ground level. Branchlets glossy, dark red; leaves strongly glaucous blue beneath; catkins very prolific arising from fat, ovoid, pointed buds, with bud scales coloured bright red towards the apex and yellow at the base before finally blackening and being discarded apically by the developing catkin within.

A specimen tree of great merit requiring ample space.

Salix daphnoides Vill. 'Pulchra ruberrima' A clone with very long, shining, dark-red young stems shown to the best advantage following coppicing; catkins pink-tinged.

Salix daphnoides Vill. 'Oxford Violet' A less vigorous clone with glabrous, green pruinose branchlets.

Salix daphnoides Vill. (Willd.) ssp. *pomeranica* Koch. A many-branched shrub with narrowly lanceolate leaves up to 12 cm long. Catkins up to 8 cm long.

Salix × dasyclados Wimm. (*S. caprea* × *Salix cinerea* × *S. viminalis*) A large vigorous shrub or small tree 3–6 m (10–20 ft) high; branchlets thick, yellowish-green, densely tomentose during their first two years, with striae on peeled wood; winter buds pubescent; leaves lanceolate, widest across the middle, 10–20 cm long and approximately six times their width, apex acute or shortly acuminate, base cuneate, margins crenate, lamina dark green and sparsely pubescent or glabrous above, densely grey lanate-pubescent beneath; stipules large, elongate-lanceolate; petioles pale green 0.5–2 cm long; catkins precocious, appearing on bare stems in March or April, 5–6 cm long; nectaries long and narrow, ovary up to 6 mm long, conical and tomentose, style long, stigma thick.

Salix × dasyclados Wimm. 'Grandis' A large, fast-growing, erect tree 6–12 m (20–40 ft) high with a shallow-fissured trunk; branches ascending steeply with thick, twiggy, branchlets. Leaves and all other organs identical to *S. dasyclados* Wimm.

Salix × dasyclados Wimm. 'Angustifolia' Differs only from the shrub form *S. × dasyclados* Wimm., in possessing narrower, more acuminate leaves.

S. × dasyclados is generally believed to be derived from the same parents as *S. × calodendron*. Although both clones embody certain features found in their parents they differ in many respects. Furthermore, *S. × calodendron* is only represented by a single female clone, whereas various clones of *S. × dasyclados* are either male or female.

Present in various biomass collections of *Salix*, it also occurs naturally in Poland and Russia. *S.* × *dasyclados* is not particularly ornamental, and can be included in a group of sallows.

Salix denticulata Anderss. = *S. elegans* Wallich. ex Anderss.   A shrub up to 3 m (10 ft), or a small tree up to 6 m (20 ft) high; branchlets glabrous dark brown; young leaves puberulent beneath at first; mature leaves 4–6 cm long, narrow-elliptic, glabrous and bright green above, glabrous and glaucous or pale green beneath, margins finely dentate; catkins coetaneous, between March and May on short leafy shoots; male catkins 4 cm long with ovate, truncate scales hairy on the upper surface; female catkins green, slender and flexuous 2–5 cm long, 4 mm wide, scales truncate; rachis hairy. Fruiting catkins up to 8 cm long; capsules 3 mm long, glabrous.

Common in forests and on open slopes from Afghanistan to central Nepal.

Salix discolor Muhl. 'American Pussy Willow'   A shrub with few main branches, or a small tree up to 8 m (26 ft) high. Branchlets stout, reddish to dark brown, pubescent becoming glabrous; buds prominent up to 10 mm long; leaves 5–12 cm long, 2–4 cm wide, mostly elliptic or obovate, sub-entire to undulate-crenate, apex acute, base acute to rounded, dark glossy green above, glaucous bluish-white with prominent venation beneath. Catkins precocious, flowering in March and April, sessile, bractless and stout; male catkins cylindrical 2.5–10 cm long and up to 2.5 cm thick; two stamens, with long glabrous filaments and bright-yellow anthers. Female catkins up to 10 cm long in fruit; ovary beaked, hairy, with a distinct style.

Indigenous in eastern states of North America and in Canada, it was introduced to Great Britain in 1811.

A very ornamental species with its striking reddish branchlets, conspicuously glaucous undersurface of the leaves and showy male anthers.

Salix drummondiana Barratt ex Hook.   A dense, many-branched shrub 1–5 m (3–16 ft) high; with dark-brown branchlets becoming greenish-yellow in their second year, glabrous or puberulent at first, becoming glossy and variably pruinose; leaves entire, margins slightly revolute, with persistent dense sericeous tomentum

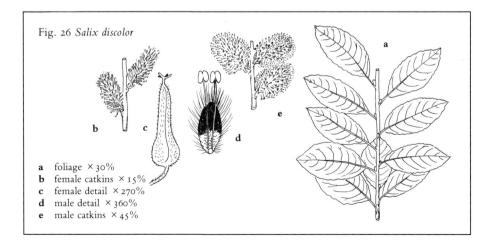

Fig. 26 *Salix discolor*

a   foliage × 30%
b   female catkins × 15%
c   female detail × 270%
d   male detail × 360%
e   male catkins × 45%

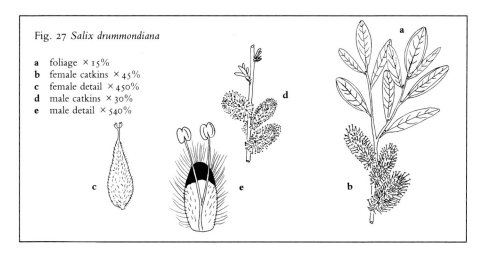

Fig. 27 *Salix drummondiana*

a   foliage × 15%
b   female catkins × 45%
c   female detail × 450%
d   male catkins × 30%
e   male detail × 540%

beneath, sparsely puberulent and soon glabrous above, narrowly or sometimes broadly elliptic or oblanceolate, 5–15 cm long, 1.5–4 cm wide; stipules narrow, small and caducous or larger and persistent on vigorous young shoots; catkins precocious to coetaneous, sessile and bractless; flower scales brown and hairy; male catkins 2.5–4 cm long, 1.5 cm thick; two stamens, filaments glabrous and often connate near the base; female catkins smaller, 2–6 cm in fruit; ovary pubescent, long, nearly sessile; style sometimes cleft above; stigmas often undivided.

Native of north-eastern North America and Canada, growing on stream banks and marshes in the Rocky Mountains, sometimes on mountain slopes.

An interesting, glossy and sometimes pruinose-stemmed species.

Salix × ehrhartiana Sm. (S. alba L. × S. pentandra L.)   A smaller tree than either parent, generally not exceeding 9 m (30 ft) high, conical or pyramidal and compact with numerous short glossy dark-brown branchlets. Leaves oblanceolate or lanceolate, serrulate, apex narrowly acuminate, base rounded or acute, young leaves sericeous, mature leaves dark glossy green with a prominent midrib above, pale green glabrous beneath; bud scale glossy dark brown; petioles pale green, glabrous 3–9 mm long; catkins appearing with the leaves in April or early May; male catkins shortly cylindrical 2–3 cm long, 1–1.5 cm thick, densely flowered; usually four stamens, with free glabrous filaments hairy towards the base; anthers golden.

A handsome tree with compact habit, dark glossy foliage and a prolific display of golden male catkins. Found in Europe, including the British Isles.

Salix elaeagnos Scop. (S. incana Schrank.) 'Hoary Willow'   A tall shrub, or occasionally a small tree up to 9 m (30 ft) high, with long, spreading, erect and graceful arching branches. Branchlets slender, grey-pubescent becoming glabrous and shining dark brown; leaves long and linear, 8–20 cm long, apex and base acute, margins involuted, serrulate particularly near the apex, young leaves grey pubescent, later glabrous dark green above, white tomentose beneath, autumn colour dark yellow; exstipulate; petioles 3–6 cm long; catkins small cylindrical, pointing outward on short leafy stems, flower scales ovate; two stamens, filaments partly connate; ovary glabrous, stalked style elongate.

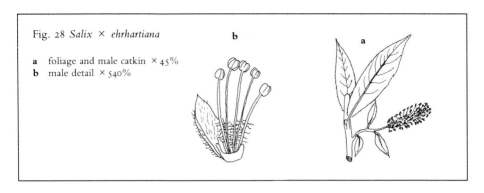

Fig. 28 *Salix* × *ehrhartiana*

a foliage and male catkin × 45%
b male detail × 540%

A native of southern and central Europe, and Asia Minor. Introduced to Great Britain in 1820 and widely planted for decorative effect.

A very graceful species, placed to the best advantage beside water, the underside of the fine linear leaves gleaming like quicksilver.

Salix elaeagnos 'Angustifolia'. *S. lavandulifolia* Koch. var. *rosmarinifolia* Hort. not L.   A shrub up to 3 m (10 ft) high, with closely upright shoots; leaves 6–12 cm long and only 3–5 mm wide, margins involuted. This variety should not be confused with the upright dwarf species *S. rosemarinifolia* L.

Salix elbursensis Boiss.   A vigorous large shrub of loose habit with long, graceful, slender, spreading branches. Older branches greyish-brown; branchlets long, arching, smoothly tapered, glabrous, glossy, dark red becoming uniformly dark shining purple in the autumn; leaves oblanceolate, oblong or narrowly elliptic, margins entire or serrate towards the apex, apex shortly and sharply acuminate, base cuneate or slightly rounded; young leaves pink-tinged; mature leaves – length six times the width, glabrous dark green above with a prominent white

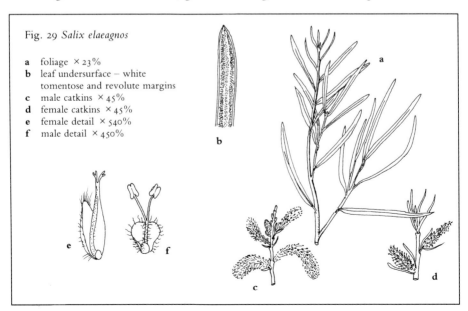

Fig. 29 *Salix elaeagnos*

a foliage × 23%
b leaf undersurface – white tomentose and revolute margins
c male catkins × 45%
d female catkins × 45%
e female detail × 540%
f male detail × 450%

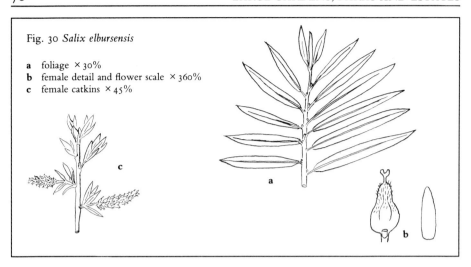

Fig. 30 *Salix elbursensis*

a foliage × 30%
b female detail and flower scale × 360%
c female catkins × 45%

midrib, glaucous and glabrous beneath; petioles purple and short, 2–5 mm long. *S. elbursensis* differs from *S. purpurea* L. in having smaller catkin buds, longer-stalked catkins, female catkin scales green or brownish and sparsely hairy.

Native of the Caucasus, Iran and eastern Anatolia, it replaces *S. purpurea* in these regions. It was introduced into Great Britain in 1972 by Roy Lancaster.

An outstandingly beautiful species in its habit, foliage and particularly in the colour of its young stems. It is also extremely hardy, tolerating hot, dry conditions.

Salix × elegantissima K. Koch. (*S. babylonica* L. × *S. fragilis* L.) 'Thurlow Weeping Willow'   A widely pyramidal weeping tree with a narrowly conical crown up to 15 m (50 ft) high; bark coarsely fissured; branches long and arching, bearing many long pendulous glossy brown branchlets; leaves 8–12 cm long, 1–2 cm wide, lanceolate, apex slender and tapering, base broadly cuneate, margins distinctly and irregularly glandular-serrate; lamina dark lustrous green above, paler and glaucous beneath; petioles 1–1.5 cm long; stipules ovate-acuminate, glandular-serrate and caducous. Catkins coetaneous, terminal on short leafy lateral shoots in April; female catkins often abnormal and androgynous, about 3 cm long and 0.5 cm thick, cylindrical and caudate, densely-flowered, flower scales uniformly pale yellow; ovary short-stalked, pubescent at the base, style short, stigma parted and outspread; either one or two nectaries; male catkins up to 5 cm long, narrowly cylindrical; two stamens, with glabrous, pubescent-based filaments, anthers golden. Female clones commoner than male.

S. × elegantissima is a very characteristic, distinct clonal hybrid, generally more hardy than any other of the large weeping *Salix* species and, in common with *S. × blanda*, is rarely subject to die-back.

The best effects are produced by treating it as a specimen tree in an exposed situation, ideally on an island in a lake, where the wind will ruffle its long pendulous branchlets to the greatest visual effect.

Salix × erdingeri. Kern. (*S. daphnoides* Vill. × S. caprea L.)   A large shrub, or usually an erect, smooth barked tree 9–12 m (30–40 ft) high, with steeply ascending branches forming a relatively compact crown. Branchlets reddish-brown, pubescent, becoming glabrous and variably pruinose; leaves obovate or elliptic, apex acute, base acute or slightly rounded, 5–8 cm long, entire or crenate, young leaves finely sericeous, becoming glabrous, glossy and dark green above, sparsely pubescent greyish green with a prominent midrib beneath; female catkins 6–8 cm long, slender, cylindrical; flower scales sericeous long-hairy, ovate; ovary pedicellate, sericeous; style elongate, stigma upright.

A hardy clone, less ornamental than *S. daphnoides.*

Salix eriocarpa Fr. and Sav., (*Salix dolichostyla* Sm.) 'Ja-Yanagi' A small tree with spreading branches; branchlets yellowish-brown, pubescent; leaves linear-lanceolate 7–12 cm long, 8–20 mm wide, acuminate, base acute, serrulate, slightly short-pilose above, glabrous and glaucous beneath, lateral nerves numerous and slender; petioles 4–7 mm long; catkins coetaneous, male catkins subsessile with small leaves at their base, 8–20 mm long, 5 mm wide, densely flowered, flower scales oblong–ovate, obtuse; ovary densely white pubescent, style short, glabrous.

A Japanese species growing in the wet lowlands in Honshu, Shikoku and Kyushu.

Salix eriocephala Michx., (*S. rigida* Muhlenb., *S. cordata* Muhlenb. non Michx.) A large shrub 3–6 m (10–20 ft) high; branchlets reddish-brown, pubescent, becoming glabrous; leaves oblanceolate to lanceolate 6–12 cm long, acuminate, scabrous serrate, base cordate or rounded, dull glabrous green above, lighter green and sparsely pubescent beneath, the distal immature leaves are sometimes laterally deflected; stipules prominent, characteristically reniform and persistent, often closely encompassing the stem; catkins precocious with leafy bracts, slender, male catkins 2–5 cm long, female catkins slightly longer; ovary 4–7 mm long, with pedicel one-quarter to one-third as long. Style 0.5–0.8 mm long. Male catkins – anthers dark orange becoming golden.

A native of North America, widespread from New Brunswick to British Columbia, south to Virginia, Montana, Colorado and California. An important willow in American basketry, hybridizing with *S. petiolaris* Sm. to produce *S.* 'Americana'.

An ornamental species with attractive male catkins.

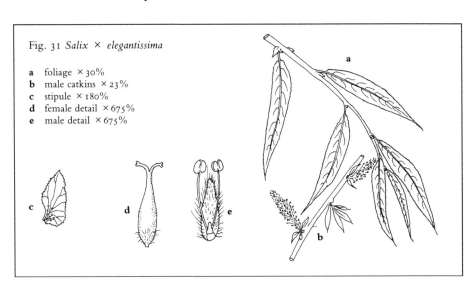

Fig. 31 *Salix × elegantissima*

a foliage × 30%
b male catkins × 23%
c stipule × 180%
d female detail × 675%
e male detail × 675%

Salix eriocephala **Michx. 'Cordata'**   A many-branched shrub to 3 m (10 ft) high. Branchlets slender, pale brown, puberulent. Immature leaves and petioles faintly pink-tinged and finely puberulent. Mature leaves lanceolate, apex narrowly acuminate, base rounded, and leaf margins coarsely serrate.

A very hardy and attractive clone.

Salix eriocephala **Michx. 'Green USA'**   An extremely vigorous tall shrub with erect habit up to 6 m (20 ft) high. Branchlets dark brown, glabrescent. Leaves oblanceolate or lanceolate 8–12 cm long, 2–3 cm wide, apex acuminate, base rounded or subcordate and often unequal, margins serrate; lamina glabrous, dark glossy green above, pale glabrous green beaneath; petioles 1 cm, finely puberulent, and with pink colouring partially continued along the midrib. Stipules prominent, ovate, acute, serrate and persistent.

A handsome, strongly growing clone ideal for incorporating into windbreaks; tolerates very poor, light soils.

Salix eriocephala **Michx. 'Pubescens'**   A widely branching shrub to 4 m (13 ft) high; branchlets and immature leaves densely pubescent and tinted pale brown; mature leaves lanceolate or oblanceolate, glabrous and glossy, sparsely pubescent above, pubescent beneath.

A hardy ornamental clone.

Salix eriocephala **Michx. 'Rouge d'Orleans'**   A vigorous shrub with a characteristic widely arching habit to 3 m (10 ft) high; branchlets long, slender, puberulent, pale green, drooping towards their extremities; leaves narrowly lanceolate to slightly oblanceolate, attenuate-acuminate, base cuneate or rounded and unequal, margins serrate; lamina glabrous dark green above, glaucous beneath; petioles pale green and puberulent, 0.5–1.5 cm long; buds flattened, bud scale yellow becoming brown; stipules ovate, serrate and persistent.

A very ornamental clone with a beautiful arching and spreading habit. It requires ample space to fully display its architectural qualities.

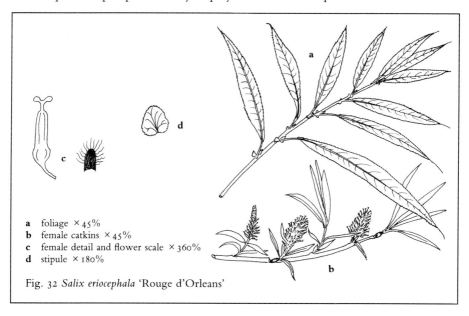

a   foliage × 45%
b   female catkins × 45%
c   female detail and flower scale × 360%
d   stipule × 180%

Fig. 32 *Salix eriocephala* 'Rouge d'Orleans'

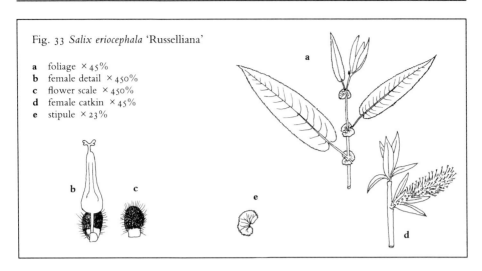

Fig. 33 *Salix eriocephala* 'Russelliana'

a foliage × 45%
b female detail × 450%
c flower scale × 450%
d female catkin × 45%
e stipule × 23%

***Salix eriocephala* Michx. 'Russelliana'**   A widely branching shrub to 4 m (13 ft) high; branchlets glabrous reddish-brown; immature leaves puberulent, translucent, purplish-red to dark purple; mature leaves lanceolate, acuminate, base cordate, margins finely serrate; lamina dark green glabrous above, pale green glabrous beneath, midrib prominent and pale yellow; petioles pink, up to 2 cm long; stipules persistent, reniform, serrate, forming a collar around the stem adjacent to the petioles.

An ornamental clone with outstandingly attractive young foliage.

***Salix* × *erythroflexuosa* Rag. (*S.* × *chrysocoma* × *S. matsudana* 'Tortuosa'; *S. matsudana* 'Tortuosa Aureopendula')**   A small tree 3–5 m (10–16 ft) high with spirally twisted, undulate and contorted, widely arching branches and branchlets. Bark of trunk and main limbs smooth, shining, golden to copper/orange; branchlets orange or pink-tinged; petioles pink or green 0.5–1 cm long; leaves twisted and undulate oblanceolate or lanceolate, attenuate-acuminate, cuneate, serrate, glabrous and glossy above, glaucous below.

A very spectacular contorted ornamental clone introduced from Argentina. Prone to die-back of young shoots caused by prolonged wet summers and severe late frosts.

***Salix exigua* Nutt., *S. argophylla* Nutt., *S. longifolia* var. *argophylla* Anderss.** **'Coyote Willow'**   A shrub to 4 m (13 ft) high or occasionally a small tree to 6 m (20 ft) high. The more usual shrub form is typical of the section *Longifoliae* with its suckering, thicket-forming habit. Branchlets long, slender, usually sericeous at first, become glabrous later; leaves 5–10 cm long, 2–8 mm wide, narrowly linear-lanceolate, nearly entire, acuminate, cuneate and subsessile with a very short petiole; leaves densely silvery sericeous on both sides when young, becoming yellow-green sparsely hairy above and persistently hairy beneath; stipules small and caducous. Catkins up to 5 cm long appearing with the leaves on short leafy stalks either from the previous season's stems, or later from the current year's lateral shoots, terminal or, in male shrubs, with additional axillary catkins; flower scales yellow, narrow, lanceolate, deciduous. Two stamens, filaments with long basal hairs, ovary pubescent or glabrous, sessile or subsessile; stigmas divided.

A North American species extending from British Columbia to California and westwards to New Mexico.

A strikingly beautiful ornamental shrub with conspicuous silver foliage. Like all members of the section *Longifoliae S. exigua* thrives best in moist sandy soils.

Salix falcata Pursh.:   (see *S. nigra* var. *falcata*)

Salix fargesii Burk.   A widely spreading shrub up to 3 m (10 ft) high; branchlets stout and glabrous, glossy green becoming glossy dark brown in their second year; winter buds conspicuously shining red; leaves elongate-elliptic to elliptic-oblong, serrulate, up to 18 cm long, 3.5–8 cm wide, glossy dark green above with deeply impressed venation, dull green below and silky-hairy, particularly on midrib and veins; 15–25 pairs of veins prominent on undersurface; petiole glossy green up to 2.5 cm long. Catkins appear in spring, are erect on short, leafy, sericeous stalks, males up to 12 cm long with 9–12 stamens, females up to 18 cm long and 6 mm wide; ovary glabrous, ovoid-cylindric, style slender, two bi-lobed stigmas, capsules subsessile; flower scales densely long-villous.

This very attractive species was introduced to Britain by E. H. Wilson in 1910, from central China in woodlands near Fang Hsien at an altitude of 1,830 m (6,000 ft). At this height it becomes a dwarf or recumbent plant, only reaching 3 m (10 ft) high in the most favoured localities. It occurs to the east of the Red Basin, in east Szechwan and Hupeh.

One of the most ornamental of all *Salix* species, with its bright-red winter buds, glossy stems, unusually large leaves, it deserves to be set in a protected position in damp, fertile soil, allowing plenty of space for lateral growth. Young shoots are liable to damage from late frosts.

S. fargesii is closely related to *S. moupinensis*. The two main differences, detailed by Schneider, being: in *S. fargesii* the catkin rachis and scales are densely long-hairy, in *S. moupinensis* they are glabrous or only sparsely hairy; in *S. fargesii* the ovary is tapered into a long style, in *S. moupinensis* it is abruptly narrowed with a shorter style. The undersurface of leaves of *S. fargesii* are more sericeous, whereas

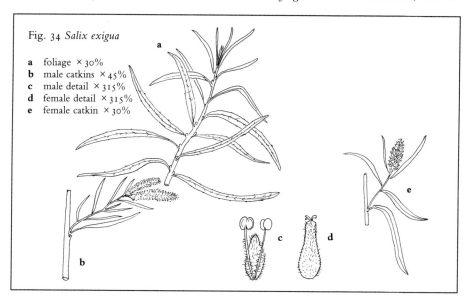

Fig. 34 *Salix exigua*

a   foliage × 30%
b   male catkins × 45%
c   male detail × 315%
d   female detail × 315%
e   female catkin × 30%

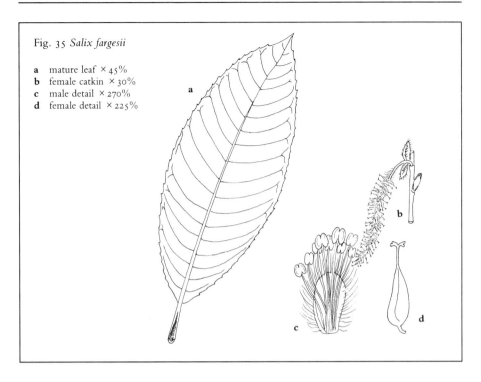

Fig. 35 *Salix fargesii*

a mature leaf × 45%
b female catkin × 30%
c male detail × 270%
d female detail × 225%

in *S. moupinensis* they are often glabrous. *S. fargesii* also tends to produce shorter stems, bigger winter buds, and longer petioles. Marginal leaf serration of *S. fargesii* is finer than in *S. moupinensis*.

Salix floridana Chapman. A large tree with a fissured dark-brown trunk; leaves elliptic, lanceolate or ovate, acute or acuminate; bud scales with free overlapping margins are sometimes fused in their lower two-thirds; catkins long and slender, male flowers with three to six, or sometimes only two stamens with free filaments. Although closely related to section *Humboldtianae* the leaves of *S. floridana* are much wider and the flower scales are persistent; female catkins – stipes 2–5 mm long.

A native of southern North America in Georgia and Florida. Chiefly of botanical interest, it is considered that *S. floridana* may be the last living species in the Americas representing a possible link between subgenus *Salix* and subgenus *Vetrix*. This species is now nearly extinct.

Salix fluviatilis Nutt. A shrub or small tree 2–6 m (7–20 ft) high; young leaves and branchlets sericeously puberulent soon becoming glabrous or sparsely hairy; stipules minute and deciduous; leaves subsessile, tapering to a 1.5 mm petiole, the lamina lance-linear, linear-elliptic or narrowly lanceolate, 7–15 times as long as wide, generally 5–15 cm long and 4–15 mm wide, light green above, glaucous with prominent midrib beneath; leaf margins with minute, widely spaced serrations or subentire; catkins flowering in June and July are serotinous on leafy stems; flower scales yellow, puberulent, deciduous; two stamens, filaments with basal hairs; female catkins 5–10 cm long when mature; capsule 5 mm long, pubescent.

A North American species found in the north-west, it is restricted to the banks of the Columbia River and lower reaches of the Williamette River. At the east end of the Columbia gorge *S. fluviatilis* hybridizes with *S. exigua*. Both species belong to the section *Longifoliae*.

The silky-hairy branchlets and young leaves combined with the light-green mature foliage create a delicately ornamental effect. Ideal in a waterside habitat. Recently introduced to Great Britain.

Salix × forbyana Sm. (S. purpurea L. × S. viminalis L. × S. cinerea ssp. oleifolia) An exceptionally vigorous bush with long tapering yellowish branchlets; leaves oblanceolate or elliptic, serrate, thick textured, glabrous, lustrous dark green above, glaucous or pale green beneath. The female catkins closely resemble those of *S. purpurea*; male clones are relatively rare.

Although of no particular ornamental value it is extremely hardy, surviving in the poorest soil, and deserves a place in sallow and osier collections.

Rods obtained by coppicing have been found useful in basketry, proving extremely flexible, tough and durable. Good clones are: *S. forbyana* 'Utilissima', 'Ferrinea', 'Brownard', and 'Red Root'.

Salix fragilis L. var. fragilis 'Crack Willow' A robust tree 12–15 m (40–50 ft) high, with a broad rounded crown and large limbs outspread from the deeply fissured, thick grey trunk. Branchlets at first thinly pubescent brownish-yellow soon become glabrous, glossy and brittle at their point of attachment; leaves lanceolate, long acuminate 10–15 cm long and 1.5–3 cm wide, dark glossy green above, glaucous below, at first adpressed-sericeous, becoming glabrous, base rounded or broadly cuneate, margins coarsely and unevenly glandular-serrate. Petiole 5–15 mm long, deeply channelled above with several glands at its laminal junction. Stipules generally narrow, acuminate, glandular-serrate and caducous. Catkins appear with the leaves in April and May on short leafy lateral shoots, rachis pubescent, both male and female catkins cylindrical 4–6 cm long and 1.5 cm wide, densely flowered; flower scales pale yellow, margins sparsely hairy; two stamens, sometimes three, filaments free or partially united, glabrous, hairy near base; anthers oblong and golden-yellow; two nectaries, two in each sex, oblong, blunt; ovary subsessile or short-stalked, flask-shaped, tapering from a rounded base, glabrous.

Widely distributed throughout Europe, and the Middle East, it is also found in the eastern states of North America, introduced during colonial times. Its natural habitat is along the river banks.

Salix fragilis L. var. furcata (Seriuge ex Gaudia). S. 'Latungensis' Identical to *S. fragilis* L. var. *fragilis* in size and habit, differing in the brighter brown, glossy branchlets and coarsely serrate leaves, up to 5 cm wide, lamina thick and coriaceous, very glossy above and glaucous blue beneath; male catkins often 5–7 cm long, approximately 1.5 cm wide and often bifurcate, dense-flowered, with long flower scales and frequently with three stamens.

Probably originally arising as a mutation from *S. fragilis* L. var. *fragilis*, var. *furcata* is represented only by a single male clone with a wide sporadic distribution throughout England and Scotland. It has also been recorded in Belgium and Switzerland.

A handsome male clone with attractive leaves and conspicuous golden catkins.

Salix fragilis L. **var.** ***russelliana*** **(Sm.) Koch. 'Bedford Willow'**   A tree resembling *S. fragilis* L. var. *fragilis* in overall appearance but generally on a much bigger scale, some mature specimens attaining a height of 24–27 m (80–90 ft) and living to a great age. *S. fragilis* L. var. *fragilis* is looser in habit with more graceful branching and finer, more flexible greenish-brown branchlets; the leaves are proportionally longer and narrower than in var. *fragilis*, 13–15 cm long and 2–2.5 cm wide, very sparsely silky pubescent, becoming glabrous, dark glossy green above and slightly glaucous beneath; leaf margins coarsely serrate with very variable size of teeth and the apex is long-attentuate. The female catkins are 4 cm long, 8 mm wide, lengthening to over 6 cm at maturity and becoming pendulous. The flower scale is more attentuate than in var. *fragilis* but is shorter than the more pedicellate ovary and is rapidly shed; the ovary is narrowly tapered to a short style.

The most frequently planted variety of *S. fragilis* throughout Great Britain and Ireland, the distribution elsewhere being uncertain. Only the female clone is known, reports of male forms usually being confused with the *S. rubens* clones of *alba/fragilis* hybrids.

S. fragilis L. var. *russelliana* is best suited to planting in deep silt with ample space on large estates.

Salix fragilis L. **var.** ***decipiens*** **(Hoffm.) Koch. 'White Welsh Willow'**   An erect tree with deeply fissured grey bark 9–15 m (30–50 ft) high. It also sometimes takes the form of a much branched shrub up to 6 m (20 ft) high. Branchlets are

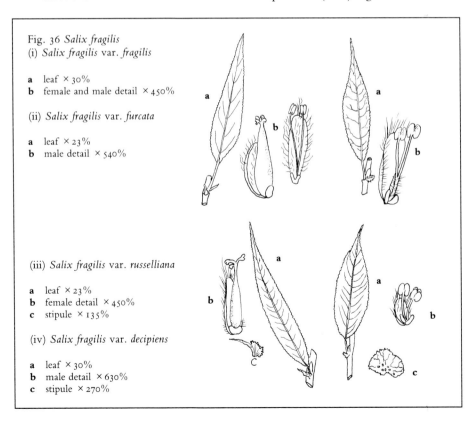

Fig. 36 *Salix fragilis*
(i) *Salix fragilis* var. *fragilis*

a   leaf × 30%
b   female and male detail × 450%

(ii) *Salix fragilis* var. *furcata*

a   leaf × 23%
b   male detail × 540%

(iii) *Salix fragilis* var. *russelliana*

a   leaf × 23%
b   female detail × 450%
c   stipule × 135%

(iv) *Salix fragilis* var. *decipiens*

a   leaf × 30%
b   male detail × 630%
c   stipule × 270%

brittle and glossy, greyish clay-coloured, quite unlike any other *fragilis* type; the youngest shoots are sometimes red-tinged; leaves entirely glabrous, shorter and wider than other fragilis varieties, usually less than 10 cm long and often 2.5–3.5 cm wide, bright glossy green above, strongly glaucous beneath, with a short acuminate apex, and coarsely serrate margins. Male catkins are usually under 3 cm long and 7 mm wide, erect on short leafy lateral shoots, flower scales densely hairy, either two or three stamens in flowers of the same catkin, staminal filaments glabrous with basal hairs, anthers oblong or suborbicular, and two oblong nectaries. Female catkins are slightly bigger than the male, with a shortly pedicellate tapering ovary.

Although only male trees occur in Britain, both sexes have been found in Germany and Austria.

The erect tree form is very distinctive and, although tall, is relatively compact, deserving a place in parks or large gardens.

Salix fragilis L. var. **bullata** Spath.   A compact, many-branched shrub rarely exceeding 4 m (12 ft) high, with pale yellowish-green branchlets. A relatively slow-growing, less vigorous variety of no special merit.

Salix × fruticosa Doell. (**S. aurita** L. × **S. viminalis** L.)   An erect, much branching shrub or small tree, usually under 5 m (15 ft) high; branchlets densely pubescent becoming glabrous, dark reddish-brown, with striae in underlying wood; leaves narrowly lanceolate up to 10 cm long and 2.5 cm wide, dull green sparsely pubescent above, ash-grey tomentose beneath, apex acuminate, base narrowly cuneate, leaf margins undulate, recurved, subentire or irregularly denticulate; nervation prominent beneath; petiole short, approximately 5 mm; stipules prominent, persistent, acuminate, undulate-serrate. Catkins precocious in April, erect, subsessile and shortly cylindrical; leafy bracts green above, densely sericeously-hairy beneath; flower scales reddish-brown, densely hairy. Male catkins – two stamens with free, glabrous filaments; anthers pale yellow; one narrow, oblong nectary. Female catkins – grey tomentose, ovary pedicellate, narrowly tapered, stigmas linear, spreading and entire.

A very hardy undemanding hybrid suitable for inclusion with the sallows in a mixed collection.

Salix futura Seem. **S. vulpinoides** Koidz. 'O-Neko-Yanagi'   A large spreading shrub with dark-brown branchlets, densely pubescent becoming sparsely hairy or glabrous; leaves narrowly oblong or elliptic 6–20 cm long, 3–6 cm wide, acuminate, margins serrate and revolute, base rounded; young leaves puberulent, dark green above, glaucous and pubescent beneath; male catkins slender, cylindrical, densely flowered and sessile; ovary pubescent, subsessile, style and stigma short.

A native of central and north-west Honshu, Japan.

An attractive willow, less well-known in Britain than the very ornamental hybrid *S. × sirakawensis* (*S. futura* × *S. integra*).

Salix 'Geminata' (**S. cinerea** L. ssp. **oleifolia** Macreight × **S. viminalis** L.)   A distinctive sallow clone in the form of a bushy shrub with pubescent branchlets and broadly lanceolate leaves, resembling *S. viminalis* in habit. Less vigorous than *S. × smithiana*, a different clone from the same parents.

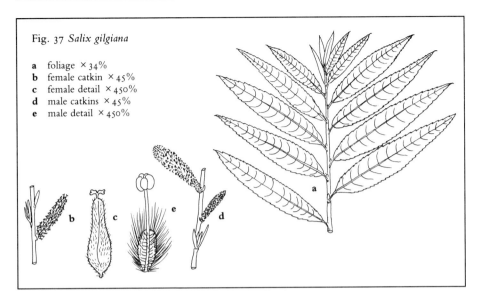

Fig. 37 *Salix gilgiana*

a foliage × 34%
b female catkin × 45%
c female detail × 450%
d male catkins × 45%
e male detail × 450%

***Salix geyeriana* Anders.** A shrub up to 4 m (12 ft) high; branchlets pruinose; leaves linear-lanceolate; closely related to *S. bebbiana* with which it shares its other characteristics.

Of North American origin, from British Columbia to Oregon, Montana and Colorado.

***Salix gilgiana* Seem. (*S. gymnolepis* Lev. and Vant. *S. purpura* spp. *gymno-lepis* Koidz., *S. purpurea* 'Sericea')** A shrub or small tree 6–9 m (20–30 ft) with long spreading branches; branchlets sericeous pubescent becoming glabrous; leaves narrowly lanceolate or almost linear, 5–12 cm long, 5–10 mm wide, serrate, acuminate, base acute, glabrous bright green above, glaucous beneath; male catkins 2.5–5 cm long, sessile with hairy obovate flower scales, staminal filaments totally connate, hairy below, with purple anthers; female catkins slightly shorter than the male, ovary pubescent, style and stigma short, bifid.

Widely distributed within Japan and Korea, it is closely related to *S. miyabeana* which differs in its more slender glabrous branchlets.

S. gilgiana is a very ornamental species, fast-growing with beautiful foliage and recently introduced into collections in Britain.

***Salix glaucophylloides* Fern. 'Dune Willow'** A shrub or shrubby tree 1–5 m (4–15 ft) high; branchlets glabrous yellowish-green, buds adpressed and yellow; leaves variable, broadly lanceolate, oblong, obovate or elliptic 5–12 cm long, 2.5–6 cm wide, thick-textured, apex acute to short acuminate, glandular-crenate-serrate, rounded to cordate or cuneate and unequal at the base, dark, glabrous, glossy green above, glabrous and strongly glaucous beneath; petioles 5–12 mm long; stipules semi-ovate, 3–5 mm long, persistent; catkins cylindrical on leafy shoots, sericeous, male 4–5 cm long, female 4–8 cm long in fruit, subprecocious or coetaneous May to July; flower scales obovate to oblanceolate 1.5–2 mm long, brownish-black, hairy, two stamens; filaments free, glabrous; capsules narrowly lanceolate 6–9 mm long, glabrous; pedicel 1–3 mm long; styles 1–1.5 mm long, entire; stigmas 0.5 mm long, bifid.

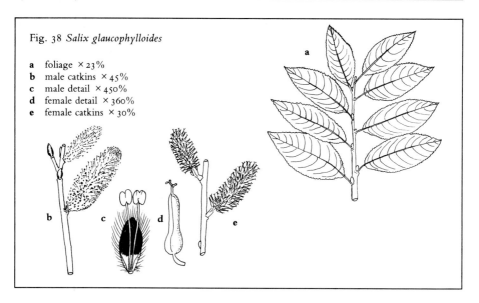

Fig. 38 *Salix glaucophylloides*

a foliage × 23%
b male catkins × 45%
c male detail × 450%
d female detail × 360%
e female catkins × 30%

A North American species widely distributed on sandy shores, calcareous slopes and swamps, from Newfoundland to Quebec and the Great Lakes area, westwards to Illinois, Wisconsin, and north to Hudson Bay.

Salix glaucophylloides var. albovestita (Ball.) Fern.   The youngest branchlets white-lanate, becoming grey-pubescent to glabrous in their second or third year; stipules reniform up to 2 cm by 1 cm; petioles pubescent, up to 2 cm long; leaves larger, up to 15 cm long and up to 8 cm wide, densely pubescent when young, persisting on the midribs.

Native from the Gaspé Peninsula to the shores of Lakes Erie and Huron.

S. 'Glaucophylloides Viminalis' (*S. glaucophylloides* Fern. × *S. viminalis* L.)
A vigorous large shrub with similar-shaped but larger leaves than *S. glaucophylloides*; branchlets pubescent; young leaves silky puberulent on both surfaces; mature leaves silky puberulent beneath; buds prominent and red; stipules ovate, denticulate 5–12 mm long.

The pure species *S. glaucophylloides* is a vigorous and ornamental shrub; its dark-green leaves are very attractive.

Salix gooddingii Ball.   A large tree closely related to *S. nigra*, but with wider lanceolate leaves, branchlets retaining yellow colour throughout the winter, and with pubescent ovaries.

A North American species, in California, south-western USA, and north Mexico.

Salix graciliglans var. nakai. (*S. Nakai* Kim. 'Chosen-Neko-Yanagi')   A large shrub with glabrous branches; branchlets silky-hairy; leaves pubescent or glabrous, lamina linear-oblanceolate or linear-oblong, serrulate, 6–10 cm long, 1–3 cm wide, apex acuminate, base acute or narrowly cuneate, glabrous above, glabrous but pubescent beneath while young; petioles 6–10 mm long; male catkins 15–25 mm long, 7–8 mm thick, sessile; flower scales oblong, acuminate to obtuse 2 mm long, glabrous except hairy at base; female catkins 3–5 cm long;

ovary pubescent, capsules densely pubescent; style 2–3 mm long, the stigma very short and bifid.

Distribution restricted to Honshu and Shikoku, Japan and Korea.

Salix gracilistyla Miq. 'Neko-Yanagi' *S. thunbergiana* Anderss. *Salix mutabilis* Hort. A widely spreading shrub with long graceful arching dark-green branches; branchlets covered with fine silky down, glabrescent; leaves 5–10 cm long, 1.5–4 cm wide, oblong, narrowly ovate or narrowly elliptic, apex acute or shortly acuminate, base obtuse or rounded, serrulate or nearly entire, pale greyish-green above, covered with appressed silky hairs at first, later confined to the midrib; glaucous and persistently sericeous beneath; veins numerous, conspicuous and parallel; petiole 5–10 mm long; stipules lanceolate up to 8 mm long; catkins precocious, produced on bare stems in March and April, flower scales densely long-hairy; males – stamens paired, nearly connate filaments with basal hairs; anthers bright red at first, turning orange, then yellow; females – ovary long-hairy, style slender, stigma bifid and very short.

Native of Japan, Korea, Manchuria and China. One of the most beautiful and well-known shrub species with a characteristic arching habit and magnificent display of male catkins.

Salix gracilistyla 'Variegata' An attractive form with white marginal leaf variegation. A Japanese cultivar.

Salix gracilistyla Miq. var. *melanostachys* (Mak.) Schneid; (*S. melanostachys* Mak. 'Kuro-Yanagi' 'Kurome') A more stiffly erect form than the species, with thicker glabrous branchlets; leaves glabrous bright green and thicker texture than *S. gracilistyla* pure species; male catkins floriferous with glabrous catkin scales mainly black, with red towards the apex; anthers dark orange becoming pale yellow when mature.

The appearance of the black male catkins on the naked stems in March with the subsequent revelation of the anthers is spectacular.

There are nine recognized hybrids, resulting from crossing *S. gracilistyla* with other Japanese species. *S. leucopithecia* is a male clone obtained by cross breeding

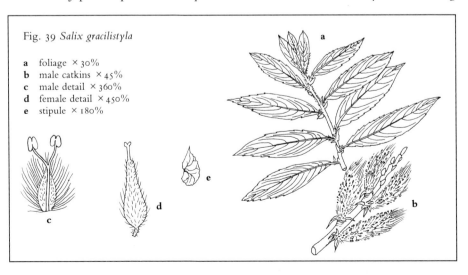

Fig. 39 *Salix gracilistyla*

a foliage × 30%
b male catkins × 45%
c male detail × 360%
d female detail × 450%
e stipule × 180%

S. gracilistyla with *S. bakko* Kimura, the Japanese counterpart of the closely related *S. caprea*. The European equivalent, originally raised at the Hague, between *S. gracilistyla* and *S. caprea* is the female clone *S.* × *hagensis*.

Salix 'Hagensis' (*S. gracilistyla* Miq. × **S. caprea L.)**   A large, vigorous, widely spreading shrub up to 6 m (20 ft) high with thick branches arising from a short trunk, or directly from soil level. Branchlets thick, brown, densely pubescent, with a few striae in the underlying wood; young leaves brown-tinged, especially near their margins, puberulent on both laminal surfaces; mature leaves obovate or elliptic, serrate, apex shortly acuminate, base obtuse or rounded, up to 10 cm long and 4 cm wide, glossy bright green above, glaucous and persistently puberulent beneath; stipules ovate 2–3 mm long; petioles 3–8 mm, puberulent; a female clone with prominent silky erect catkins up to 5 cm long, many flowered, stigmas bifid and very distinct.

An ornamental clone with a good display of female catkins and attractive foliage, well worth inclusion in large gardens.

Salix *harmsiana* Seem. 'Tsukushi-Yama-Yanagi'   A large shrub or small tree; branchlets sericeously pubescent becoming glabrous later; leaves oblong or broadly elliptic, acute, margins with incurved teeth, sparsely pubescent; male catkins 3–4 cm long, 5–6 mm wide, short stalked, a single stamen, filament with basal hairs, flower scales ovate, obtuse with long brown hairs on both sides; female catkins up to 3 cm long, 5 mm wide, ovary densely pubescent; style short; stigmas bifid.

A Japanese species from Kyushu.

Salix *heterochroma* Schneid.   A large shrub or tree to 15 m (50 ft) high; branchlets glabrous or pubescent at first becoming totally glabrous later, yellow to purple-brown; leaves elliptic-ovate or elliptic to oblong-lanceolate, 5–12 cm long, acuminate, entire, dark glabrous green above, glaucous beneath and sericeous, becoming glabrous; petioles 5–15 mm long; stipules minute or exstipulate, catkins on short leafy stalks, coetaneous or produced shortly before the leaves; male catkins 5–10 cm, females 10–15 cm long; flower scales oblong, extremely hairy, pale yellow/brown; ovaries pubescent, 5 mm long; pedicel approximately four times as long as nectary; style one-third as long as ovary, with narrow-oblong bifid stigmas.

An attractive large-leafed species, native of central China.

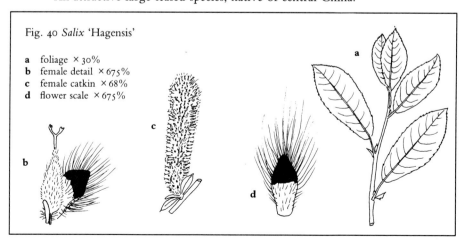

Fig. 40 *Salix* 'Hagensis'

a foliage × 30%
b female detail × 675%
c female catkin × 68%
d flower scale × 675%

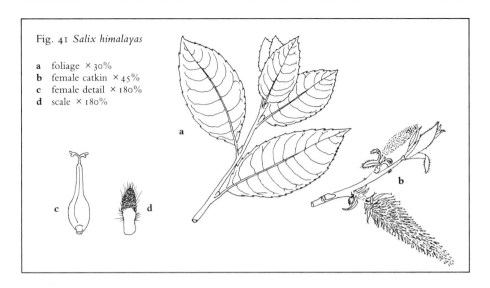

Fig. 41 *Salix himalayas*

a   foliage × 30%
b   female catkin × 45%
c   female detail × 180%
d   scale × 180%

Salix × *heterandra* Dode. (*S. pentandra* L. × *S. purpurea* L.)   A large shrub or small tree; branchlets glabrous brown; leaves lanceolate, glabrous dark green above, glabrous and glaucous beneath, margins remotely serrate; three to five stamens, partly connate.

An uncommon hybrid, occurring sporadically in Europe.

Salix *hidewoi* Koidz. 'Ezo-Miyama-Yanagi'   A large vigorous erect shrub with thick grey branches; branchlets glabrous purple turning dark brown later; leaves oblong or obovate 1–5 cm long, 0.5–2.5 cm wide, glabrous dark green above, paler or glaucous beneath, apex obtuse or rounded, base obtuse, margins undulate-serrate; petioles 5–10 mm long; catkins on short peduncles, male catkins loosely flowered, hairy, 2–3 cm long; female catkins densely flowered, 3–3.5 cm long, rachis villous, scales oblong with rounded apex, yellowish and densely hairy; style short, stigmas bifid; catkins in fruit 4–4.5 cm long; capsules 6–7 mm long, puberulent, glabrescent.

A native of Hokkaido, Japan.

Salix *himalayas* Heybr.   A large shrub or small erect tree, stiffly branching, up to 6 m (20 ft) high; branchlets slender, glabrous, glossy, bright red to dark brown, minutely pubescent towards their extremities; young leaves puberulent, pink, orange and red-tinged; mature leaves 10–15 cm long, 3–7 cm wide, elongate-elliptic or broadly oblong, irregularly serrate, apex acute or shortly acuminate, base acute or cuneate, light green glabrous and glossy above, puberulent glaucous whitish-grey beneath; axillary buds compressed, bright red; petioles 1–1.5 cm long, pubescent pink; midrib pink; stipules small or exstipulate.

Collected from the warm temperate forest region of the Himalayas in 1965 by Dr Hans Heybroek of the Dutch Forest Research Institute, Dedorschkarp.

An extremely ornamental, colourful large-leaved species. It is also frost-hardy.

Salix *hippophaefolia* Thuill.:   (see *S. mollissima*)

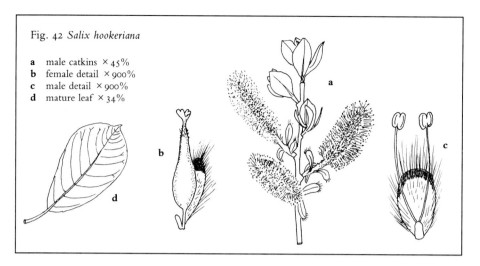

Fig. 42 *Salix hookeriana*

a male catkins × 45%
b female detail × 900%
c male detail × 900%
d mature leaf × 34%

***Salix hirsuta* Thunb.**   A small erect tree to 3 m (10 ft) high with spreading branches; leaves broadly ovate or narrowly elliptic 2–5 cm long, 0.5–2 cm wide, apex acute to obtuse, base rounded or acute, pubescent beneath.
Confined to the Cape Peninsula, South Africa,
Not hardy in temperate climates.

***Salix* × *holosericea* Willd. (*S. viminalis* L. × *S. cinerea* L. var. *cinerea*)**   An upright shrub with spreading branches up to 5 m (16 ft) high. Branchlets persistently and densely pubescent; wood beneath bark showing striae; leaves oblong-ovate to lanceolate or oblanceolate, 5–15 cm long, crenulate, dull green pubescent above, pale grey and sericeously-pubescent beneath; stipules ovate-lanceolate, subentire; catkins 3–5 cm long; pedicel as long as nectary; style of equal length to stigmas.
A European clonal cultivar.

***Salix hookeriana* Barratt**   An ornamental species exhibiting great variations in form and height, from a small densely-branched shrub, to a tree up to 10 m (32 ft) high, with a short smooth trunk divided into several thick main limbs from

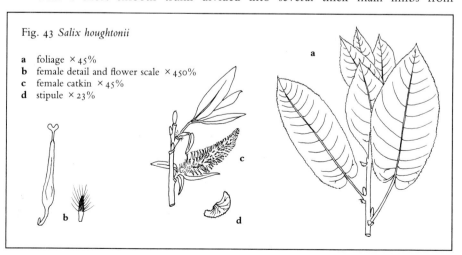

Fig. 43 *Salix houghtonii*

a foliage × 45%
b female detail and flower scale × 450%
c female catkin × 45%
d stipule × 23%

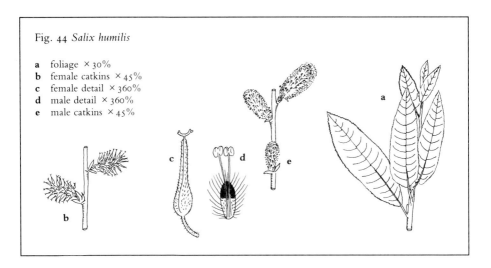

Fig. 44 *Salix humilis*

a foliage × 30%
b female catkins × 45%
c female detail × 360%
d male detail × 360%
e male catkins × 45%

which many ascending branches rise to form a rounded crown. Branchlets are thick, green and faintly brown, densely tomentose and very brittle; leaves oblong to oblong-obovate, apex varying from shortly cuspidate or acute to rounded or obtuse, base rounded or cuneate; young leaves puberulent above, lanate beneath; mature leaves 5–15 cm long, sparsely silver-pubescent or dark glossy green above, remaining persistently white-pubescent beneath; petioles pubescent 0.5–3 cm long; stipules small or absent; catkins erect, subsessile with basal bracts, male 4–6 cm long, thick, white, woolly, with golden anthers when mature, female 8–12 cm long in fruit.

A native of western coastal regions of North America, from Alaska southwards to California.

Outstandingly ornamental either as a shrub or as a tree, with silver-white broad leaves and very attractive male catkins, it grows rapidly in deep fertile soil. The leaves greatly increase in size when coppiced as a small shrub. It is never far from the sea in its original habitat and should be successful in exposed seaside gardens elsewhere.

Salix houghtonii A bushy, branching shrub or occasionally a small tree, up to 6 m (20 ft) high; branchlets stiff, pubescent, pale green, turning brown in the autumn; buds compressed, red and puberulent; leaves thin 6–10 cm long, 2–3.5 cm wide, broadly lanceolate, serrulate, apex acute or shortly acuminate, base cordate and unequal; lamina glabrous, bright green above, glabrous paler green beneath; immature leaves brown-tinged; petioles glabrous 1.5–3 cm long; stipules prominent, reniform and persistent. Catkins slender, male 3–5 cm, female 3.5–7 cm long.

A North American species with attractive foliage exhibiting similar characteristics to *S. eriocephala*.

Salix hultenii Flod. var. ***angustifolia*** Kim. A large shrub or small tree, closely related to *S. bakko* Kimura, differing in its branches, which become purple during their second year, longitudinal striae are not generally present under the bark and the leaves are narrow, obovate or oblong.

A native of Japan.

Salix humboldtiana Willd. A large tree with fastigiate form, long lanceolate leaves, bud scales with free overlapping margins, and male flowers with up to 12 stamens bearing very small anthers.

A native of South America, it is also present in other subtropical regions.

It is rather coarse, without any special ornamental quality and is very susceptible to frost.

Salix humilis Marsh. 'Prairie Willow'   A medium to large shrub up to 3 m (10 ft) high, with considerable lateral spread; branches long, ascending and arching; branchlets yellowish-green, pubescent; young leaves thin, translucent, brownish-red and puberulent; mature leaves 5–12 cm long, 1–3 cm wide, lanceolate or oblong-lanceolate, undulate-serrulate, slightly revolute, apex shortly acuminate or acute, base rounded or cordate, glabrous and dark green above; glaucous, pubescent and rugose becoming glabrous beneath; midrib pink on upper surface; petioles pink, pubescent, 1–1.5 cm long; stipules reniform or ovate, serrulate and persistent; catkins slender, sessile, precocious, 1.5–4 cm long, flower scales oblanceolate 1.5–2 mm long, puberulent, styles and stigmas of equal length, each 0.2–0.4 mm long, stigmas red. Male catkins – two stamens with free glabrous filaments, anthers red turning yellow.

A North American species common in open woodlands, exposed regions and prairies ranging from Newfoundland, southern Quebec, to the east in North Dakota, and south to Florida and Texas.

A good ornamental shrub with beautiful widely arching habit, most attractive young leaves and autumn colours. It requires ample space.

Salix hypoleuca Seem.   A shrub to 5 m (16 ft) high with yellowish-brown branchlets; leaves oblong, ovate or elliptic, 3–5 cm long, acuminate or acute, base cuneate or rounded, serrate or subentire, glabrous dark green above, glabrous and glaucous beneath; catkins on short leafy stems, slender, cylindrical, 3–6 cm long, flower scales oval, glabrous; two stamens, with filaments free, hairy at base; ovary sessile and glabrous; stigmas subsessile and bifid.

A graceful species with neat, compact foliage.

Salix integra Thunb. (S. purpurea var. multinervis (Franch. & Sav.) Koidz.; S. purpurea ssp. amplexicaulis var. multinervis (Franch. & Sav.) Schneid. 'Axutime', 'Inu-Kori-Yanagi')   A large shrub or small tree, with long glabrous shining branches; branchlets drooping, glabrous, glossy, reddish-brown; young leaves glabrous, translucent, tinged with orange and pink; mature leaves usually paired, subsessile, oblong, thin, glabrous and bright green above, apex obtuse or rounded, base obtuse or cordate, entire or partially serrate towards apex, glaucous greyish-white beneath; catkins precocious, on bare polished branchlets in early April, cylindrical 1.5–2.5 cm long, flower scales obovate and hairy, staminal filaments glabrous; ovary sessile and sericeous; style and stigmas short; capsule up to 0.5 cm long, densely hairy.

A native of Japan and Korea.

A rapidly-growing graceful and very elegant species with delicately tinted young foliage. Ideally suited to a waterside position.

Salix integra Thunb. 'Pendula'   A very attractive and vigorous Japanese cultivar with the characteristics of S. integra Thunb. combined with disproportionally long pendulous, trailing branches. The branchlets become glossy dark red during winter, with small bright-red buds.

It can be left as a loosely trailing low shrub or can be trained upwards, removing laterals, to form a small weeping tree. Alternatively, if quick results are

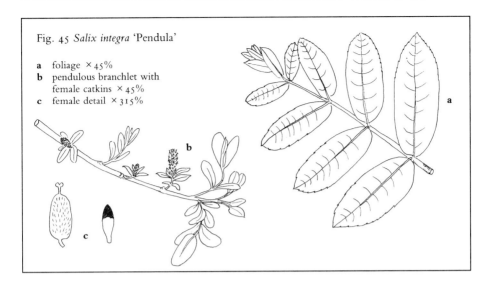

Fig. 45 *Salix integra* 'Pendula'

a foliage × 45%
b pendulous branchlet with
  female catkins × 45%
c female detail × 315%

required a scion can be effectively grafted onto a strongly growing straight rootstock, preferably of *S. purpurea* species. Very decorative effects can be produced by planting in a large urn several feet above ground level, or by positioning behind a retaining wall, encouraging its long pendulous branchlets to trail down over the edge.

Salix interior Row. (longifolia Gray.) 'Long Leaf Willow', or 'Sand Bar Willow'   A thicket-forming shrub suckering over wide areas, with branches arising vertically from very long, spreading surface roots. Occasionally found growing as a small tree; height 1–5 m (4–16 ft); branchlets leafy, slender, glabrous, glossy, reddish-brown; leaves linear or linear oblanceolate 8–15 cm long, acute to acuminate at both ends, subsessile, remotely and irregularly denticulate, glabrous bright green above, glaucous and paler beneath, young leaves sericeous. Catkins serotinous, flowering in April and May and sometimes again in late summer, from 3–8 cm long, lax, borne on the tips of leafy lateral shoots. Flower scales lanceolate, puberulent, pale yellow and deciduous; two stamens, filaments free with basal hairs. Ovaries variably hairy, shortly pedicellate, styles indistinct; stigmas divided and short.

Commonly found on sand bars and moist alluvial soil around estuaries in North America extending from New Brunswick to Yukon and Alaska, south and westwards across the Great Plains.

An interesting species with striking varnished branchlets, but because of its vigorous suckering habit, requiring considerable space. It should not be planted in the vicinity of smaller ornamental shrubs.

Salix interior Row. var. pedicellata (Anderss.) Ball.   Leaves only 3–6 mm wide, often with longer marginal teeth. Commonest on the Great Plains.

Salix interior Row. var. wheeleri Row.   Leaves short and broad, 3–5 cm long, 1.5–2 cm wide, more densely and persistently pubescent. Concentrated in sandy situations with the species around the Great Lakes.

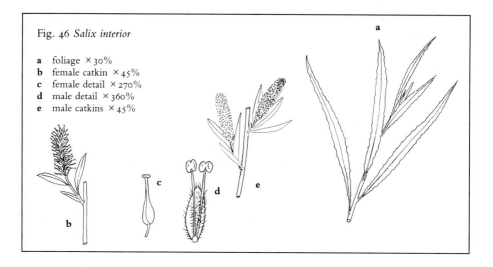

Fig. 46 *Salix interior*

a   foliage × 30%
b   female catkin × 45%
c   female detail × 270%
d   male detail × 360%
e   male catkins × 45%

Salix irrorata Anderss.   An upright shrub with a spreading, bushy habit, up to 6 m (20 ft) high; branchlets slender, glabrous, reddish-brown, markedly pruinose; leaves oblong to oblanceolate or narrowly elliptic, 6–10 cm long. up to 1.5 cm wide, acuminate, cuneate, bright green and glossy above, glaucous beneath, remotely serrate or entire; petiole yellow 3–10 mm long; catkins subsessile, without leafy bracts, short and compact 1.5–2.5 cm long, concentrated mainly towards the ends of the stems, flower scales densely white-villous; male anthers brick-red changing to yellow at maturity; female – style short; stigmas short and thick.

A North American species, from Colorado to New Mexico and Arizona.

An ornamental species characterized by the white bloom on young stems, the silver-haired catkins and, in the male, the beautiful colour shades of the anthers.

S. canariensis is closely related. For basic differences, see *S. canariensis*.

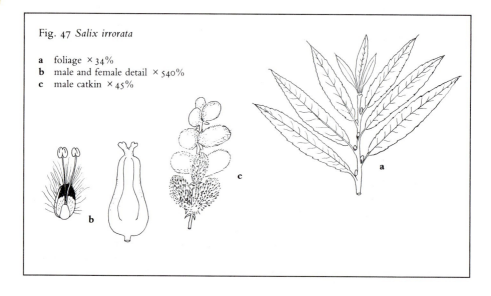

Fig. 47 *Salix irrorata*

a   foliage × 34%
b   male and female detail × 540%
c   male catkin × 45%

***Salix japonica* Thunb. 'Shiba-Yanagi', (*S. babylonica* var. *japonica* (Thunb.) Anderss.)** A shrub or small tree up to 4 m (13 ft) high with slender brown branches; branchlets pale yellowish-green, pubescent becoming glabrous; young leaves sericeous puberulent; mature leaves glabrous, lanceolate, 5–9 cm long, 1–2.5 cm wide, margins with finely appressed teeth, apex acuminate, base rounded or obtuse, vivid green above, glaucous beneath; male catkins 4–8 cm long, slender, cylindrical and loosely flowered, two stamens, filaments free with basal hairs; female catkins short-stalked, linear, loose flowered, 7–12 cm long, flower scales ovate and sparsely pubescent, ovary glabrous, style short, stigmas oblong. Flowers of each sex possess one nectary.

A Japanese native from the hills of Honshu. A beautiful, graceful species with arching branches, bright-green foliage and long slender catkins.

***Salix jessoensis* Seem. (*S. hondoensis* Koidz.) 'Shiro-Yanagi'** A large tree up to 24 m (80 ft) high with a girth of 4 m (13 ft) or more in Japan; bark lightly fissured; branches brown; branchlets grey-pubescent; leaves lanceolate, glabrous when mature, lamina dark green above, glaucous blue beneath; stipules ovate, serrulate; coetaneous, catkins on short leafy stalks; flower scales with basal hairs. Male catkins 2.5 cm long, two stamens with thick filaments. Female catkins up to 5 cm long with persistent scales when in fruit. Ovary sessile, sericeous; style short; stigmas entire and oblong.

A very impressive tree found in Hokkaido and Honshu, Japan, not attaining its full stature in the West.

***Salix kangensis* Nak.** A tall erect tree, closely related to *S. daphnoides*. Of purely botanical interest, the young branchlets being devoid of the attractive bloom of *S. daphnoides*.

This species is a native of Korea, the Ussuri region of Russia, and north-east China.

***Salix karelinii* Turcz.** A small shrub or tree up to 5 m (16 ft); leaves elliptic to ovate, finely dentate, 4–5 cm long, lanate at first becoming glabrous above and beneath when mature; catkins precocious flowering between May and July; male catkins stout, silky-haired, 3–4 cm long; female catkins stout, very silky-hairy, to 5 cm long, with blackish spathulate bracts; fruiting catkins to 9 cm; capsules 5 mm long.

A species extending from Afghanistan to central Nepal and central Asia; common on open mountain slopes and along streams in the drier regions of Kashmir.

***Salix kinuiyanagi* Kim. ('Kishu')** A very vigorous large shrub, often a small tree and occasionally a medium-sized tree up to 15 m (50 ft) high, with a fissured grey-barked trunk dividing into widely spreading branches; branchlets thick, grey, villous with short internodes; leaves of *S. viminalis* type, narrowly lanceolate, 10–20 cm long, 1.5–2 cm wide, attenuate-acuminate or caudate-acuminate base obtuse to acute, with indistinctly undulate and slightly recurved margins; lamina silky puberulent above when young, becoming dark green and glabrous later, remaining silver appressed villous beneath; catkins ovoid 2.5–3 cm long, 1.5–2 cm thick, sessile, densely packed together towards the tips of the branchlets; flower scales broadly lanceolate, silky-hairy; staminal filaments free and glabrous with yellow anthers. Only the male form is known.

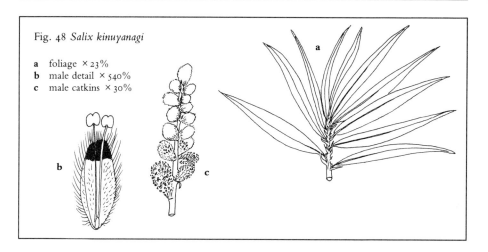

Fig. 48 *Salix kinuyanagi*

a   foliage × 23%
b   male detail × 540%
c   male catkins × 30%

Extensively cultivated in Honshu, Shikoku and Kyushu, Japan, where it is coppiced and used for coarse basketry.

When planted in good soil and left unpruned this willow can become a very attractive specimen tree. Adequate space must be given to allow for its widely spreading branches and to fully apreciate the beauty of the silver undersurface of its leaves and densely crowded catkins. It is one of the last species to lose its leaves, in the late autumn.

A cultivated hybrid of *S. kinuiyanagi* with *S. gracilistyla* is *S.* × *thaumastu* Kimura.

Salix 'Kioryu'; *S. sachalinensis* 'Kioryu'   A slender medium-sized shrub or small erect tree, with graceful spreading branches and slender glabrous, glossy dark-brown branchlets. Similar to *S. sachalinensis* 'Sekka', but differing in its more erect habit and lack of fasciation of the branchlets. The leaves are narrowly lanceolate, entire, narrowly acuminate, glabrous dark green above, glabrous and glaucous beneath.

An elegant female clone of Japanese origin.

Salix koreensis Anderss. 'Korai-Yanagi'   A large tree up to 20 m (65 ft) in its native habitat, closely related to *S. jessoensis*, with a more deeply fissured trunk and light-grey or greyish-green branches. Branchlets and leaves are more glabrous than those of *S. jessoensis*. The young leaves of *S. koreensis* are very thin, translucent and attractively brown-tinged.

A native of Korea and Manchuria.

An elegant, erect and relatively small tree when grown in the West. The young shoots are tender and can suffer from late frost.

Salix koriyanagi Kim. *S. purpurea* var. *japonica* Nakai.   A large, erect, many-branched shrub up to 4 m (13 ft) high; branches glabrous, yellowish-grey; branchlets long and slender, glabrous, pale green, very flexible, and yellow under the bark; leaves opposite or alternate, linear-lanceolate 5–10 cm long, 5–12 mm wide, apex acuminate, base rounded or obtuse, faintly serrate, thin-textured, glabrous dark green above, glaucous beneath, with numerous lateral nerves; youngest leaves pale shades of pink and brown. Male catkins, cylindrical, densely flowered, 2–3 cm long, flower scales obovate, long-hairy, staminal filaments connate, anthers dark purple at first, becoming red, orange, and yellow progressively; female catkins 2–3.5 cm long, subsessile, dense-flowered, scales long-hairy, ovary sessile, densely hairy, style short, stigma short and bifid.

Of Korean origin, extensively grown in Japan for fine basketry.

A very graceful and extremely hardy shrub with beautiful young leaves and male catkins. The oldest branches can be pruned hard back to just above ground level every three or four years to promote new growth without radically altering the general form.

The hybrid *S. koriyanagi* × *S. gracilistyla* is *S.* × *yoitiana* Kimura.

Salix 'Koten'   A medium-sized shrub or small tree up to 6 m (20 ft) high with a curving trunk. Branches spreading, greyish-brown; branchlets pale grey, pubescent; buds adpressed, pale brown pubescent; petioles puberulent 5–15 mm long; stipules small, lanceolate, caducous; leaves 5–14 cm long, 1.5–2 cm wide, lanceolate or narrowly elliptic, finely acuminate or acute, base narrowly cuneate or acute, leaf margins entire, lamina dark green, glabrous and glossy above, glabrous and glaucous beneath. Male catkins loosely flowered, 5–8 cm long, 3–4 cm wide, staminal filaments long, free and glabrous; anthers golden-yellow, immature catkins silky hairy.

An ornamental clone, especially suited to a waterside habitat, believed to be of Japanese origin.

Salix 'Kurome' and Salix 'Kuroyanagi':   (see *S. gracilistyla* var. *melanostachys*)

Salix laggeri Wimm. (S. albicans Bonj.; S. pubescent Schl.)   A shrub up to 4 m (13 ft) high, with spreading branches; branchlets thick, gnarled, dark grey-brown, woolly tomentose becoming glabrous after the second year; leaves narrowly elliptic to oblong-lanceolate, pubescent above and brown-tinted towards the base when young, becoming glabrous dark green above and densely pubescent beneath when mature; stipules semi-saggitate, serrate. Catkins large, up to 4 cm long, 1.5 cm diameter, filaments free with long basal hairs, anthers yellow. Ovary pedicellate, densely white-lanate.

A species found in the Austrian and Swiss Alps, partial to sandy, well-drained soil.

Salix lasiandra Benth. (S. lancifolia Anderss. S. lyallii Heller.)   A several-stemmed, vigorous shrub or a strongly growing tree 6 m (20 ft) to 18 m (60 ft) high, similar to *S. pentandra*, the 'Bay Willow'; the trunk is smooth at first and grey-barked becoming dark and fissured in larger specimens; branchlets and leaves puberulent when young, later becoming glabrous; mature leaves glossy dark green above and glaucous or pale green beneath, lanceolate or narrowly elliptic, evenly tapered attenuate-acuminate 5–18 cm long, 1–5 cm wide, considerably larger on young shoots; leaf margins regularly serrulate or almost entire; stipules prominent, rounded, glandular-serrate, deciduous; petiole 3–15 mm long with glands on the upper surface near the junction with the lamina; catkins coetaneous, rachis hairy, flower scales yellow, deciduous. Male catkins 2–6 cm long, 1–1.5 cm wide; three to eight stamens, usually five, filaments with basal hairs; female catkins 5–12 cm when mature, ovary subsessile; style short; stigmas broad and blunt.

A big tree, attaining its greatest stature in the alluvial silt beside rivers in western North America.

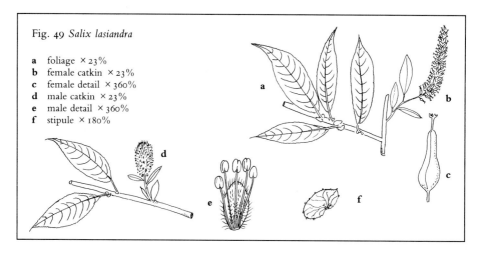

Fig. 49 *Salix lasiandra*

a   foliage × 23%
b   female catkin × 23%
c   female detail × 360%
d   male catkin × 23%
e   male detail × 360%
f   stipule × 180%

A spectacular, fast-growing species. The foliage, dark glossy green above and glaucous beneath, is very attractive.

Salix lasiolepis Benth.   A strongly-growing, loosely branching shrub or small tree 2–6 m (7–20 ft), up to 12 m (40 ft) high in its most southern habitats; branchlets long whip-like, very flexible, typically yellowish-olive, usually downy-pubescent at first; stipules minute, lanceolate, deciduous; leaves variable, mainly narrowly oblanceolate to narrowly oblong or elliptic-oblong, 6–15 cm long, 0.5–2.5 cm wide, thick, revolute margined, entire, occasionally shallow-toothed; lamina dark green above, distinctly paler and glaucous beneath, densely puberulent when young; mature leaves usually glabrous above, puberulent beneath or completely glabrous; catkins precocious, sessile or on short leafy stems; flower scales blackish, persistent, densely hairy; male catkins 2–5 cm long, two stamens, filaments glabrous; female catkins 2.5–6 cm long, ovaries glabrous, subsessile; style short, stigmas short, broad and indistinctly bilobed.

A native species of northern and western America, along streams to moderate altitudes in mountains in Alaska, the Yukon, Mackenzie, and southwards to California, New Mexico and South Dakota. Two distinct varieties occur in different localities:

S. lasiolepis var. *sandbergii* Ball. The more hairy extreme, in the north.

S. lasiolepis var. *bracelinae* Ball. The narrow-leaved phase of the southern part of the range of the species.

A very hardy species, the long, light olive-green young branches being very conspicuous and decorative throughout the winter months. One of the ornamental species most easily propagated from cuttings.

Salix 'Latifolia' (S. caprea L. × S. myrsinifolia Salisb.)   A sallow hybrid exhibiting characteristics of both parents, not particularly ornamental, of botanical interest in a mixed sallow collection.

Salix 'Latungensis':   (see *S. fragilis* L. var. *furcata*)

Salix × laurina Sm. (S. caprea L. × S. phylicifolia L.);   (see *S. wardiana* White.)   A large shrub or small tree with widely spreading branches forming a

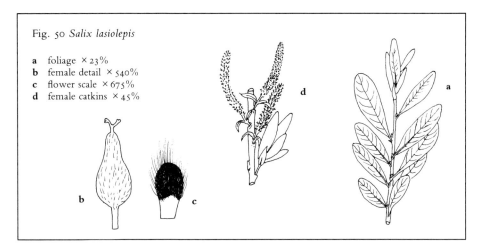

Fig. 50 *Salix lasiolepis*

a   foliage × 23%
b   female detail × 540%
c   flower scale × 675%
d   female catkins × 45%

rounded crown; branchlets glabrous, shining, reddish-brown; leaves obovate, oblong or elliptic 5–10 cm long, apex acute or shortly acuminate, glossy dark green above, conspicuously glaucous beneath; catkins precocious, narrowly cylindrical 3–5 cm long, ovaries white, tomentose; style distinct; stigmas linear-oblong and cleft to the base. Only the female form in cultivation.

A good sallow clonal hybrid with attractive foliage.

Salix × leucopithecia Kimura. 'Furi-Sode-Yanagi' (*S. gracilistyla* Miq. × *S. bakko* Kim.)   A large, vigorous, thick-branched, spreading shrub, up to 6 m (20 ft) high; a male clone almost identical to the female European clone *S.* × *hagensis*.

It is cultivated in Japan for its large ornamental catkins.

Salix livida Wahlenb.   A low shrub or sometimes a small erect tree up to 8 m (25 ft); branchlets glabrous and glossy; leaves obovate to oblong-lanceolate, up to 6 cm long, apex acute, entire or crenate, glabrous dark green above, paler beneath; petioles 2–6 mm long; flower scales obtuse, yellow, dark at apex; pedicel as long as ovary; style short.

Present in Europe and northern Asia, of no special merit.

Salix longifolia Gray.:   (see *S. interior* Row.)

Salix longipes Hook.   A tree to 9 m (30 ft) high, with spreading or slightly drooping branches; branchlets sparsely puberulent or glabrous; leaves thin, lanceolate to oblong-lanceolate 6–15 cm long, lamina light green above, whitish and sparsely puberulent beneath, margins partially serrulate, apex acuminate, base unequal, subcordate to broadly cuneate; young leaves brown and pink-tinged towards the base; stipules foliaceous, acute; petioles glandless, 1.5–2 cm long, pink or pale green; catkins 5–9 cm long; three to seven stamens, capsules slender-pedicellate.

A North American species, extending from Virginia to Florida. It is also present in Cuba.

An attractive willow with bright, translucent young leaves.

Salix lucida Muhlenb. 'Shining Willow'   A large shrub or small tree, up to 6 m (20 ft) high; branchlets glabrous, very glossy light brown; leaves ovate-lanceolate

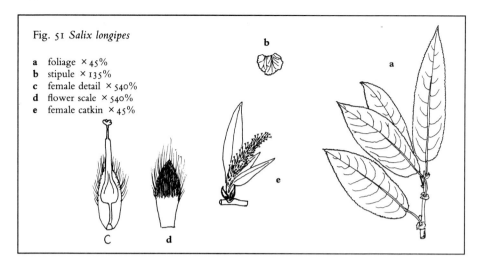

Fig. 51 *Salix longipes*

a foliage × 45%
b stipule × 135%
c female detail × 540%
d flower scale × 540%
e female catkin × 45%

to lanceolate 6–14 cm long, typically long-acuminate, base broadly cuneate to rounded, glandular-serrulate, dark green glabrous and glossy above, paler green glabrous and glossy beneath; petiole 5–10 mm long, glandular; stipules semi-cordate, glandular and persistent; catkins coetaneous in April on leafy shoots; male catkins 3–5 cm long, female 6–8 cm long, densely flowered; usually five stamens, filaments hairy to the middle; stigmas subsessile.

A North American native, distributed from Newfoundland to the north-west Territories, and southwards to New Jersey, Kentucky and Nebraska. It is also cultivated in Europe and Great Britain.

A very conspicuous species with particularly beautiful shining foliage and branchlets. The golden anthers of the male catkins coinciding with the leaves are also very attractive.

Salix lutea Nutt.:   (see *S. rigida*)

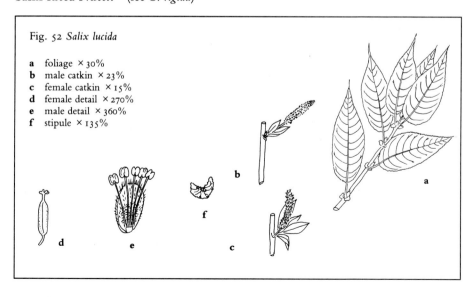

Fig. 52 *Salix lucida*

a foliage × 30%
b male catkin × 23%
c female catkin × 15%
d female detail × 270%
e male detail × 360%
f stipule × 135%

Salix maccalliana **Row.** An erect shrub 1–5 m (4–16 ft) high, with dark reddish-brown, glabrous, glossy branches and branchlets; mature leaves coriaceous, narrowly elliptic to oblong, 5–7 cm long, 1–2 cm wide, apex acute or acuminate, base acute to rounded; lamina glabrous glossy on both sides, paler non-glaucous beneath, margins glandular-serrulate; immature leaves sericeously hairy and red-tinged; catkins coetaneous on short leafy branchlets. Male catkins – two stamens, filaments free with basal hairs, nectaries typically cup-like, surrounding the stamens, with four to six lobes. Female catkins – pistils long and densely sericeous with white hairs, styles 1 mm long, stigmas 0.5 mm long, a single nectary, flower scales yellowish and hairy.

Recently introduced to Great Britain from the Yukon. It is also found on river margins and marshes in British Columbia, south in the Rocky Mountains to Alberta and eastwards across Canada.

An interesting, very distinctive and relatively invariable species.

Salix mackenziana **Raup:** (see *S. rigida mackenziana*)

Salix macroblasta **Schneid.** A large spreading shrub to 6 m (20 ft) high; branchlets yellow to yellowish-brown, pubescent; winter buds oblong, twice as long as petioles; leaves narrow-lanceolate 1.5–3 cm long, base acute, rounded or sub-cordate, glabrous, glaucous beneath; fruiting catkins 2.5–3 cm long; ovary glabrous, style very short, stigmas short and emarginate.

A native of western China, related to *S. hypocleuca.*

Salix **'Maerd Brno'.** (*S. magnifica* **Hemsl.** × *S. erdingeri* **Kern.)** A female clone represented as a large shrub or small erect tree 6–9 m (20–30 ft) high, with steeply ascending branches; branchlets light green glabrous and slender; leaves broadly oblanceolate or oblong-elliptic, serrate, apex shortly acuminate or acute, base cuneate or acute; lamina thin, light green glabrous and glossy above, glaucous and glabrous with prominent venation beneath, 8–12 cm long, 5–6 cm wide; petioles pubescent 1.5–2 cm long; stipules absent or small. Catkins ovoid, precocious, in April; flower scales red-tinged and densely silky-hairy.

An attractive large-leaved female clone with remarkably beautiful silver-pink immature catkins.

Salix magnifica **Hemsl.** A shrub or small tree 2–6 m (7–20 ft) high, entirely glabrous throughout. Branchlets thick, purple and glossy with conical purple buds; leaves elliptic or slightly obovate, magnolia-like, thick, up to 20 cm long and 10 cm wide, distinctly blue-green above, paler green beneath, apex ending in a short blunt tip; base rounded or slightly cordate; petiole stained purple 1.5–3.5 cm long; catkins erect, serotinous, flowering in May; male catkins 10–18 cm long, two stamens; female catkins up to 25 cm long.

Discovered by E. H. Wilson in 1903 in Szechwan, western China. In the wild the branchlets turn red during the first winter, remaining so for several years.

A most spectacular species. Late spring frosts can severely cut back young shoots, especially after a mild winter.

Salix **'Mamus Brno'.** (*S. magnifica* **Hemsl.** × *S. muscina* **Dode.)** An erect, small tree 3–5 m (10–16 ft) high, with stiff ascending branches; branchlets thick, greyish, glabrous; leaves elliptic, up to 20 cm long and 12 cm wide, apex acute or shortly acuminate, base acute; lamina glabrous olive green above, glabrous pale green beneath with prominent slightly hairy venation; leaf margins subentire, unevenly dentate or scabrous at intervals of 0.5–1 cm; petioles purple, 1.5–2 cm long; stipules small or absent. A female clone with stiff, erect catkins to 15 cm long.

An ornamental clone with large leaves and neat habit.

Salix matsudana Koidz. 'Peking Willow'   A medium-sized tree 12–18 m (40–60 ft) high; branches steeply ascending and spreading; branchlets slender, drooping, minutely puberulent, yellow-grey becoming brownish-grey and glabrous; leaves linear-lanceolate 5–12 cm long, 1–1.5 cm wide, apex attenuate-acuminate, base obtuse, serrulate, bright green and glabrous above, glaucous and puberulent beneath becoming glabrous; petiole 2–6 mm long; stipules lanceolate, serrulate, caducous; catkins cylindrical 1.5–3 cm long, two stamens, filaments with basal hairs; flower scales ovate, pale green; ovaries sessile, glabrous or sparsely hairy, two nectaries, stigma dark and sessile.

Originally native of north China, Mongolia and Korea, it is now cultivated in many countries, thriving in dry soils and withstanding drought conditions.

An ornamental tree with slender tapering foliage.

Salix matsudana 'Caradoc' (S. m. 'Tortuosa' × S. alba var. vitellina)   Similar to *S. m.* 'Tortuosa', but more attractive, with yellow branchlets, brighter green foliage and less tendency to die-back.

Salix matsudana 'Pendula'   An erect tree with spreading pendulous branchlets, exhibiting all the characteristics of the species; commonly cultivated in northern China for its ornamental effect; represented by a female clone in Great Britain.

A very elegant weeping tree with beautiful form, the bright upper surface of the leaves being more visible than in the upright species.

Salix matsudana 'Tortuosa'   A small erect tree 6–9 m (20–30 ft) high; branches, branchlets and leaves undulate and spirally twisted.

A contorted sculptural tree, prone to die-back.

Salix matsudana 'Umbraculifera'   A variety with a flat, widely spreading, semi-pendulous crown, commonly cultivated around Beijing, China.

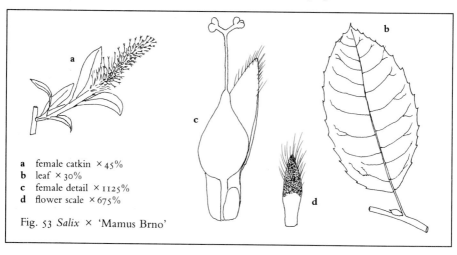

a   female catkin × 45%
b   leaf × 30%
c   female detail × 1125%
d   flower scale × 675%

Fig. 53 *Salix* × 'Mamus Brno'

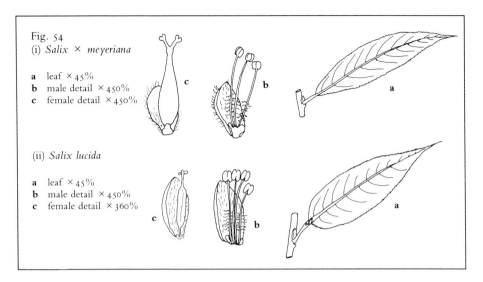

Fig. 54
(i) *Salix* × *meyeriana*

a leaf × 45%
b male detail × 450%
c female detail × 450%

(ii) *Salix lucida*

a leaf × 45%
b male detail × 450%
c female detail × 360%

Salix matsudana 'Golden Curls' A clone with bright copper/gold curling branchlets.

**Salix matsudana 'Tortuosa' (Salix alba L. var. vitellina Stokes ×
S. babylonica L.):** (see *S.* × *erythroflexuosa*)

Salix matsudana Koidz. × Salix alba L. var. alba A vigorous, large erect shrub
or tree combining the best qualities of both species. The branchlets are long and
slender, steeply ascending and drooping terminally.
  Robust male and female clones are in cultivaton.

Salix medemii: (see *S. aegyptiaca*)

**Salix melanopsis Nutt. (S. melanopsis var. gracilipes Ball.; S. exigua ssp.
melanopsis Nutt.)** A thicket-forming, suckering, colonial shrub 2.5–3 m
(8–10 ft) high, or occasionally a slender tree to 8 m (25 ft) high; closely related to
S. exigua but with serrulate, relatively wider, less hairy leaves bearing callous or
glandular teeth, branchlets and leaves soon becoming glabrous; ovary and capsule
glabrous, flower scales broad and blunt.
  Present in sandy river banks in western North America.
  Lacking sericeous foliage, it is less ornamental than *S. exigua*.

Salix melanostachys: (see *S. gracilistyla* var. *melanostachys*)

**Salix × meyeriana Rostk. ex Willd. (S. pentandra L. × S. fragilis L.) S.
cuspidata Schultz.** A strongly-growing large tree often reaching 24 m (80 ft)
high, with widely spreading branches and rounded crown; branchlets light brown,
glabrous and brittle; leaves up to 12 cm long, to 5 cm wide, oblong-elliptic,
glandular serrulate, apex acute or acuminate, base broadly cuneate or acute, glossy
dark green above, glaucous beneath; catkins 3–4 cm long; three or four stamens,
anthers golden; ovary glabrous, pedicel two to three times as long as ventral nectary.
  In general appearance it resembles *S. pentandra*, but *S.* × *meyeriana* is usually a
bigger tree, with thinner, narrower leaves, glaucous-blue beneath; the male
flowers have fewer stamens and the flower scales are more hairy; the female
catkins are more slender and tapering. It occurs with the parents in the wild in
Great Britain and Europe.

A vigorous and extremely ornamental species, a specimen tree worthy of a prime site.

Salix microstachya Turcz.   A large shrub with long, slender, spreading branches; branchlets finely tapering and glabrous; leaves linear, entire, 1.5–3 cm long, not exceeding 3 mm wide, silky-hairy at first, becoming glabrous; catkins slender on leafy stalks, anthers yellow, ventral nectary of male flower half as long as scale; ovary glabrous.

A graceful shrub very similar to, but more glabrous than *S. wilhelmsiana* Bieb.

Salix mielichhoferi Sauter.   A large shrub or occasionally a small tree, with numerous stiff branches; resembling *S. myrsinifolia* (*S. nigricans*), but branchlets thicker and more nodose, sparsely hairy at first soon becoming glabrous; leaves oblanceolate to obovate, entire or partially serrate, dark green above, paler green with prominent reticulate venation beneath; stipules large, ovate; catkins coetaneous on short leafy stalks, ovoid, flower scales brown and hairy; two stamens, filaments pubescent; ovaries pedicellate, style short, stigma tip parted.

Native of the eastern Alps in Europe.

Of no particular ornamental merit.

Salix missouriensis Bebb.   A large shrub or tree up to 15 m (50 ft) high, with spreading branches; branchlets pubescent; leaves lanceolate to ovate-oblong, rarely obovate 5–15 cm long, glaucous beneath; female catkins 5–10 cm long; capsules 8–10 mm long.

A North American species from Kentucky to Iowa and Nebraska.

A vigorous willow with attractive foliage.

Salix miyabeana Seem. (S. dahurica Turcz., S. sapporoensis Lev.,) 'Ezo-No-Kawa-Yanagi'   An erect shrub or small tree to 6 m (20 ft) high, with light-grey branches; branchlets slender, glabrous, pale brown; leaves lanceolate to linear-lanceolate, 5–18 cm long, acuminate at both ends, undulate-serrate, glabrous light green above, glaucous beneath; petioles 3–8 mm long; male catkins 3–5 cm long, sessile, densely flowered, the filaments completely connate; anthers yellow; female catkins 5–8 cm long, short-stalked, flower scales ovate, pubescent; ovary sessile, villous; stigma undivided, sessile, very short.

Native of Honshu and Hokkaido, Japan.

The main eastern counterpart of *S. purpurea*, which it closely resembles.

A very graceful ornamental species.

Salix × mollissima Hoffm. ex Elwert, (S. triandra L. × S. viminalis L.)   A large group of clonal hybrids resulting from centuries of crossbreeding in osier beds, clearly exhibiting inherited qualities, and classified in accordance with their most dominant traits.

Salix × mollissima Hoffm. ex Elwert var. undulata (Ehrh.) Wimm.   A tall shrub 3–6 m (10–20 ft) high, or a small erect tree with flaking bark, as in *S. triandra*, with olive-brown or reddish, glabrous or glabrescent branchlets; leaves dark glossy green above, paler or glaucous beneath, with coarsely serrate margins; leaf apex attenuate-acuminate, unlike *S. triandra*, giving rise to a narrow-lanceolate leaf blade 10–12 cm long and up to 1.5 cm wide; the leaf is subtended by two small stipule-like auricles; stipules conspicuous and persistent, gland-dotted, finely

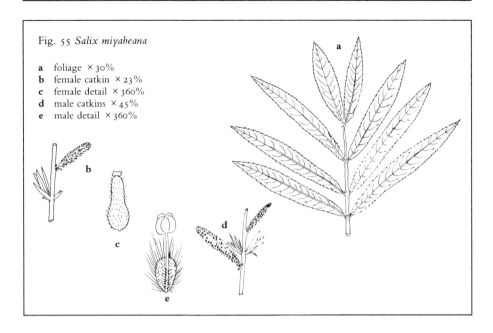

Fig. 55 *Salix miyabeana*

a　foliage × 30%
b　female catkin × 23%
c　female detail × 360%
d　male catkins × 45%
e　male detail × 360%

serrate, acuminate; a female clone, catkins coetaneous in April and May; narrowly cylindrical 3–4 cm long with pale, sparsely hairy flower scales; ovaries glabrous and subsessile; style short and equal to the stigmas.

A relic of osier-holts, being a valuable basket-willow, it is a common hybrid in southern England, easily recognized by its long acuminate leaves.

An attractive, very erect clone occupying relatively little ground area. If preferred it can be regularly coppiced to produce long, shining olive-green rods.

Salix × mollissima Hoffm. ex Elwert var. *hippophaefolia* (Thuill.) Wimm.

A robust shrub 3–5 m (10–16 ft) high, with glabrescent branchlets and acuminate puberulent buds; leaves resemble *S. viminalis*, being linear or linear-lanceolate up to 15 cm long and 1.5 cm wide, apex long-acuminate, margins entire or minutely glandular-serrate; the lamina, unlike *S. viminalis*, is soon glabrous, glossy, dark green above, dull and paler beneath; male and female plants equally common; catkins coetaneous in April and May; male catkins subsessile, to 3.5 cm long, 1 cm wide, with densely hairy yellowish scales, two to three stamens, with yellow anthers. Female catkins slender up to 5 mm wide, stalked, ovaries glabrescent; styles short; two stigmas, cleft.

It occurs sporadically in England, south of Nottingham and Derby. Apart from leaf indumentum it resembles *S. viminalis* more than *S. triandra*.

As a group *S. × mollissima* is both useful and ornamental.

Salix × mollissima Hoffm. ex Elwert 'Trevirani'

A vigorous large shrub with erect habit; glabrous bright green, lanceolate, acuminate leaves; coetaneous with long, erect male catkins with golden anthers in April.

A distinctive ornamental male clone.

Salix monticola Bebb.

A large shrub to 7 m (24 ft) related to *S. glaucophylloides*, but leaves glabrous, not glossy above, ovate or obovate and only 3–5 cm long, leaf margins closely and finely toothed to subentire; catkins subsessile and slender, in fruit up to 4.5 cm long.

A native of western North America, found to the east of the Cascade Mountains.

Salix *moupinensis* Franch.   A shrub or tree 3–6 m (10–20 ft) high with stiff, thick, reddish-brown branches; branchlets yellowish to orange, glabrous, and more slender than in *S. fargesii*; winter buds 6–12 mm long, dark red and glossy; young leaves reddish-purple; mature leaves oblong or narrow-elliptic 6–20 cm long, apex acute or short-acuminate, base rounded, margins sharply glandular-serrulate, glabrous dark green above, paler, reticulate and usually glabrous beneath; petioles 1–1.5 cm long; exstipulate; catkins on short leafy branchlets, male catkins 6–9 cm long, female catkins up to 15 cm long and loose flowered; flower scales glabrous, yellow-brown and persistent; ovary glabrous, short stalked. Only the female in cultivation.

Introduced from west Szechwan, China by Ernest Wilson in 1910.

An exceptionally ornamental large-leafed species often confused with *S. fargesii* – for distinguishing features see also under *S. fargesii*.

Salix *mucronata* Thunb.   A tall tropical tree 6–15 m (20–50 ft) high; branchlets glabrous; leaves dimorphic, small spring leaves deciduous, followed by larger summer leaves, in common with other species of South African *Salix* (see also explanation under *S. wilmsii*). Spring leaves obovate, 2–2.5 cm long, 4–8 mm wide, entire, apex mucronate, base cuneate; petioles 1 mm long; summer leaves ovate, 4–5 cm long, 1–1.5 cm wide, apex acuminate, base acute or obtuse, margins serrulate; petioles 2–3 mm long; stipules small and caducous; five to six stamens; ovaries pedicellate.

A South African species of river banks and mud flats with a range extending in a wide belt across the most southern part of the Cape Province.

Not hardy in western cold temperate conditions.

Salix *mucronata* Thunb. var. *integra* Davy.   A tall, many-branched tree; branchlets densely tomentose; summer leaves longer and wider than the species; leaf margins entire or subserrulate.

Mainly confined to the head waters of the Sunday River in the Cape Province, South Africa.

Salix *mucronata* Thunb. var. *caffra* Davy.   A tall, many-branched tree with long pendulous branchlets; spring leaves very small, only 2–3 mm wide, apex mucronate; summer leaves narrowly linear-lanceolate, 3–3.5 mm long and only 3–5 mm wide, apex long-acuminate or acute.

Confined to rivers of the Eastern Cape and Transkei, South Africa.

Salix × *multinervis* Doell. (*S. cinerea* L. var. *oleifolia* Macreight, or var. *cinerea* × *S. aurita* L.)   An erect, many-branched shrub or small tree, up to 6 m (20 ft) high; branchlets slender grey-pubescent becoming glabrous, dark reddish-brown, peeled wood with many striae; leaves oblong or obovate 1.5–2 cm long, 0.5–2.5 cm wide, dull green above, persistently densely grey or rusty pubescent with prominent nervation beneath, apex obtuse or shortly acute, the tip sometimes twisted, margins undulate-serrate; petiole short 3–5 mm; stipules large, persistent, auricular and rugose; catkins precocious in April and May, erect, sessile, shortly cylindrical 1.5–3 cm long, scales brown or reddish, densely hairy; male catkins – two free stamens, filaments glabrous or with basal hairs, anthers yellow or red-tinged, nectary oblong; female catkins densely pubescent, pedicellate, style very short, stigmas sometimes two – cleft.

A common hybrid in Great Britain and Europe. In Great Britain *S. cinerea* var. *oleifolia* (*atrocinerea*) is usually a parent, but is replaced by *S. cinerea* var. *cinerea* throughout Europe. *S. multinervis* is distinguishable from both the varieties of *S. cinerea* by the prominent, persistent stipules and dull wrinkled leaves remaining pubescent beneath. *S. aurita* is a much smaller, more twiggy bush with smaller, more wrinkled leaves.

Not very ornamental. Mainly of botanical interest.

***Salix* × *myricoides* Muhlenb. (*S. cordata* Muhlenlb. × *S. sericea* Marsh.)**   A medium-sized shrub to 4.5 m (15 ft) high, with long, spreading branches; branchlets pubescent; leaves lanceolate, acuminate, cuneate, serrulate, puberulent at first, becoming glabrous bright green above, glaucous or glabrescent and glabrate or variably silky beneath; stipules small; capsules silky when young.

A North American hybrid from Massachusetts to Wisconsin and Kansas.

A shrub willow with attractive foliage.

***Salix* 'Myricoides Hastata' (*S.* × *myricoides* × *S. hastata* Muhlenb. L.)**   A shrub to 3.5 m (12 ft) high, with loosely spreading, arching branches; branchlets yellow-green, red-tinged, pubescent at first becoming glabrous and glossy; leaves thin, lime-green and very glossy above, glabrous and glaucous beneath, up to 10 cm long and to 5 cm wide, broadly ovate or broadly ovate-lanceolate, scabrous-serrate, apex shortly acuminate, base cordate; petioles 5–10 mm long; stipules prominent, reniform, dentate, persistent, forming a collar round the youngest shoots.

North American origin.

A hybrid with outstandingly attractive glossy, broad hastate leaves.

***Salix myrsinifolia* Salisb. (*S. nigricans* Sm.) 'Dark Leaved Willow'**   A variable shrub, low and sprawling, but frequently a large open bush exceeding 3 m (10 ft) in height, and sometimes with a dark-grey trunk that is smooth or lightly fissured; twigs dull brown, sometimes black, or green, thickly pubescent,

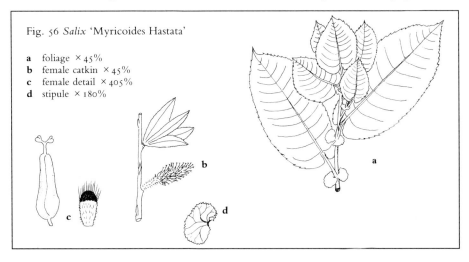

Fig. 56 *Salix* 'Myricoides Hastata'

a   foliage × 45%
b   female catkin × 45%
c   female detail × 405%
d   stipule × 180%

becoming glabrous or glossy in their second year, striae visible in the wood of peeled twigs; leaves thin, obovate, elliptic or oblong 2–8 cm long, 1.5–5 cm wide, dull and dark green above, glaucous below, turning black when dried, sparsely pubescent above, becoming glabrous later, the midrib retaining pubescence below; apex shortly acute or rounded, base cuneate or rounded; leaf margin irregularly serrate; petiole less than 1 cm long; stipules variable, often well developed and persistent, sometimes small and caducous or absent, auricular, pubescent with small scattered, sessile glands. Coetaneous, catkins appearing with the leaves in April and May, usually terminal on short lateral shoots, cylindrical 1.5–5 cm long, 1–2 cm wide; bracts variably pubescent; flower scales fuscous, sparsely hairy. Male catkins with two free stamens; filaments totally glabrous or hairy towards their base, up to 1 cm long; anthers oblong and golden-yellow, nectary shortly oblong and truncate. Female catkins longer and narrower than the male, ovary flask shaped, glabrous or pubescent; pedicels pubescent, 1 cm long; style usually distinct; stigmas suberect or spreading 0.5 mm long, sometimes oblong and entire, but frequently cleft into four lobes.

S. myrsinifolia is scattered throughout the British Isles, but is mainly concentrated in the north of England and Scotland. In Europe it is found as far east as Siberia, usually on river banks at low altitudes. The triple hybrid clone S. myrsinifolia × S. caprea × S. cinerea is included in some salicta.

There are several ornamental and extremely hardy clones of S. myrsinifolia and one subspecies often incorrectly shown under the old-standing species name nigricans.

Salix myrsinifolia ssp. alpicola   A densely branching compact medium-sized shrub or small tree up to 3 m (10 ft) high, with a wide flat crown; branchlets, petioles and bud scales glabrous, dark red; leaves coriaceous, ovate or elliptic 2–5 cm long, 1–2 cm wide, apex acute, base acute or obtuse, serrate; lamina glabrous, glossy dark green above, paler and glaucous beneath. Catkins coetaneous 2–3 cm long, 1–1.5 cm wide, in May. Male and female forms in cultivation. Male catkins prolific with bright-golden anthers.

A very attractive subspecies thriving in relatively dry soil on hillsides, suitable for large or small gardens.

Salix Myrsinifolia 'Bief Froid':   a small male clone similar to S. nigricans ssp. alpicola.

Salix myrsinifolia 'Faucille' and S. nigricans 'St. Antonien'   are female clones.

Salix 'Napoleonis':   (see S. babylonica 'Annularis', S. b. 'Crispa')

Salix neotricha Goerz.   A large fast-growing shrub or small tree with erect habit. Branches smooth; branchlets flexible, finely tapered, glabrous, glossy, pale brownish-green at first, becoming ochreous and orange-tipped during the autumn; buds bright pink. Leaves 6–11 cm long, 1–3 cm wide, lanceolate, acuminate, base cuneate or rounded; lamina dark green glabrous and glossy above, paler green and glabrous beneath; leaf margins glandular-serrate. Stipules absent or minute, petioles light green 3–15 mm long.

A vigorous ornamental species with very striking autumn stem colour.

Male specimens have been recently introduced to Great Britain from the Salictum of the Agricultural University of Brno, Czechoslovakia.

***Salix nigra* Marsh. 'Black Willow'**   A large tree exceeding 30 m (100 ft) in height in its native habitat, but elsewhere a medium-sized or small tree, often with several trunks. Bark dark brown and deeply fissured; branches spreading and slender; branchlets yellow-tinged becoming brown by the autumn, puberulent at first, soon glabrous; leaves linear-lanceolate to lanceolate, 8–12 cm long, 7–20 mm wide, acuminate, cuneate, serrulate, glabrous, pale green, venation sometimes pubescent beneath; petioles 3–6 mm long; stipules semi-cordate, persistent; catkins on leafy branchlets; male catkins 3–5 cm long and slender, stamens three to seven; female catkins 4–8 cm long; ovary glabrous; pedicel longer than nectary; stigma subsessile.

A North American species extending from New Brunswick to western Ontario and California.

***Salix nigra* var. *falcata* Pursh.**   Leaves narrower than the species, only 4–6 mm wide, falcate, totally glabrous green on both sides. A native of eastern North America.

S. nigra is an elegant species, perfectly hardy, not usually exceeding 12 m (40 ft) in Europe.

***Salix nigricans* Sm:**   (see *S. myrsinifolia* Salisb.)

***Salix oleifolia*:**   (see *S. cinerea* ssp. *oleifolia*)

***Salix opaca*:**   (see *S. sachalinensis*)

***Salix oxica* Dode.**   A strongly growing erect tree with widely spreading branches; branchlets reddish-brown, sericeously pubescent at first, becoming glabrous; leaves lanceolate or lanceolate-elliptic, 10–15 cm long, coarsely serrate, apex acuminate, base cuneate, lamina pale green above, silky-hairy and glaucous beneath; ovaries subsessile and glabrous, scales lanceolate.

A native of Turkestan, Bukhara, Russia.

***Salix paraplesia* Schneid.**   A small tree to 7 m (23 ft) high; leaves glabrous, glossy, ovate to elliptic-obovate or elliptic-lanceolate, 5–10 cm long, pale green or glaucous beneath. Closely related to *S. pentandra*.

A native of west China.

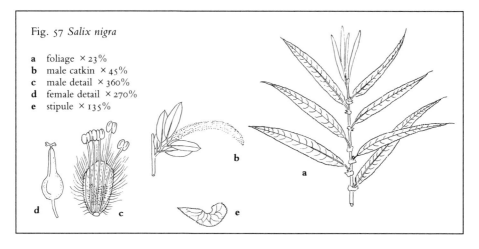

Fig. 57 *Salix nigra*

a   foliage × 23%
b   male catkin × 45%
c   male detail × 360%
d   female detail × 270%
e   stipule × 135%

***Salix pedicellata* Desf.**   A tall shrub or tree up to 9 m (30 ft) high; branchlets grey-pubescent becoming glabrous later, peeled bark revealing numerous prominent striae; leaves oblong or obovate-lanceolate, serrate, crenate or subentire, glabrous above, sparsely pubescent beneath; lateral veins, 10–12 pairs, prominent and reticulate beneath, impressed above; stipules conspicuous, semi-cordate, serrate, caducous; scales pubescent; catkins precocious, elliptic, 3–5 cm long, 1–1.5 cm wide, ovary glabrous; pedicel 3–5 mm; style variable, distinct; stigma short.

Widespread in the Mediterranean region, from Spain to Asia Minor.

***Salix pella* Schneid.**   A large shrub or small tree to 6 m (20 ft) high; leaves elliptic-oblong to elliptic, 5–15 cm long, acute or obtuse, serrulate, with silky-pubescent veins beneath; petiole 6–15 cm long; catkins in fruit 5–10 cm long; scales glabrous, rachis pubescent.

An ornamental large-leafed species from western China, related to *S. magnifica*.

***Salix pellita* Anderss.**   An erect shrub or small tree 3–5 m (10–16 ft) high; branchlets brittle, yellowish to reddish-brown, pubescent to glabrous, frequently with pruinose bloom. Exstipulate; petioles up to 10 mm long; leaves linear-lanceolate, linear-oblanceolate or lanceolate, 5–12 cm long, 10–22 mm wide, apex acuminate, base acute or obtuse, margins slightly revolute, entire or undulate-crenulate; lamina glabrous with impressed veins above, glaucous and sericeously pubescent becoming glabrous beneath; leaf veins numerous and closely parallel. Catkins sub-precocious to coetaneous, 2–5 cm long, subsessile or on short leafy stalks; scales oblanceolate 1–2 mm long, obtuse, blackish, long-hairy, two stamens, filaments free and glabrous; capsules lanceolate 4–6 mm long, subsessile, densely pubescent; styles 0.5–1.5 mm long, deeply cleft; stigmas entire to partly divided.

Originally a native of Europe, it was introduced to North America for basketry and ornamental use many years ago, occasionally escaping into the eastern states and southern Canada.

An attractive species flowering in April and May, very variable after centuries of cultivation.

***Salix pentandra* L. 'Bay Willow'**   A large shrub in the wild, or a tree 9 m (30 ft) to 18 m (60 ft) high in cultivation, with lightly fissured grey bark; branches widely spreading to form a broad, rounded crown; branchlets very glossy brown or

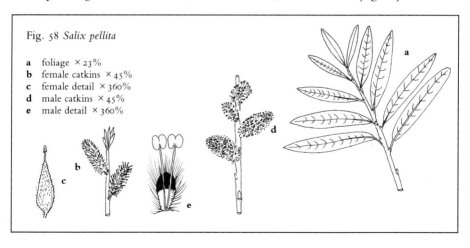

Fig. 58 *Salix pellita*

a   foliage × 23%
b   female catkins × 45%
c   female detail × 360%
d   male catkins × 45%
e   male detail × 360%

reddish and supple; buds small, ovoid, pointed, glossy dark brown; leaves ovate-elliptic, broadly lanceolate or obovate, 5–12 cm long, 2–5 cm wide, base rounded or broadly cuneate, apex cuspidate-acuminate or acute, margin minutely and regularly glandular-serrulate; lamina thick, glabrous, glossy dark green above, paler and glabrous beneath; petiole under 1 cm long with several sessile apical glands; stipules small, ovate, deciduous. Catkins coetaneous, appearing with the leaves in May or June on the tips of short leafy lateral shoots; rachis and upper part of peduncle densely pubescent; male catkins cylindrical 2–5 cm long, 1–1.5 cm wide, dense flowered; scales uniformly pale yellow, oblong, obtuse, 2 mm long, pubescent at the base, glabrous above; generally five to eight stamens, less often four or rarely up to 12; filaments free, with long basal hairs; anthers suborbicular and rich golden-yellow; two nectaries; female catkins usually shorter than the male; ovary glabrous, narrowly flask shaped, attenuate, 6 mm long, 1–1.5 mm wide; style short, indistinct; stigmas spreading, shortly two – cleft or subentire; two nectaries, smaller than the male; capsule up to 10 mm long, ripening in July.

Widely distributed throughout northern and central Europe, the Bay Willow is absent from most of southern Europe and the Mediterranean region. In Great Britain it is common in the wild by streams, and in moist soil at low levels in the north, but is not indigenous in counties south of Yorkshire, North Wales and Northern Ireland. In southern England most specimens are male, planted for their ornamental value.

S. pentandra is one of the most beautiful of all *Salix* species, with its strikingly glossy, broad leaves, varnished branchlets and golden male anthers.

Salix petiolaris Sm. A large shrub to a several-stemmed small tree 3–7 m (10–24 ft) high; branchlets long, arching and slender, puberulent at first becoming glabrous and purple; leaves narrowly lanceolate or narrowly oblanceolate 5–15 cm long, 1–3 cm wide, acute to acuminate, subentire to glandular-serrulate, base acute, lamina dark green and glabrous above, glaucous and glabrous beneath; stipules very small or absent; petioles slender, 5–15 mm long; catkins coetaneous 1–3.5 cm long, 2–2.5 cm wide, lax, subsessile or on short peduncles, scales oblanceolate, brown, sparsely hairy; staminal filaments free, glabrous or with basal hairs. Capsules lanceolate-rostrate 5–9 mm long, finely sericeous; pedicels 2.5–5 mm long, puberulent; styles short, entire to divided.

An eastern North American native frequently found on the banks and in the

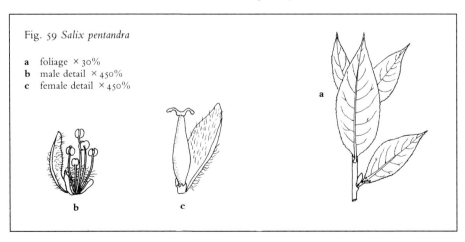

Fig. 59 *Salix pentandra*

a foliage × 30%
b male detail × 450%
c female detail × 450%

shallows of streams and in water meadows from New Brunswick to New Jersey, westwards to James Bay, Alta. Also present in Montana and Colorado, and to the north in Nebraska; sporadic in Vancouver and Oklahoma.

Used in basketry, hybridizing with *S. eryocephala* to produce *S.* 'Americana'.

Flowering in April and May, *S. petiolaris* is a very ornamental arching species with long, slender, purple young stems.

Salix petsusu Kim. (*S. viminalis* sensu auct. Japan., non L.; *S. yezoensis* (C. K. Schn.) Kim. 'Ezo-No-Kino-Yanagi') A vigorous small to medium-sized widely spreading tree 9–12 m (30–40 ft) high; closely resembles *S. kinuiyanagi*, differing in the more slender branches, which are less densely hairy with shorter pubescence, the branchlets greyish-brown, densely white-pubescent while young; leaves lanceolate to oblong-lanceolate 10–20 cm long, 1.5–2 cm wide, apex long-acuminate, base acute to obtuse, entire, glabrous above, with a dense covering of sericeous appressed hairs beneath; petioles pubescent 10–15 mm long. Male catkins short-cylindric or ovoid, 2–3.5 cm long, 1–1.5 cm wide, sessile; female catkins cylindric 3.5–6 (− 12) cm in fruit, scales 2–2.5 mm long, dark brown above, white-hairy on back.

A Japanese species growing in Hokkaido and Honshu. Also in Sachalin.

A very handsome tree grown, in common with *S. kinuiyanagi*, for ornamental purposes and basketry in Japan.

Salix phanera Schneid. A large shrub or tree to 12 m (40 ft) high; branches densely pubescent at first, becoming glabrous; leaves ovate-lanceolate or broadly elliptic-lanceolate 8–20 cm long, apex shortly acuminate or acute, base rounded, leaf margins crenate-denticulate, sparsely puberulent or glabrous with impressed reticulate venation above, densely pubescent becoming glabrous and reticulate beneath, the midrib and numerous parallel veins glabrate and yellowish; petiole 1–2 cm long; stipules semi-cordate, glandular-serrate; male catkins 10–15 cm long; slender; rachis hairy; staminal filaments with basal hairs; scales ovate, rounded, yellow-brown, hairy on both sides.

An impressive species with large leaves, native of western China.

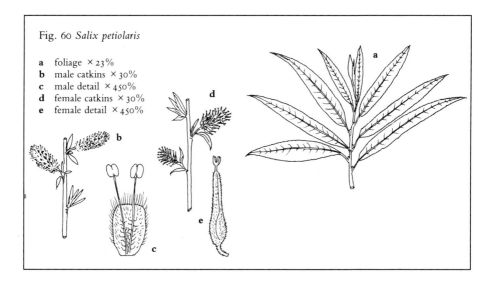

Fig. 60 *Salix petiolaris*

a   foliage × 23%
b   male catkins × 30%
c   male detail × 450%
d   female catkins × 30%
e   female detail × 450%

Salix phylicifolia **L. 'Tea-Leaved Willow'**   A strong-growing, densely branching shrub or tree 2–3 m (7–10 ft) high, rarely up to 6 m (20 ft); bark grey, lightly fissured; twigs bright reddish-brown, lightly pubescent at first, rapidly becoming glabrous and glossy; striae usually absent in the wood of peeled twigs; leaves rigid and coriaceous, bright glossy green above, glossy below, not becoming black when dried, oblong, ovate, or elliptic in shape, 2–5 cm long, 1–5 cm wide, sparsely pubescent, becoming glabrous on both surfaces; apex acute or obtuse, base cuneate or rounded, margins very variable from entire to sharply serrate; petiole up to 1 cm long; stipules tiny, auricular, caducous or lacking. Catkins, coetaneous, with the leaves in April and May on short lateral shoots, cylindrical 2–4 cm long, 1–2 cm wide; two to four leaf-like bracts, pubescent below and glabrous above; flower scales fuscous, variably hairy. Male catkins with two free stamens, up to 1 cm long, anthers oblong and yellow, nectary shortly oblong, truncate. Female catkins of equal length to the male, ovary flask-shaped, thickly pubescent and tapering; pedicel short or almost absent; style 1 mm long stigmas usually spreading and cleft into four lobes.

The distribution of *S. phylicifolia* tends to overlap that of *S. myrsinifolia* within the British Isles. It is widespread in northern Europe, from Iceland and Scandinavia to Russia, and is scattered in central Europe, in Germany, Austria and Czechoslovakia.

Both *S. myrsinifolia* and *S. phylicifolia* are very similar, but *S. phylicifolia* is less variable and is usually recognizable by its shining twigs and bright green, glossy thicker leaves. A triple hybrid clone *S. phylicifolia* × *S. caprea* × *S. cinerea* is present in some collections.

Salix pierotti **Miq.**   A shrub, or occasionally a small tree to 5 m (16 ft) high; branchlets dark brown and glabrous; leaves lanceolate or oblanceolate 6–15 cm long, broadest below the middle, serrulate, glaucous blue beneath, finely puberulent at first, soon becoming glabrous; catkins – male 2–3.5 cm long, sessile, female – 3–5 cm long in fruit on short leafy stalks; style half as long as ovary.

An ornamental Japanese species closely related to *S. miyabeana*.

Salix pierotti **Miq. 'Pendula'**   An attractive pendulous cultivar of *S. pierotti*.

Salix piperi **Bebb.**   Closely related to *S. hookeriana* (Barratt.), a large shrub to 6 m (20 ft) high, similar but less hairy; branchlets villous–puberulent initially becoming glabrous; stipules usually well-developed and foliaceous; leaves entire to serrate or crenate-serrate, up to four times as long as wide, puberulent when very young in shoots, rapidly becoming glabrous and glossy above, strongly glaucous beneath; male catkins more slender than in *S. hookeriana*, often 1.5 cm thick; staminal filaments with basal hairs; capsules 4–6 mm long and slightly hairy at apex. Catkins flowering in March and April.

A North American species found on stream banks, swamps and roadside ditches. It is distributed to the west of the Cascade Mountain summits in Oregon, Washington and adjacent British Columbia, southwards to California. Unlike *S. hookeriana*, with which it hybridizes, *S. piperi* is not confined to maritime habitats.

A vigorous and ornamental willow, less silver in overall appearance than *S. hookeriana* but retaining its other attractive characteristics.

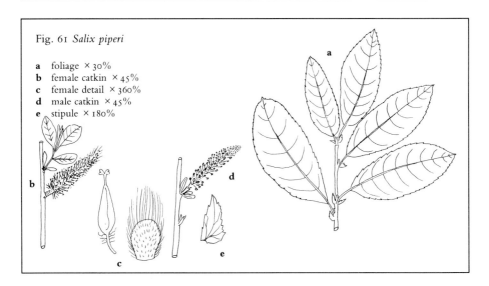

Fig. 61 *Salix piperi*

a foliage × 30%
b female catkin × 45%
c female detail × 360%
d male catkin × 45%
e stipule × 180%

Salix planifolia Pursh.   A shrub 1–4 m (3–13 ft) high; branchlets purple-tinged, often with pruinose bloom; leaves elliptic to lanceolate or oblong-ovate 2–5 cm long, 1–1.5 cm wide, margin entire or glandular serrulate, glabrous above, glabrous and glaucous beneath; pedicels longer than the nectary; capsules 5–6 mm long.

An attractive North American species closely related to S. *phylicifolia* but with smaller catkins. Its distribution extends from Labrador to Alberta, southwards to Colorado and California.

Salix pomeranica: (see S. *daphnoides* ssp. *pomeranica*)

Salix × pontederana Willd. (S. × sordida Kern., S. cinerea L. × S. purpurea L.)   An erect or spreading many-branched shrub up to 5 m (16 ft) high; branchlets rather slender and sparsely pubescent soon becoming glabrous and glossy reddish-brown. Leaves obovate or oblong-elliptic, 4–6 cm long, 1.5–2 cm wide, thinly pubescent on both surfaces at first, becoming glabrous and shining green above, remaining sparsely pubescent and grey beneath or with a few hairs along the midrib and nerves, apex shortly cuspidate or acute, margins irregularly glandular-serrulate or subentire; nervation conspicuous and reticulate; petioles up to 5 mm long; stipules narrowly ovate, acute, serrulate; catkins precocious in March or April, erect, cylindrical, sessile, 2–3.5 cm long, 5–7 mm wide; scales ovate, acute, red-tinged at the base and hairy; male catkins – two free or partly connate stamens, filaments glabrous, anthers red, becoming bright orange and finally turning yellow on dehiscence; female catkins densely grey-pubescent, short-stalked, narrowly ovoid ovaries, the pedicel shorter than the oblong nectary, style absent or indistinct, stigmas erect and entire.

A very hardy hybrid thriving in relatively dry soils. Widespread throughout Europe, occurring in the wild, often with transitional forms, wherever the parents are found together. In Great Britain the typical form has been confirmed in various regions, particularly in Scotland.

A beautiful shrub worthy of a place in a large garden. The male catkins on the bare shining reddish-brown stems in late March or early April are very spectacular.

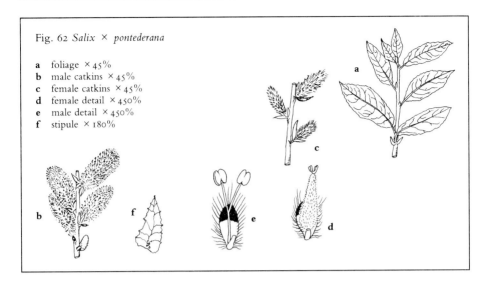

Fig. 62 *Salix* × *pontederana*

a   foliage × 45%
b   male catkins × 45%
c   female catkins × 45%
d   female detail × 450%
e   male detail × 450%
f   stipule × 180%

Salix praecox: (see *S. daphnoides*)

Salix pruinosa: (see *S. acutifolia*)

Salix pseudopentandra Flod.   The Asian form of the European *S. pentandra*. The branchlets and leaves are exceptionally lustrous, even more glossy than those of *S. pentandra*.
  A native of eastern Russia, Manchuria, and Mongolia.
  It is hardy and has recently been introduced to Great Britain.

Salix pubescens: (see *S. laggeri*)

Salix purpurea L. 'Purple Willow'   A shrub of variable habit, sometimes a small many-branched bush, frequently a vigorous, erect, somewhat arching large shrub or an erect small tree up to 5 m (16 ft) high. The bark is pale grey, smooth, yellow internally and very bitter-tasting; branchlets slender, flexible, tough and glabrous, usually greyish-yellow, sometimes tinged with red or purple; buds elongate, ovoid, acute, yellow or red. Leaves frequently opposite or subopposite and extremely variable in length and width, 2–10 cm long, 0.5–3 cm wide, oblanceolate, obovate or linear–oblong; lamina glabrous dark green above, paler or glaucous beneath, immature leaves sometimes thinly pubescent, apex acute, base cuneate, margins subentire or indistinctly serrate in the apical half; petioles very short; stipules small, narrowly oblong, caducous or absent; catkins appear before the leaves in March or April, distributed laterally along the branchlets, often opposite, sessile, erect or curved, narrowly cylindrical, densely flowered, 1.5–3 cm long, 3–7 mm wide, with two or three leaf-like bracts; rachis densely hairy; scales small, ovate, up to 1.5 mm long, hairy, blackish at the base; a single oblong nectary; male flowers – staminal filaments totally united and glabrous; anthers purple, becoming red and eventually pale yellow at dehiscence; female flowers – ovary small, sessile, pubescent; style short and indistinct; stigmas shortly ovate, spreading, sometimes bifid. Capsule ovoid up to 4 mm long and 2.5 mm wide.

There are two fundamentally different forms of *S. purpurea*. A recognizable distinction can be drawn in respect of the narrow-leaved *S. purpurea* L. ssp. *purpurea* and the broad-leaved *S. purpurea* L. ssp. *lambertiana* (Sm.). In Europe the narrow-leaved variants of *S. purpurea* predominate. In Britain the prevailing variant is *S. purpurea* var. *helix* which is one of a series of cultivars connecting the narrow and broad-leaved forms.

S. purpurea has a wide distribution throughout Europe, to a lesser extent in Russia, and is absent from Scandinavia. Several closely related species exist in Asia and Japan. In North America *S. purpurea* and several of its clones were introduced in colonial times for basketry. The clones are very numerous and have been used for the finest quality basketry over the centuries in many parts of the world. Many are very ornamental and are planted in large and small gardens. (*See* Fig. 4.)

Salix purpurea var. amplexicaulis: (see *S. amplexicaulis*)

Salix purpurea L. 'Angustifolia'   A cultivar with long-linear or linear-lanceolate leaves.

Salix purpurea 'Eugenii'   A male clone in the form of a large many-branched shrub 3–5 m (10–16 ft) high, the branches typically ascending from ground level or from a short trunk. Branchlets glabrous, long, slender, arching and very flexible; leaves subopposite and thin, youngest leaves pale brown and translucent; mature leaves linear-lanceolate or narrowly oblong-elliptic, length approximately nine times the width, apex acuminate, base cuneate, lamina dark glabrous green above, glaucous beneath, margins entire or partially and minutely serrate towards the apex; petioles pale green, glabrous, 1–3 mm long, bud scales light grey. Catkins 2–3 cm long, 5–6 mm wide, cylindrical, anthers purple, turning red and finally very pale yellow.

An outstandingly ornamental clone, benefitting from coppicing every third year. Very hardy and vigorous. Ideal for parks or large gardens.

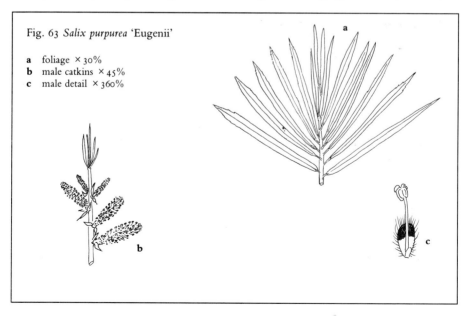

Fig. 63 *Salix purpurea* 'Eugenii'

a   foliage × 30%
b   male catkins × 45%
c   male detail × 360%

***Salix purpura* 'Gold Stones'**   A handsome broad-leaved clone; leaves subopposite, length four times their width, dark green above, glaucous beneath.

***Salix purpura* var. *gracilis* (var. *nana*):**   (see p.163, 164)

***Salix purpurea* var. *helix* (L.) Koch.**   The commonest British form; branchlets pale greenish yellow; leaves opposite, obovate, the length six times their width, apex shortly acuminate or acute, bright glabrous green above, paler and glaucous beneath, margins entire or serrulate towards the apex; exstipulate; petioles short 1–2 mm. Catkins 1.5–2 cm long, 4–6 mm wide, cylindrical.

Exceptionally hardy, tolerating dry situations; the colour changes of the male catkins are striking.

***Salix purpurea* 'Irette'**   An ornamental narrow-leaved clone; leaves subopposite, linear-lanceolate, length ten times the width, apex acuminate, base cuneate, glabrous bluish-green above with prominent nervation, glabrous and glaucous beneath, margins entire.

***Salix purpurea* var. *japonica* Nakai:**   (see *S. koriyanagi* Kimura)

***Salix purpurea* ssp. *lambertiana* Sm. (*S. purpurea* var. *latifolia* Kern.)**   A large shrub or small erect tree up to 6 m (20 ft) high, with steeply ascending thick dark-brown branches; branchlets glabrous, light brown and stout; leaves subopposite broadly oblong or obovate, apex acute, base obtuse, dark glabrous green above, glabrous and strongly glaucous beneath, margins serrate or subentire, length four times the width.

An attractive, vigorous broad-leaved clone.

***Salix purpurea* var. *multinervis*:**   (see *S. integra* Thunb.)

***Salix purpurea* 'Nancy Saunders':**   (see p.164)

***Salix purpurea* 'Nicholsonii Purpurascens'**   A large shrub with ascending grey branches; branchlets long and slender, glabrous, pale green, tinged with red; leaves thin subopposite and narrow, linear-lanceolate, length 12 times the width, apex attenuate-acuminate, base narrowly cuneate, dark bluish-green and glabrous above, glabrous and glaucous beneath, margins entire; young leaves pale brown or purple-tinged; bud scales pink; stipules small or absent; petioles 1–4 mm long.

An extremely graceful ornamental narrow-leaved clone.

***Salix purpurea* 'Pendula':**   (see p.163, 164)

***Salix purpurea* 'Procumbens'**   A totally procumbent clone with branches fanning out widely from the central base; branchlets pale reddish-brown; young leaves purple; mature leaves broadly oblanceolate or obovate, length five times the width, apex acute, base rounded or obtuse, margins partially and minutely serrate towards the apex; stipules small or absent, petioles purple 3–5 mm long.

An interesting clone with characteristic habit and conspicuous young foliage. Requires ample ground space and light. If crowded it will become erect.

Salix purpurea **'Richartii'**   A medium-sized, rounded, bushy shrub; branchlets slender, glabrous dark red becoming glossy dark brown during the winter; immature leaves, thin, translucent, in pale shades of pink to orange; mature leaves blue/green above, glaucous beneath, narrow linear-lanceolate, apex acute or shortly acuminate, base cuneate.

Male and female clones are in cultivation.

An exceedingly beautiful and graceful shrub throughout the year, worthy of a good position in large or small gardens.

Salix purpurea **var.** ***sericea*** **Koch.**   A shrub with the branchlets and leaves covered in a silky tomentum at first, becoming glabrous later.

Salix purpurea **'Uralensis'**   A large shrub with long ascending branches; branchlets glaucous, pale green; buds brown and compressed; leaves alternate or suboppo-site, oblanceolate, lanceolate-elliptic or obovate, length four times the width, glabrous dark green above, glabrous glaucous blue below, marginal serrations more distinct than in usual *S. purpurea* forms, apex shortly acuminate at the tip, base cuneate; petioles short 1–2 mm long.

A handsome broad-leaved clone.

Salix pyrifolia **Anderss. (*S. balsamifera* Barratt.) 'Balsam Willow'**   A large, vigorous, widely-branched shrub or small tree to 9 m (30 ft) high; branchlets glabrous, very glossy dark red or reddish-brown; leaves broadly ovate-lanceolate, with a long tapering apex, base acute or rounded, 9–12 cm long, 2–4 cm wide, glabrous very glossy deep brown above, glabrous light green and less glossy beneath with reticulate venation, margins regularly serrulate; petioles pale green 5–15 mm long. Catkins coetaneous, male 2–3 cm long, female up to 9 cm in fruit, loosely flowered, ovaries glabrous and beaked; style distinct; stigma short and broad.

A very ornamental species from eastern North America with strikingly glossy foliage and winter stems. Distinctly aromatic, balsam-scented.

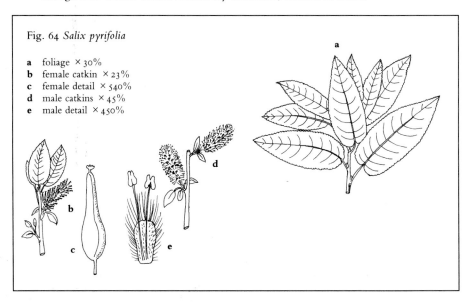

Fig. 64 *Salix pyrifolia*

a   foliage × 30%
b   female catkin × 23%
c   female detail × 540%
d   male catkins × 45%
e   male detail × 450%

Plate 1   *Salix × aegma Brno*. Female catkins.

Plate 2   *salix alba* var. *aurea*. Striking golden foliage against a blue sky.

Plate 3   *Salix alba* var. *aurea*. Female catkins and immature leaves.

Plate 4   *Salix alba* var. *aurea* and *S. alba* var. *sericea*. Good contrasting foliage.

Plate 5 *Salix alba* var. *vitellina*.
September stem colour.

Plate 6 *Salix alba* var. *vitellina*.
November stem colour.

Plate 7   *Salix alpina*. An ideal glossy-leaved shrublet for a rock garden.

Plate 8   *Salix appenina*. Male catkins very prolific. A vigorous large shrub or small tree.

Plate 9   *Salix arenaria (S. repens* var. *arge tea)*. Male catkins in early spring.

Plate 10   *Salix × ausserdorferi (S. glaucosericea × S. retusa)*. Female catkins and glossy leaves. An elegant ground-hugging hybrid.

Plate 11 *Salix × balfourii (S. caprea × S. lanata)*. A widely spreading grey-leaved hybrid with large golden male catkins.

Plate 12 *Salix × basfordiana (S. alba var. vitellina × S. fragilis)*. A fast-growing tree with glossy orange-yellow branchlets and long, pendulous golden male catkins.

Plate 13 *Salix × boydii*. A very hardy slow-growing, grey-leaved dwarf shrub, for an exposed site in the rock garden.

Plate 14 *Salix breviserrata*. Colourful male catkins. A hardy ground-hugging dwarf species.

Plate 15 *Salix caesia* ('Blue Willow'). Male catkins and immature leaves.

Plate 16 *Salix caesia* ('Blue Willow'). Striking blue mature foliage.

Plate 17 *Salix caprea* ('Goat Willow').
Male catkins on a young tree in March.

Plate 18 *Salix caprea* ('Goat Willow').
Male catkins.

Plate 19 *Salix chaenomeloides*. Blue/green leaves and next year's prominent, pink, male catkin buds.

Plate 20 *Salix × chrysocoma*. A beautiful weeping tree with young leaves, in April.

Plate 21 *Salix daphnoides*. A mature specimen tree.

Plate 22 *Salix daphnoides*. 'Continental Purple'. Shining red branchlets and developing male catkins.

Plate 23 *Salix elaeagnos*. A fine shrub with arching stems and linear leaves.

Plate 24 *Salix × elegantissima*. An extremely vigorous and hardy, large weeping hybrid

Plate 25 *Salix eriocephala*. 'Russelliana'. Colourful young leaves and female catkins.

Plate 26 *Salix fargesii*. Unfolding spring buds.

Plate 27 *Salix fragilis* var. *russelliana*. A very big tree with a widely spreading, loosely branched crown.

Plate 28 *Salix glabra*. Female catkins and glossy foliage. An attractive shrub for the small garden.

Plate 29   *Salix glaucosericea*. Immature male catkins and leaves. A very handsome small shrub.

Plate 30   *Salix gracilistyla*. A graceful shrub with arching habit. The red anthers of the male catkins subsequently turn yellow.

Plate 31 *Salix hastata.* 'Wehrhahnii'.
Mature male catkins.

Plate 32 *Salix hastata.* 'Wehrhahnii'.
Immature male catkins.

Plate 33 *Salix helvetica*. Male catkins with red anthers and silver/grey young leaves. An exceptionally beautiful dwarf species for the small garden.

Plate 34 *Salix hibernica*. ('Irish Willow'). Female catkin and glossy leaves.

Plate 35 *Salix hookeriana*. Mature male catkins. A very ornamental shrub or small tree.

Plate 36 *Salix hookeriana*. Characteristic white pubescent broad leaves.

Plate 37 *Salix humilis* ('Prairie Willow'). Female catkins and colourful translucent young leaves.

Plate 38 *Salix integra.* 'Pendula'. Delicately tinted young foliage.

Plate 39 *Salix irrorata*. The male catkins are concentrated towards the tips of the branchlets.

Plate 40 *Salix kinuiyanagi*. Densely crowded male catkins. A very vigorous and outstandingly attractive tree with widely spreading branches.

Plate 41 *Salix kitaibeliana*. Male catkin
and glossy green leaves. A hardy,
procumbent dwarf species.

Plate 42 *Salix koriyanagi (S. purpurea
japonica)*. Male catkins with richly
coloured anthers. Branchlets are long
and finely tapered.

Plate 43 *Salix lapponum* 'Grayii'. A beautiful mound-forming low shrub with silver/grey leaves.

Plate 44 *Salix lindleyana*. A compact, Himalayan, carpet-forming dwarf shrub thriving in an exposed rocky situation. Similar to creeping forms of *S. hylematica* (*S. furcata*). Differences listed under *S. lundleyana*.

Plate 45 *Salix lucida* ('Shining Willow').
An elegant small tree, glossy-leaved,
with golden male anthers.

Plate 46 *Salix magnifica*. An attractive
species with broad magnolia-like leaves
and purple branchlets.

Plate 47 *Salix matsudana* 'Pendula'. An ornamental weeping tree, thriving in relatively dry conditions.

Plate 48 *Salix melanostachys (S. gracilistyla* var. *melanostachys)*. The black male catkin scales are very striking on the naked branchlets in early spring. Anthers are dark orange, becoming pale yellow when mature.

Plate 49 *Salix moupinensis*. A very ornamental shrub with glossy branchlets and large, broad leaves.

Plate 50 *Salix myrtilloides* 'Pink Tassels'. An attractive dwarf male clone with bright purplish-pink anthers.

Plate 51 *Salix × onusta*. Male catkins with bright-orange anthers becoming golden-yellow. A low, spreading shrub.

Plate 52 *Salix polaris*. A procumbent dwarf arctic alpine species best cultivated in a sink garden.

Plate 53 *Salix purpurea* 'Eugenii'. An ornamental male clone of *S. purpurea*, best planted in a large garden or park.

Plate 54 *Salix reinii*. A vigorous small tree with attractive male catkins and dark glossy green leaves.

Plate 55 *Salix repens* var. *subopposita*. An ornamental, compact, hebe-like Japanese dwarf shrub. Male catkins crowd the tips of the branchlets before the leaves appear.

Plate 56 *Salix retusa*. An attractive ground cover in the rock garden.

Plate 57 *Salix rosemarinifolia*. An ornamental small shrub with slender upright branchlets and linear leaves. Very hardy and trouble-free.

Plate 58 *Salix sachalinensis* 'Sekka'. Characteristic fasciation of the stem and golden male catkins. A rapidly growing large shrub.

Plate 59 *Salix schraderiana (S. bicolor)*. Male catkins and lustrous foliage.

Plate 60   A selection of clones, demonstrating stem colours.

Plate 61   *Salix tatrae*. An ornamental alpine shrub.

Plate 62 *Salix × wimmeriana.* A bushy shrub with abundant conspicuous male catkins.

Plate 63 *Salix yezo-alpina (S. Nakamurana* var. *yezo-alpina).* Immature leaves and male catkins.

Plate 64 *Salix yezo-alpina*, with mature, shining dark–green leaves.

Plate 65 *Salix yezo-alpina*, showing striking autumnal foliage colour.

Salix pyrolifolia Ledeb.   A large shrub or small tree to 7 m (24 ft) high; branchlets stout, reddish-brown, glabrous and glossy or sparsely puberulent; leaves ovate to elliptic, dark green and glabrous above, puberulent with prominent pink midrib and venation beneath; petioles pink, up to 3 cm long; stipules reniform, prominent, 1–1.5 cm wide; catkins dense-flowered, small and subsessile, capsule 3–4 mm long, glabrous, brown; style 1 mm; stigma short.

A European species, native in northern Finland, northern Russia and the Urals.

Salix rehderiana Schneid.   A large shrub or usually a tree up to 9 m (30 ft) high, with an erect fissured grey trunk. Branchlets sparsely pubescent or glabrous, reddish-brown; leaves 5–12 cm long, lanceolate, apex shortly acuminate, base rounded to broadly cuneate, margins irregularly glandular-serrate, sometimes subentire, lamina glabrous dark green above; greyish-white and sericeous becoming glabrous and glaucous beneath; petioles 3–9 mm long, pubescent; catkins sessile or subsessile in April with two or three basal leaf bracts; scales oblong, obtuse, puberulent; staminal filaments glabrous with basal hairs; anthers purple, becoming yellow; ovary glabrous and subsessile; stigmas short and emarginate.

A hardy ornamental tree from western China.

Salix × reichardtii Kern. S. polymorpha Host. (S. caprea L. × S. cinerea L.)   A large many-branched shrub or small tree to 6 m (20 ft) high or sometimes more, exhibiting typical characteristics of both parents. Branchlets generally slender, pubescent, dark brown like those of *S. cinerea*; leaves broad, rugose-margined, with a soft indumentum beneath similar to *S. caprea*. Catkins of the hybrid are usually smaller and more slender than those of *S. caprea*. The wood of the branchlets is often marked with longitudinal striae characteristic of *S. cinerea*. In the late summer a few scattered rufous hairs are present beneath the leaves of *S. × reichardtii*. These hairs are coarse when compared with the soft pubescence of the undersurface of leaves of *S. caprea*. Pure *S. caprea* is becoming much rarer than is generally accepted; normally it grows at the edge of woodlands on well-drained soil; where trees have been cut down or the habitat has been disturbed, the hybrid and *S. cinerea* often replace *S. caprea*.

The incidence of *S. × reichardtii* is very widespread, occurring wherever the parents are found growing together, and is often accompanied by the presence of a series of intermediate forms.

Salix reinii Fr. and Sav., (S. kakista Schneid. 'Miyama-Yanagi', 'Mine-Yanagi')   A large glabrous shrub or small erect tree to 5 m (16 ft) or more high, with thick dark-brown branches. Branchlets glabrous, glossy yellowish-brown; leaves obovate or elliptic, 2–6 cm long, 1.5–3.5 cm wide, rounded and mucronate, apex abruptly acute, with incurved, undulate-serrate teeth, base rounded to obtuse, thick-textured, dark green and very glossy above, glabrous and glaucous beneath, the lateral nerves slender; petioles lime green, 0.5–1.5 m long; male catkins short-stalked, slender 3–4 cm long, loose flowered, rachis hairy, scales broadly lanceolate to narrowly ovate, sparsely hairy below and marginally; female catkins narrowly cylindric, 3–6 cm long; capsules glabrous; style slender; the stigmas shortly bifid.

A Japanese species, common in Hokkaido and Honshu.

A very elegant, ornamental species; vigorous, with broad, remarkably glossy, dark-green leaves. The male anthers are very attractive, bright red at first, changing to pale yellow.

Salix reinii Fr. and Sav. var. *eriocarpa* Kimura. 'Ke-Miyama-Yanagi' Branchlets and young leaves sericeously hairy; ovaries densely white pubescent.
Confined to mountain slopes in Honshu, Japan.

Salix × reuteri Moritzi. (*S. elaeagnos* Scop. × *S. daphnoides* Vill.) A large shrub with spreading branches, or often a small tree to 6 m (20 ft) high. Branchlets grey-pubescent, becoming glabrous with a pruinose bloom later; leaves lanceolate or narrow-lanceolate, apex attenuate-acuminate, base cuneate, dark green glabrous above, sericeously pubescent beneath; stipules small, lanceolate; catkins subsessile; scales dark brown towards the apex; staminal filaments partially connate at the base.
An uncommon, very ornamental European cultivar.

Salix rigida Muhl. A large shrub or small tree up to 4 m high; branches reddish-brown, glabrous and glossy; branchlets reddish-brown to yellowish-green, glabrous and shining or with a very fine puberulent covering. Leaves narrowly oblong-obovate, 5–10 cm long, 1–2 cm wide, apex acuminate or acute; base round or cuneate; margins serrulate; immature leaves red-tinged, translucent, densely to sparsely pubescent; mature leaves glabrescent above with the midrib often remaining softly puberulent, glaucous and glabrescent beneath; petioles 8–20 mm long, pink-tinged; stipules narrowly elliptic to ovate 5–12 mm long, margins serrulate; bud scales frequently separating and left attached to the base of shoot. Catkins precocious to coetaneous, on short floriferous branchlets. Male catkins 1.5–3 cm long; stamens two, filaments connate at the base, glabrous; female catkins 3–5 cm long; pistils slender, red or green-tinged, glabrous, capsules 4–6 mm long; styles short, stigmas small; stipes 1–2 mm long, glabrous, one nectary, adaxial; flower scales narrowly elliptic, apex acute, 1–2 mm long, yellowish to deep brown and sparsely hairy.
A widely distributed North American species, sporadic in southern Yukon and

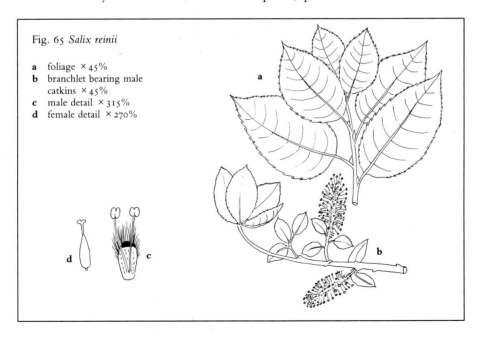

Fig. 65 *Salix reinii*

a foliage × 45%
b branchlet bearing male
      catkins × 45%
c male detail × 315%
d female detail × 270%

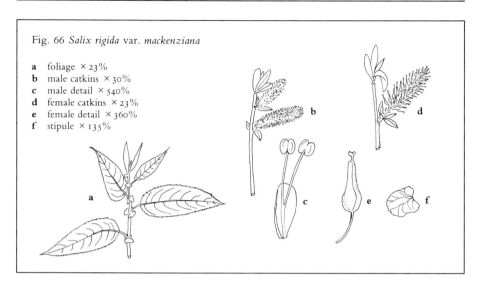

Fig. 66 *Salix rigida* var. *mackenziana*

a   foliage × 23%
b   male catkins × 30%
c   male detail × 540%
d   female catkins × 23%
e   female detail × 360%
f   stipule × 135%

adjacent British Columbia; southward to Washington, California and Arizona; eastward to Newfoundland and Virginia.

A very hardy species living on sand bars along rivers. The shining foliage and branchlets are attractive.

Salix rigida Muhl. var. *mackenziana* (Raup) Cronq; (*S. mackenziana* Raup; *S. lutea* Nutt., *S. cordata* Muhl. var. *mackenziana* Hook.)   A large, thick-branched, widely spreading shrub, often a small tree 9 m (30 ft) high, with a wide crown and several thick limbs arising from a very short base; branchlets long, slender and flexible, glabrous, glossy yellowish-green; immature leaves glabrous, glossy bright green; mature leaves obovate, broadly lanceolate or narrowly elliptic, coarsely serrate, apex acuminate or acute, base round or cuneate, 5–12 cm long, 1–3 cm wide, three to five times as long as wide; lamina dark green, and glabrous above, pale green beneath; stipules 6–12 mm long, persistent, narrowly elliptic, acute, serrulate. Catkins precocious to coetaneous, terminating short lateral branchlets with leafy basal bracts; rachis densely lanate; flower scales glabrous, brown or blackish, persistent. Male catkins 2–5 cm long, 1–1.5 cm thick; stamens two, filaments glabrous, connate below, frequently to above the middle; female catkins 3–6 (9) cm long when mature, stipes 3–4 mm long; capsules glabrous 3–7 mm long; style short but distinct; stigmas short, subentire.

A North American transcontinental variety with a distribution corresponding to that of the species, *S. rigida* Muhl. The tough, flexible branchlets have been widely used for basketry.

An ornamental variety with dark glossy foliage and shining yellow/green branchlets.

Salix rorida Lacksch. (*S. daphnoides* sensu auct. Japan., non Vill.; 'Ezo-Yanagi')   A tall, erect, smooth-barked tree varying from 9 m (30 ft) to 18 m (60 ft) high, with glabrous, glossy reddish branches; branchlets dark red and slightly pruinose; leaves 5–12 cm long, 7–30 mm wide, lanceolate, long-acuminate, base acute to obtuse or rounded, lamina glabrous, glaucous beneath, leaf margins serrulate; petioles 2–8 mm long; male catkins subsessile, 1.5–3.5 cm long,

12–14 mm diameter, very densely flowered, two stamens, the filaments free and glabrous; scales narrowly obovate, 2–2.5 mm long, with glandular margins and densely long silvery-hairy; female catkins 2–4 cm long, 1–1.5 cm diameter, very densely flowered; ovaries glabrous, pedicellate; style long and slender; stigmas short, bifid.

A Japanese native of Hokkaido and Honshu; also present in Sakhalin, Amur, Ussuri, and Korea.

A beautiful tree, closely related to *S. daphnoides*.

Salix rorida var. ***roridaeformis*** **(Nakai) Ohwi.; (*S. rorida* var. *eglandulosa* Kimura) 'Ko-Ezo-Yanagi'** A similar form to the species, differing in the catkin scales which are without glands.

Salix rossica **Nasarov. (*S. viminalis* L. var. *serotina*)** A large shrub or small tree 3–5 m (10–16 ft) high; branchlets long, flexible, slender, pale brown or yellowish, generally glabrous; buds obtuse and conspicuously larger than in *S. viminalis*; leaves narrowly oblanceolate, base narrowly rounded, lamina sparsely hairy and greyish-green above, sericeously pubescent beneath, leaf margins revolute, with prominent glands; lateral veins 12–30 pairs. Catkins appear after the leaves (serotinous); style shorter than the stigmas.

A useful basket willow, largely replacing *S. viminalis* L. in the former USSR.

Salix rowleei **Schn.** Closely related and similar to *S. lasiolepis*; an endemic species in Mexico.

Salix × rubens **Schrank (*S. alba* L. × *S. fragilis* L.)** A large erect tree 20–30 m (65–100 ft) high, with a broad trunk and roughly fissured bark; branches widely spreading to form an extensive rounded crown; branchlets smoothly rounded, pubescent at first, soon becoming glabrous dull olive-brown. Leaves lanceolate or linear-lanceolate, usually long-acuminate, margins serrulate or irregularly serrate, lamina sericeously pubescent beneath. Catkins spreading or suberect, narrowly cylindrical 4–6 cm long, generally less than 8 mm in diameter; both peduncle and rachis pubescent. Male catkins frequently loose-flowered, scales blunt, hairy and much shorter than the stamens; ovary subsessile, glabrous and flask-shaped.

The name *S. × rubens* includes a wide range of variants, from *S. alba* L. var. *coerulea* (Sm.) at one end of the scale, to *S. fragilis* L. at the other. Many of these clones are very impressive in stature and form; some also have attractive yellow, orange or red-tinged branchlets.

Salix rubens **Schrank *basfordiana* (Scaling ex Salter) Meikle.:** (see *S. × basfordiana*)

Salix × rubens **Schrank *basfordiana* (Scaling ex Salter) Meikle. var. *sanguinea*** A variable-sized bushy shrub or less commonly small tree, considerably smaller and less vigorous than *S. × basfordiana* and with darker-red branchlets and bright scarlet-red catkin bud scales; leaves up to 10 cm long, less than 1.5 cm wide, narrowly lanceolate attenuate-acuminate, base narrowly cuneate; lamina densely pubescent at first, remaining sparsely pubescent when mature, leaf margins shortly serrate. The female catkins are narrowly cylindrical, spreading or erect, 3–4 cm long, up to 6 mm diameter; peduncle and rachis sparsely pubescent, glabrescent; catkin scales 3 mm long and up to 1 mm wide. Ovaries narrow, 3–4 mm long; style short; stigmas short and bifid.

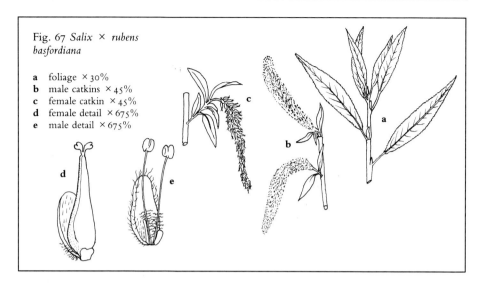

Fig. 67 *Salix* × *rubens basfordiana*

a foliage × 30%
b male catkins × 45%
c female catkin × 45%
d female detail × 675%
e male detail × 675%

Only female forms are in cultivation. Not known outside Great Britain.

This shrub is distinctive, with low, spreading slender branchlets and conspicuous bright-red catkin bud scales, particularly beautiful in the early spring.

Salix × rubra Huds. (S. purpurea L. × S. viminalis L.)   A tall shrub or small tree 3–6 m (10–20 ft) high, with fissured bark and loosely spreading branches; branchlets very flexible, long, slender, tough, glabrous and lustrous yellowish-green. Leaves linear or narrowly lanceolate 5–15 cm long, 1–1.5 cm wide, densely pubescent becoming glabrous and dark shining green above, paler green and usually remaining sparsely pubescent beneath; apex usually finely acuminate, base narrowly cuneate; leaf margins narrowly revolute, undulate or flat, frequently minutely serrulate mainly towards the apex; stipules linear, glandular-serrulate and caducous. Catkins precocious in mid-March or early April, frequently concentrated towards the extremities of the branches as in *S. viminalis*, sessile, shortly cylindrical, 2–4 cm long, 0.8–1 cm thick; catkin scales short, black and hairy as in *S. purpurea*, occasionally brown-tinged as in *S. viminalis*; two stamens, free or partly connate, glabrous, or sparsely hairy filaments; anthers red or yellow; ovary ovoid or nearly spherical, densely pubescent; style short; two linear stigmas, united, twice as long as the style.

A very common hybrid in Great Britain and throughout Europe. It is represented in cultivation by a wide range of cultivars and is frequently a relic of osier beds. The rods, being long, flexible and very durable have for many centuries been used in basketry. Clones well known to basket makers are known as 'Mawdesley's Long Skein', 'Tulip Willow', 'Continental Osier', 'Harrison's Seedling' and 'Pyramidalis'. The hybrid is readily identified, the green lower surface of the leaves distinguishing it from *S. viminalis* and the pubescent branchlets and immature leaves preclude *S. purpurea*.

Salix rupifraga Koidz 'Koma-Iwa-Yanagi'   A large shrub with dark-brown glabrous branches; branchlets light greyish-brown with long grey appressed hairs; leaves ovate-oblong to oblong 4–7 cm long, 1.5–3 cm wide, apex acuminate to acute, base acute or obtuse and sometimes rounded, margins irregularly serrate, lamina of immature leaves sericeously pubescent becoming glabrous except for the midrib above, glaucous below; petioles 5–10 mm long; male catkins cylindrical, 2–3 cm long, 5–6 mm thick, shortly pedunculate, scales elliptic or ovate, long-pubescent, 1–1.5 mm long; female catkins up to 5 cm long in fruit, dense-flowered; ovaries glabrous and shortly pedicellate; styles short; stigmas short and bifid.

A Japanese species confined to the mountains of Honshu.

Salix russelliana: (see *S. fragilis* L. var. *russelliana* (Sm.) Koch)

Salix sachalinensis F. Schmidt. (S. opaca Seem.) 'Onoe-Yanagi'   A voluminous large shrub or small tree 4 m (13 ft) to 6 m (20 ft) high, typically arising from several trunks bearing long very widely spreading branches; branchlets numerous, sparsely pubescent becoming glabrous, glossy and reddish-brown; leaves lanceolate 5–10 cm long, 1–2 cm wide, apex acuminate, base cuneate, margins entire or slightly recurved and undulate, lamina glabrous dark green above, paler and slightly glaucous beneath, with silky pubescence while young. Catkins precocious or coetaneous; male catkins subsessile, densely flowered, cylindrical, 2–4 cm long, 5–8 mm in diameter, scales lanceolate, brown towards apex, obtuse with long marginal hairs, filaments glabrous. Female catkins densely flowered, 2.5–5 cm long; ovaries pubescent, pedicel distinct; style long, slender, up to 1.5 mm long; stigma entire, oblong and short.

A native of Japan common in Hokkaido, Honshu and Shikoku; also occurs in Amur, Ussuri, Sachalin, Kamchatka, and Kuriles.

Salix sachalinensis F. Schmidt 'Sekka'; (S. sachalinensis var. ligulata Kim., S. 'Setsuka' Hort.); 'Dzyariu-Yanagi' 'Dragon Willow'   A vigorous male clone with long, very widely spreading branches; branchlets shining mahogany-red with characteristic broad fasciation (bundling and flattening) and a tendency to curl round in the fasciated sections; leaves lanceolate, 6–12 cm long, 1–2 cm wide, bright glossy green above, white pubescent beneath; catkins precocious, very prolific, 4.5–8 cm long, 0.5–1 cm in diameter, densely flowered, with bright golden anthers.

Widely cultivated in Japan and introduced to Holland in 1950.

A hardy and outstandingly ornamental clone, requiring ample space in a large garden. In addition to its attractive stems and catkins, which are ideal for use in floral decorations, its leaves change from glossy green to a rich yellow in the autumn.

This clone deserves to be more widely grown in the West.

Salix safsaf Forsk.   A tall tropical tree; the leaves are dimorphic, in common with other tropical African species, with very small deciduous and entire spring leaves, followed by much larger serrulate summer leaves. In the case of *S. safsaf* the summer leaves are lanceolate, 5–10 cm long, 1–1.5 cm wide, apex long-acuminate, base cuneate, margins indistinctly serrulate; petioles 1–1.5 cm long; five stamens, filaments free with basal hairs; ovaries oval, pedicellate and glabrous, stigma subsessile, thick and bifid.

Unlike other tropical African *Salix* species, which are all local in distribution, *S. safsaf* has a wide range extending from Syria and Egypt to Angola. It follows the Nile and the great lakes to the south along the Congo-Zambezi watershed to the Zambezi and Cunene Rivers, from Eritrea to Zimbabwe. It hybridizes with *S. woodii* Seem. All the African *Salix* species show the closest affinity with *S. acmophylla* in Syria.

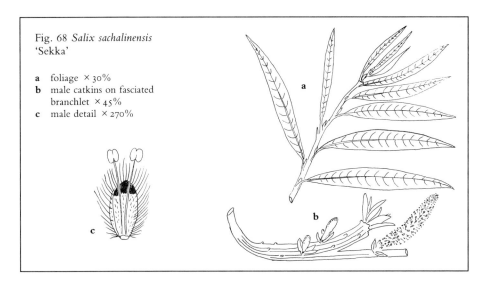

Fig. 68 *Salix sachalinensis*
'Sekka'

a foliage × 30%
b male catkins on fasciated
  branchlet × 45%
c male detail × 270%

This species is purely of botanical interest. It does not survive outside its tropical habitat.

***Salix × salamonii* Carr. (*S. alba* L. var. *alba* × *S. babylonica* L.)** A large, extremely vigorous tree often exceeding 18 m (60 ft) high, with a wide, rounded crown and strong ascending branches thickly covered in dense foliage. Branchlets semi-pendulous, less slender than in *S. babylonica*, sericeously pubescent at first, becoming glabrous later; leaves 6–12 cm long, 1–2 cm wide, less pubescent than *S. alba* when young, becoming glabrous green above, bluish-white beneath, leaf margins finely serrulate. Leaf fall is often delayed, sometimes until December. A female clone, the catkins are sometimes androgynous, 4–5 cm long, borne on peduncles 2–2.5 cm long; scales ovate, apex obtuse, pubescent and deciduous; ovary ovoid, glabrous and sessile; style short.

Salix × salamonii is the western European cultivar of *S. × sepulchralis* (Simonk.), the latter representing a group of hybrids occuring naturally where *S. alba* var. *alba* is native and *S. babylonica* is still generally cultivated in central Asia, Turkey and Palestine.

One of the most significant and vigorous of all willows, exhibiting the firmness and greater height of *S. alba* combined with extremely graceful form, less pendulous than *S. babylonica*. An ideal specimen tree for parks or estates.

Often misquoted as being synonymous with *S. × chrysocoma* (*S. alba* L. var. *vitellina* × *S. babylonica* L.).

***Salix salvaefolia* Brot. 'Salvia-Leaved Willow'** A tall shrub or sometimes a small tree up to 8 m (26 ft) high; branches and branchlets remaining grey-tomentose, peeled branchlets revealing longitudinal striae; leaves linear-lanceolate to linear-oblong, three to five times as long as wide, apex shortly acuminate or rounded, base cuneate; lamina sparsely pubescent above, densely white pubescent beneath; margins finely serrate or subentire; multiple lateral veins; petioles 4–6 mm long; stipules semi-cordate, serrate; catkins precocious and elliptic, two stamens, filaments with basal hairs; fruiting catkins 3–5 cm long, 1 cm in diameter; capsules tomentose; pedicel short; style very short.

A native of river banks in Spain and Portugal, with attractive foliage.

***Salix* × *sanguinea*:**   (see *S. rubens* var. *sanguinea*)

***Salix schraderiana* Willd. (*S. bicolor* Willd.)**   A large shrub or small many-branched tree up to 4 m (13 ft) high; branchlets like *S. phylicifolia* but with striae on peeled wood, sometimes greenish-yellow and glabrous; buds short, yellowish or orange, bud scales persistent after opening of the bud. Leaves obovate-lanceolate, ovate or narrowly elliptical, obtuse; immature leaves sericeously pubescent above and beneath; mature leaves glabrous, shining dark green above, paler bluish-green beneath; catkins coetaneous, 2–3 cm long, 1 cm diameter, anthers red becoming yellow.

Growing wild in mountains of Europe from central Germany to northern Spain and Bulgaria. It is not present in the Alps.

An ornamental bushy species with attractive and prolific catkins towards the ends of the branchlets. Very hardy.

***Salix* × *schroederi* (*S. purpurea* L. × *S. pyrolifolia* Ledeb.)**   A medium-sized bushy shrub with thick ascending branches; branchlets slender, glabrous dark green or red-tinged; leaves ovate to elliptic 2–5 cm long, 1–3 cm wide, apex acute or obtuse, base acute or rounded, dark glossy green above, paler green and glabrous beneath, margins serrulate or subentire; catkins ovoid 2–3 cm long, 1 cm diameter, stamens with bright golden anthers.

An uncommon male cultivar with conspicuous catkins.

***Salix scouleriana* Barr.**   A shrub 3–6 m (10–20 ft) high or tree 10–20 m (33–65 ft) high; branches dark reddish or yellowish brown, glossy, staying pubescent two years; branchlets brown, pubescent to lanate. Leaves elliptic or obovate, 5–8 cm long, 2–3 cm wide; apex acute to round with acute tip, acuminate in the more narrowly elliptic leaves; base cuneate; margins generally entire and remotely glandular to irregularly glandular serrulate, revolute; young leaves sericeous to lanate; lamina of mature leaves glabrescent, dark green and glossy, glaucous beneath with variable pubescence and white or rusty hairs; petioles 5–15 mm long sparsely pubescent reddish-brown; stipules tiny up to 1–3 mm long, semi-ovate, glandular serrulate; catkins precocious on short leafy branchlets. Male catkins 1.5–4 cm long, two stamens, filaments 5 mm long, glabrous or with basal hairs;

Fig. 69 *Salix schraderiana*

a foliage × 45%
b male detail × 450%
c male catkins × 45%

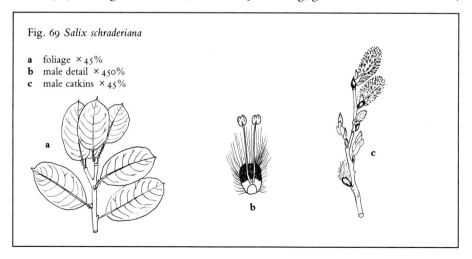

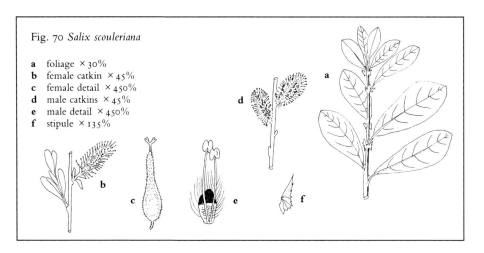

Fig. 70 *Salix scouleriana*

a foliage × 30%
b female catkin × 45%
c female detail × 450%
d male catkins × 45%
e male detail × 450%
f stipule × 135%

female catkins 1.5–5 cm long, ovaries densely pubescent, capsules 5–10 mm long with elongate slender beak, sericeous, hairs covering the seeds often rusty; styles up to 0.5 mm long; stigmas 0.6–1.2 mm long with two lobes, twice as long as the style; pedicels sericeous, 1–2 mm long; one nectary, adaxial, up to half as long as pedicel; scales narrowly elliptic, 2–4 mm long, dark brown, villous with long straight hairs, twice as long as the scale.

A North American species with a wide distribution in woodlands and meadows near rivers. Common in disturbed areas. Present in Alaska and the Yukon; south to British Columbia, California and New Mexico; eastward in boreal forest to Manitoba and South Dakota.

A very hardy species, surviving in most soils, with attractive foliage.

Salix × sericans Tausch. ex Kern. (S. caprea L. × S. viminalis L.) A large vigorous shrub or small tree to 9 m (30 ft) high with shallow-fissured bark and spreading branches; branchlets red-tinged, densely puberulent becoming glabrous and shining later; peeled branchlets do not show striae on the underlying wood; leaves broadly lanceolate or ovate-lanceolate 6–12 cm long, 1.5–3 cm wide, dull green and glabrescent above, densely tomentose with soft, grey hairs beneath; nervation prominent, apex gradually acuminate, base rounded, margins often undulate, slightly revolute, with small distant teeth or subentire. Petioles 1–1.5 cm long; stipules auricular, serrate, small and caducous. Catkins precocious in March or early April, numerous and sessile, mainly towards the tips of the branchlets. Male catkins shortly cylindrical, 2–3 cm long, 1 cm diameter, scales ovate-elliptic 2 mm long, 1 mm wide, brownish, darker at the apex, densely hairy; filaments to 1 cm long, glabrous; anthers golden. Female catkins up to 5 cm long, under 1 cm diameter, ovary narrow and densely pubescent, pedicel short, style distinct, stigmas larger than the style, bifid.

A common hybrid in Great Britain, sometimes spontaneous but usually a clone with distinct uniform features; a relic of cultivation when it was originally grown for coarse basketry many years ago. It is mainly of botanical interest. See also under *S. × smithiana* Willd. with which *S. × sericans* is often confused.

Salix sericea Marsh. (S. grisea Willd.) 'Silky Willow' A large shrub or occasionally a small tree up to 4 m (13 ft) high; branchlets purplish, long, slender,

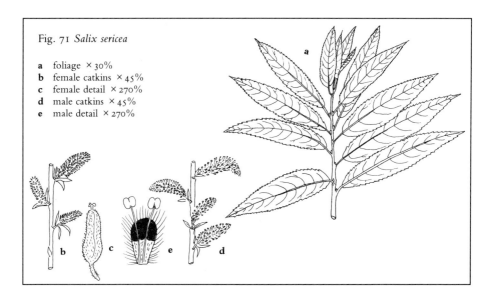

Fig. 71 *Salix sericea*

a foliage × 30%
b female catkins × 45%
c female detail × 270%
d male catkins × 45%
e male detail × 270%

puberulent when young, becoming glabrous; leaves lanceolate to narrowly lanceolate, 5–12 cm long, 1–3 cm wide, apex acuminate, base cuneate to rounded, margins serrulate; lamina sericeously puberulent above and beneath at first, becoming dark green and glabrous above and glaucous with persistent sericeous puberulence beneath when mature; stipules lanceolate to semi-ovate, 4–10 mm long, deciduous; petioles slender, puberulent, 5–10 mm long. Catkins precocious between February and May, 1–5 cm long, 6–10 mm wide, subsessile; scales obovate-oval, obtuse, blackish and hairy. Two stamens, filaments free, glabrous above with basal hairs, pedicel about one-third as long as the ovoid–oblong, obtuse puberulent ovary; stigmas short and sessile.

A native of eastern North America from Nova Scotia and New Brunswick to Michigan and eastern Indiana; south to Georgia and south-eastern Mexico.

A very elegant species with long arching branchlets, usually found near or often in running water. Ideal for a waterside situation in a large garden.

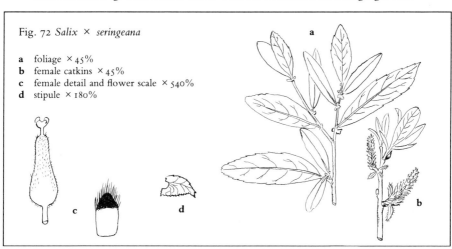

Fig. 72 *Salix × seringeana*

a foliage × 45%
b female catkins × 45%
c female detail and flower scale × 540%
d stipule × 180%

***Salix* × *seringeana* Gaud. (*S. elaeagnos* Scop. × *S. caprea* L.)** A medium-sized shrub or a small erect tree up to 4 m (13 ft) high; branchlets straight, slender, pale grey, tomentose; leaves lanceolate or oblong-lanceolate, 3–9 cm long 1–2.5 cm wide, apex rounded, shortly acuminate or acute, base cuneate or rounded, leaf margins revolute and irregularly serrate or subentire, lamina densely white sericeously pubescent on both surfaces of young leaves, becoming sparsely silver-white pubescent above and persistently dense silver-white pubescent beneath mature leaves, nervation prominent on under surface; leaves subsessile, petioles 1–2 mm long; stipules auricular, pubescent, small and often persistent. Catkins precocious, peduncle 3–4 mm long, leaf bracts silver hairy beneath; stamens connate and hairy at the base of the filaments; pedicel about half as long as the ovary; style short.

A very handsome and hardy European hybrid, strikingly silvery-white in overall appearance. An exceedingly beautiful shrub for large or small gardens.

***Salix serissaefolia* Kim. 'Kogome-Yanagi'** A large shrub or small tree to 6 m (20 ft) or more high with ascending pale-brown branches; branchlets long, slender, greyish puberulent at first becoming glabrous and shining; leaves lanceolate to broadly lanceolate 4–8 cm long, 8–12 mm wide, apex tapering long-acuminate, base obtuse, margins serrulate, lamina glabrous and glossy bright yellowish-green above, paler beneath, the lateral nerves slender, spreading, paler coloured and prominent above; female catkins slender, 1–2 cm long, shortly pedunculate, dense-flowered, sericeously pubescent; style short; stigmas linear; capsules ovoid, about 25 mm long.

A Japanese species, native of Honshu.

A vigorous and very ornamental species with unusually glossy bright-green foliage on slender arching branchlets.

***Salix serissima* (Bailey) Fern. 'Autumn Willow'** A large shrub up to 4 m (13 ft) high with olive-brown branches; branchlets and bud scales yellowish-brown, glabrous and glossy; exstipulate; leaves lanceolate, elliptic-lanceolate to oblong-lanceolate, 6–10 cm long, 1–3.5 cm wide, apex shortly acuminate or acute, base cuneate or rounded, leaf margins regularly and minutely glandular-serrulate, lamina glabrous and conspicuously shining green above, paler bluish-green

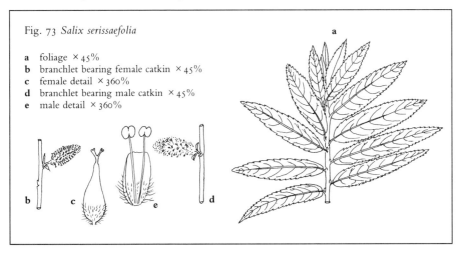

Fig. 73 *Salix serissaefolia*

a foliage × 45%
b branchlet bearing female catkin × 45%
c female detail × 360%
d branchlet bearing male catkin × 45%
e male detail × 360%

beneath. Petioles slender, glandular near the laminal junction. Catkins serotinous, appearing long after the leaves in late summer, the fruit being retained from July until September. Catkins cylindrical or cylindric-oval, 1–3 cm long, up to 2 cm diameter, on leafy lateral stalks 1–4 cm long; male catkins – three to five stamens, or more; filaments free with a few basal hairs; scales obovate, yellow, with white hairs, deciduous. Female catkins – capsules narrowly conical, 7–12 mm long, brown, thick-walled and glabrous; pedicels thick, 1–2 mm long; styles short; stigmas very short and bifid.

A North American species thriving in swampy ground from Newfoundland to James Bay, west to Saskatchewan and Alberta, south to New Jersey and Indiana and centrally in Minnesota, North Dakota and Montana. Less common in South Dakota and Colorado.

A beautiful large shrub, adapted to boggy conditions, with very shiny glossy leaves and branchlets. Closely related to *S. pentandra* and *S. lucida*.

Salix sessilifolia Nutt. (*S. sessilifolia* var. *villosa* Anderss.)   A large shrub or small erect tree up to 8 m (26 ft) high, with a narrow trunk; branchlets, immature leaves and capsules markedly villous or villous-puberulent; mature leaves lanceolate, narrowly elliptic or oblong, 3–10 cm long, 1–3.5 cm wide, leaf margins with widely-spaced small sharp teeth or entire, lamina sparsely villous or glabrescent above, remaining villous beneath; petioles 1–5 mm long; stipules minute and caducous; catkins serotinous, between May and July, on leafy lateral branchlets; scales yellow, hairy; two stamens, filaments free with basal hairs; female catkins 4–10 cm long; capsules 3–5 mm long and occasionally with three valves; style distinct; stigma lobes long and slender.

A member of the North American section *Longifoliae* with characteristic suckering, thicket-forming habit and narrow leaves. In this species, however, branchlets, leaves and capsules are conspicuously hairy. It is closely related to *S. fluviatilis*, with which it hybridizes.

Found in or beside streams flowing to the west of the Cascade Mountains, its range extending from south British Columbia to the Umpqua Valley in Oregon, and up the Columbia to the east end of the gorge.

Salix sieboldiana Bl. 'Yama-Yanagi'   A large shrub or often a small tree up to 6 m (20 ft) high with a fissured trunk and slender, arching, dark-brown, glabrous

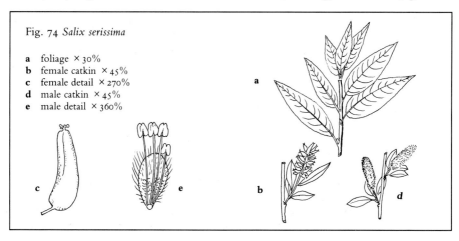

Fig. 74 *Salix serissima*

a   foliage × 30%
b   female catkin × 45%
c   female detail × 270%
d   male catkin × 45%
e   male detail × 360%

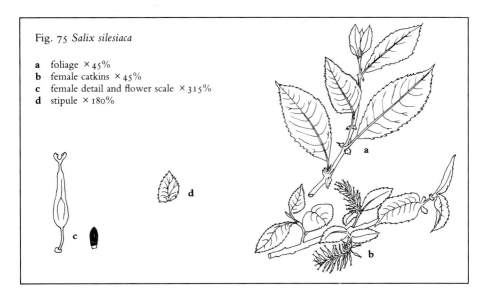

Fig. 75 *Salix silesiaca*

a foliage × 45%
b female catkins × 45%
c female detail and flower scale × 315%
d stipule × 180%

branchlets; immature leaves white-pubescent; mature leaves lanceolate-oblong or elliptic, 4–12 cm long, 1.5–4 cm wide, apex shortly acuminate, base obtuse, leaf margins bearing incurved undulate serrations; lamina glabrous above, glaucous and glabrous with pubescence confined to the midrib beneath; petioles 1–1.5 cm long; male catkins 3–3.5 cm long, 5–7 mm diameter, shortly pedunculate, densely flowered, scales ovate, obtuse and long-haired. Two stamens, filaments with basal hairs; style short, stigma bifid.

An ornamental Japanese species growing in Kyushu.

Salix silesiaca Willd.   A large shrub or small tree up to 6 m (20 ft) high with ascending and spreading branches; branchlets dark brown slightly pubescent at first, soon becoming glabrous, peeled wood sometimes revealing striae; immature leaves reddish-brown, thin, densely white villous beneath, sparsely pubescent above; mature leaves glabrous on both sides, broadly lanceolate or oblanceolate, apex triangular or shortly acuminate, base broadly cuneate or rounded, leaf margins serrate, crenate or subentire, lamina light green above, bluish-green beneath with prominent reticulation; stipules reniform and glandular; catkins precocious or coetaneous in March or April, shortly pedunculate, peduncle 4–5 mm long, pubescent; leaf bracts two to four glabrous above, sericeously puberulent beneath; catkins 2–4 cm long, 1–1.5 cm in diameter; male – two stamens – free, glabrous, anthers red at first; female – ovary glabrous; scales oblong, apex dark red, rounded and bearded with long white hairs.

A native of the Balkans, Carpathians and Sudetanland, but absent from the Alps and western Europe.

An attractive member of the sallow group, with beautiful young foliage and graceful, somewhat spreading habit.

Salix × sirakawensis Kim. (S. futura Seem. × S. integra Thunb.)   A large shrub or small tree up to 5 m (16 ft) high; trunk short and smooth; branches olive green, smooth and widely spreading; branchlets long, slender, arching, olive or red tinted, glabrous and glossy; immature leaves thin and translucent, conspicuously orange and glabrous; mature leaves oblong or oblong-elliptic, apex obtuse or rounded, base broadly cuneate or rounded, finely serrulate or subentire; lamina glabrous on both sides, bright green above, paler green beneath; catkins coetaneous in March or April, shortly pedunculate, peduncle 3–4 mm long, puberulent; 3–6 narrowly elliptic leaf bracts, sericeously pubescent beneath, at base of peduncle. Male catkins 2–3.5 cm long, 1–1.5 cm wide, densely flowered, two stamens, filaments free with basal hairs; anthers red, turning orange and finally golden yellow; rachis hairy; flower scales narrowly oblong, yellowish, apex blackish, acute and hairy.

An exceptionally beautiful Japanese hybrid with graceful arching habit and very attractive foliage and catkins.

Salix × smithiana Willd. (S. cinerea L. × S. viminalis L.)   A vigorous large shrub or small erect tree up to 9 m (30 ft) high, very closely resembling S. × sericans ('Tausch. ex Kerner) but with the following fundamental differences:

The branchlets of S. × smithiana remain densely pubescent throughout the first year and their underlying peeled wood is striated. The leaves are generally smaller and narrower than S. × sericans and are transiently sericeously pubescent, becoming almost glabrous beneath when mature. The leaves of S. × smithiana are more distinctly serrulate, with many small teeth. Stipules are prominent, auricular, acuminate and persistent, sometimes with small basal appendages. The stipules of S. sericans are small and caducous.

A common Salix hybrid in Great Britain and Ireland, it is also widely distributed throughout Europe. It is less common in Great Britain than S. × sericans but, unlike the latter, is more often spontaneous than deliberately introduced.

It is of no special merit apart from the ornamental catkins crowding the extremities of the branchlets in March.

Salix × sordida Kern.:   (see S. × pontederana Willd.)

Salix spaethii Koop.:   (see S. wilhelmsiana Bieb.)

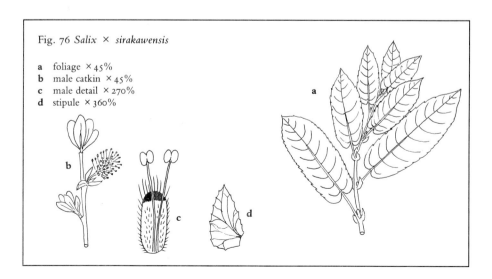

Fig. 76 Salix × sirakawensis

a   foliage ×45%
b   male catkin ×45%
c   male detail ×270%
d   stipule ×360%

***Salix stipularis* Sm.**   A large shrub with long erect branches and branchlets, up to 6 m (20 ft) high; similar to *S. viminalis* but with broader leaves, and stipules denticulate, foliaceous and longer than the petioles; branchlets densely lanate; leaves lanceolate 12–20 cm long; catkins 3–4 cm long; ovaries subsessile or sessile; stigmas linear and undivided, equal to or larger than the style.

A European cultivar of no particular ornamental merit.

***Salix stipulifera* Fold.**   A shrub with spreading branchlets and obovate or oblanceolate leaves, apex rounded or obtuse; lateral veins five to seven pairs; stipules prominent, lanceolate and persistent; capsule 8–12 mm long.

A native of northern Scandinavia and Arctic Russia.

***Salix* × *strepida.* Forb. non Scheicher *S. vaudensis* Forb. (*S. cinerea* L. var. *oleifolia* × *S. myrsinifolia* Salisb.)**   A small to medium-sized relatively slow-growing, rather gnarled shrub; branchlets thick, dark-grey pubescent with short internodes; leaves coriaceous, 2–5 cm long, 1–3 cm wide, elliptic, ovate or obovate, glabrous dark green and dull above, sparsely pubescent greyish beneath.

A somewhat diminutive sallow hybrid of little ornamental value.

***Salix syrticola* Fern. (*S. adenophylla* Hort. non Hook.)**   A medium-sized shrub up to 4 m (13 ft) high, widely branched; branchlets sericeously pubescent; leaves ovate to oblong-ovate, 4–10 cm long, finely glandular serrate with teeth 1 mm apart, apex abruptly acuminate, lamina densely sericeously villous above and beneath; petioles 4–6 mm long; stipules prominent and persistent; catkins coetaneous, pedunculate with basal small, under-developed pubescent leaf bracts; female catkins 5–8 cm long.

A very similar shrub to *S. adenophylla* (Hook.) but differing in the spacing of teeth, 2 mm apart in *S. adenophylla*. The latter species also differs in being acuminate in the basal half of the leaf, possesses longer petioles and has fully developed leaves at the base of the male catkins.

A very hardy species, native of north-eastern North America.

***Salix taraikensis* Kim. 'Taraika–Yanagi'**   A large shrub with sericeously pubescent branchlets and young leaves, becoming glabrous later; leaves thin-textured, narrowly obovate or oblong-elliptic, 5–10 cm long, 2–3.5 cm wide, apex acuminate to acute, indistinctly serrulate, base acute; lamina broadest at or just above the middle, glabrous dark glossy green above, glabrous and glaucous beneath with silky hairs on nerves; male catkins elliptic or shortly cylindrical, densely flowered, 2–3 cm long, pedunculate, scales oblong, obtuse and densely hairy; ovaries white-villous, pedicellate; style short; stigma bifid with short, thick lobes; capsules 7–10 mm long.

An ornamental Japanese species, native of Hokkaido; also present in Sakhalin, Manchuria and Mongolia.

***Salix tatrorum* Zap.**   A small erect tree with spreading branches; branchlets glabrous light brown at first, becoming darker brown later; buds somewhat triangular and adpressed, reddish; leaves elliptic or obovate, apex acute, base acute or cuneate, margins shallowly crenate-serrate, lamina glabrous on both surfaces, bright green with impressed venation above, very pale and whitish beneath; stipules absent; catkins coetaneous or serotinous; male catkins 2–3 cm long, female catkins 3.5–5 cm long; two stamens, staminal filaments glabrous.

An ornamental small tree originally from the Tatra Mountains in Czechoslovakia, morphologically similar to *S. phylicifolia*, but much less bushy and brighter
green on the upper surface of the leaves.

Salix taxifolia Kunth.   A large shrub with long, variably pubescent branchlets;
leaves small or very small, linear or linear-lanceolate, subentire or entire, rarely
more than 3 cm long and up to 3.5 mm wide; petioles subsessile or up to 2 mm
long; stipules minute, caducous or absent; male catkins 5–13 (− 18) mm long and
about 8 mm in diameter, two stamens, filaments long with dense basal hairs,
anthers very small, globose or elliptic, one dorsal nectary, scales yellowish; female
catkins short with few flowers, up to 2 cm long in fruit, stigmas divided into
linear-lanceolate lobes, four to five times as long as thick.

An attractive native of western and northern Mexico along river margins; also occurs in
southern California, south-eastern Arizona, southern New Mexico, and south-
western Texas. *S. taxifolia* and and *S. taxifolia* var. *microphylla* are the most
southern representatives of the section *Longifoliae* in the Americas.

Salix taxifolia Kunth. var. *microphylla* Schneid.   A large shrub, differing from
the species by its densely villous-pubescent branchlets and shorter, broader, more
distinctly denticulate leaves; stipules distinct, ovate-lanceolate or lanceolate; the
nectary of the male flower is usually ventral.

This variety is very closely related to the typical *S. taxifolia*. Its range extends
from central Mexico to Guatemala and Puerto Rico.

Salix × tetrapla Walker (*S. phylicifolia* L. × *S. myrsinifolia* L.)   A large, erect
many-branched variable shrub exhibiting the characteristics of both parents;
branchlets grey, pubescent, later becoming glabrous; young leaves pubescent;
mature leaves glabrous on both surfaces, broadly lanceolate, oblanceolate or
elliptic, entire or partially and indistinctly crenate, glossy bright green above,
paler green beneath, blackening when dried; petioles 0.5–1 cm long, purplish;
stipules prominent, lanceolate; male catkins – staminal filaments with basal hairs;
female catkins – ovaries frequently only partially pubescent.

An attractive hybrid occurring in the wild where mixed populations of the
parents are found together, in Great Britain and northern Europe.

Salix × thaumastu Kim. (*S. gracilistyla* Miq. × *S. kinuiyanagi* Kim.)   A large
shrub with widely spreading branches and loosely arching habit, possessing characteristics of both parents. Leaves lanceolate and silky pubescent beneath; catkins
concentrated mainly towards the ends of the branchlets are very ornamental.

An elegant Japanese hybrid.

Salix tinctoria Sm: (see *S. × meyeriana*) (*S. fragilis* L. × *S. pentandra* L.)

Salix triandra L. (*S. amygdalina* L.) 'Almond-Leaved Willow'   A robust bushy
shrub or small erect tree up to 10 m (33 ft) high, with smooth greyish-brown bark
exfoliating in large irregular patches exposing an orange-brown underlayer;
branchlets glabrous, shining olive-brown; buds compressed, tapering to a narrow
apex, puberulent at first, becoming glabrous; leaves lanceolate, oblong-lanceolate
or narrowly elliptic, 5–12 cm long, 1–3 cm wide, apex acute or long-acuminate,
margins prominently and regularly serrate; lamina glabrous, dark glossy green

above, greenish or glaucous beneath; petioles 1–1.5 cm long, glandular at apex; stipules auricular, large and persistent, 5–10 mm long, 3–6 mm wide, irregularly glandular-serrate, the upper surface gland dotted. Catkins coetaneous or sometimes precocious in April and May, a few occasionally appearing later during the summer, erect on short leafy or bracteate lateral shoots; rachis and peduncle pubescent. Male catkins very fragrant narrowly cylindrical 4–8 cm long, 0.5–1 cm diameter, catkin scales shortly lingulate, pale yellow, sparsely hairy or pubescent mainly towards the base; three stamens, filaments free, about 5 mm long, with basal hairs; anthers golden-yellow; two nectaries, the adaxial one shorter and thicker than the abaxial nectary. Female catkins shorter and more densely flowered than the male; ovaries glabrous, broadly flask shaped, distinctly pedicellate, pedicels up to 3 mm in fruit; styles very short; stigmas short, spreading, usually bifid; one nectary, oblong, shorter than the pedicel.

One of the most important basket-willows with very many named varieties or clones in cultivation. A large number of those found growing in the wild have descended from the cultivars grown in osier beds over many centuries. The resultant polymorphic forms are present in Great Britain, throughout Europe, extending eastwards through Turkey and Iran to central Asia. Closely related species also exist in China and Japan.

An outstandingly attractive, hardy, vigorous willow with exceedingly good glossy foliage and a spectacular display of prolific, fragrant, 'candle-like', golden male catkins.

Deserves much wider recognition as a garden shrub. (*See* Fig. 3.)

Salix triandra L. var. hoffmanniana Bab. A many-branched bush, somewhat pyramidal and usually less than 4 m (13 ft) high; branchlets numerous, ascending, slender and glabrous; leaves uniformly smaller than in typical *S. triandra*, 2–5 cm long, 1–1.5 cm wide, lanceolate, regularly serrate, dark glossy green above, paler green below; petioles short, 4–7 mm long; stipules prominent, persistent, broad, blunt and sometimes suborbicular. Catkins (commonly male) smaller than in the species, rarely exceeding 7 cm long and 7 mm in diameter.

Very localized distribution. In Great Britain male plants are common in Dorset, Surrey, and Sussex, and sporadically in more northern counties. In Europe male and female specimens have been found at high altitudes near the snow line in the Pyrenees.

A very hardy twiggy, glossy-leaved shrub with showy erect golden male catkins in May. Ideal for inclusion in small or large gardens.

Salix triandra L. 'Semperflorens' A very erect male clone with conspicuous erect catkins bearing flowers with pale-yellow anthers. Fresh catkins keep appearing towards the extremities of the glabrous branchlets from April onwards throughout the summer.

Salix × tsugaluensis Koidz. (S. integra Thunb. × S. vulpina Anderss.) 'Ginme'
A vigorous large shrub with long, smooth, light-grey, widely spreading branches; branchlets slender, glabrous and shining olive-green; immature leaves red-tinged and translucent; mature leaves oblong or obovate, 5–9 cm long, 1.5–3 cm wide, margins entire or partially and indistinctly serrulate, apex obtuse or very shortly acuminate at the tip, base unequal and broadly cuneate; lamina glabrous and apple-green above, glabrous and glaucous beneath; petioles 2–3 mm long; stipules ovate, entire; female catkins cylindrical and very silver, precocious in March or

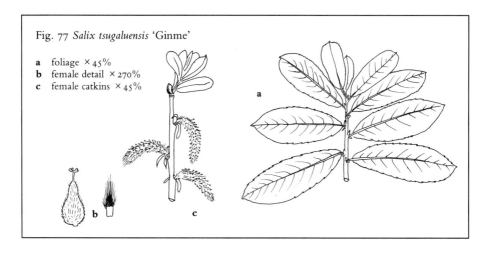

Fig. 77 *Salix tsugaluensis* 'Ginme'

a foliage × 45%
b female detail × 270%
c female catkins × 45%

April, 1.5–4 cm long, 5–8 mm in diameter, evenly distributed along the branchlets, attached by peduncles 4–6 mm long with two to four basal leaf bracts silky-
hairy beneath. The catkins become characteristically recurved at maturity, their
apex reaching below the level of attachment of their peduncle. Some are finally
parallel with and pointing down the branchlet to which they are attached. Catkin
scales narrowly oblong, black towards the apex and bearded with long silver
hairs.

A very ornamental Japanese clonal hybrid, requiring ample space in a large
garden or park.

**Salix urbaniana Seem. *Toisusu urbaniana* (Seem.) Kimura; *S. cardiophylla*
Trautv. & Mey. ssp. *urbaniana* (Seem.). Skv.; *Toisusu cardiophylla*
var. *urbaniana* (Seem.) Kim.**   A massive spectacular tree up to 30 m (100 ft)
high and 3 m (10 ft) in diameter, with deeply fissured bark; branchlets bright
crimson with pruinose bloom; leaves elliptic to oblong-ovate, 6–15 cm long,
5–8 cm wide, shortly acuminate, base usually rounded, glabrous above, glaucous and reticulate beneath, leaf margins glandular-serrate; petioles 1–3 cm
long; catkins borne on leafy lateral shoots; male catkins 5–8 cm long, filaments
glabrous and free; female catkins up to 10 cm long; ovary shortly-pedicellate
and glabrous; style distinct, deciduous and cleft at apex; stigmas slender, deeply
cleft; two nectaries present in both sexes, placed laterally in the female, one on
each side of the ovary (as opposed to the normal anterior and posterior
positions).

A magnificent ornamental tree, native of river valleys in Japan and Korea. A
few specimens are present in European collections, although these have not
achieved the stature of those in their natural habitat.

Salix vaudensis Forb.:   (see *S. × strepida*)

Salix viminalis L. 'The Osier'   A vigorous tall shrub or small tree 3–6 m (10–20 ft)
high and occasionally up to 9 m (30 ft); bark grey, fissured; branches erect
forming a narrow or somewhat rounded crown; branchlets typically straight,
long and flexible, densely grey-pubescent at first, becoming smooth and shining
yellowish or olive-green; buds ovoid, pubescent becoming glabrous yellow,

brownish or red-tinged. Leaves linear or narrowly linear-lanceolate 10–16 cm long, 0.5–2.5 cm wide, apex gradually tapered and long-acuminate, base narrowly cuneate, margins entire, narrowly recurved or revolute and frequently undulate; lamina dull green and sparsely pubescent above, shining silver beneath with a dense covering of adpressed silky hairs; petioles up to 1 cm long, pubescent; stipules narrowly lanceolate, sometimes indistinctly glandular-toothed, up to 10 mm long and rarely exceeding 2 mm wide, caducous or sometimes absent. Catkins precocious in late February or March, sessile or subsessile, thickly crowded towards the tips of the branchlets, erect, ovoid or cylindrical 1.5–3.5 cm long, 0.5–1 cm wide, densely flowered and often lacking leaf bracts or with two or more tiny densely silver-hairy lanceolate bracts; rachis densely hairy; catkin scales about 2 mm long, narrowly elliptic, densely hairy, brown or blackish; one nectary, narrowly oblong, truncate. Male flowers – two stamens, filaments free, glabrous, up to 1 cm long; anthers yellow. Female flowers – ovary densely pubescent, 2 mm long, 1 mm wide; style distinct, 1 mm long; stigmas linear, undivided or rarely two – cleft and spreading; capsule pubescent, 5–6 mm long and 2 mm wide.

A common early-flowering species in Great Britain, the male plant being very easily recognized by its long erect branchlets characteristically crowded with yellow catkins silhouetted against a bleak wintery landscape.

In Great Britain and western Europe *S. viminalis* is usually either deliberately planted or is a relic of former osier beds. In North America it was introduced from Europe in colonial times for coarse basketry. In Russia it is indigenous and very widespread, extending from tundra to the desert-steppe region, forming deep thickets along many river banks. It is one of the oldest recorded species used in basketry. Taxonomically significant is the frequency with which *S. viminalis* hybridizes with other *Salix* species. Hybridizing with *S. triandra*, it links species of subgenus *Salix* with sallows of subgenus *Caprisalix*.

A popular ornamental willow, producing attractive shining rods when coppiced and thriving beside water. (*See* Fig. 5.).

Salix viminalis Clones   Large numbers of different clones have been grown over many generations for their special qualities in basketry. Some well-known examples of these are: 'Aquatica Gigantea', 'Black Osier', 'Yellow Osier', 'Irish Rod', 'English Rod', 'Black Satin', 'Brown Mirriam', 'Gigantea Korso', 'Mealy Top', 'Reader's Red', 'Stricta', 'Utelescens', and 'Superba'.

Salix vitellina L.:   (see *S. alba* var. *vitellina* L. Stokes)

Salix wardiana White: (see *S.* × *laurina*)

Salix wilhelmsiana Bieb. (S. angustifolia Willd., non Wulf.)   A large shrub with long, slender, flexible branchlets, arching and widely spreading, silky pubescent; leaves linear 1.5–5 cm long, up to 4 mm wide, entire or very finely glandular-serrulate, pubescent on both sides at first, becoming more or less glabrous; petioles very short; stipules small and caducous or absent; catkins on leafy lateral shoots, 2–4 cm long, cylindrical and slender, catkin scale pale yellowish; stamens with basal hairs; anthers yellow; ovaries sericeously pubescent; stigmas sessile.

A native of Russia, ranging from the Caucasus to eastern Asia.

An extremely graceful shrub with arching habit and attractive linear foliage.

Salix wilhelmsiana Bieb. var. microstachya Herd., (S. microstachya Turcz. ex Trautv.) Very similar to the species but with glabrous branchlets; leaves pubescent at first, becoming totally glabrous; the ventral nectary of the male flower half as long as the catkin scale; ovary glabrous.

From western Siberia to Mongolia.

Salix wilmsii Seem. A large tropical shrub or small erect tree 3–6 m (10–20 ft) high; *spring leaves small elliptic, 1.5–1.8 cm long, 3–4 mm wide, apex acute, base obtuse; *summer leaves lanceolate, 7–12 cm long, 1–1.3 cm wide, usually entire or occasionally remotely serrulate, apex acute or shortly acuminate, base cuneate; stipules small and caducous; ovaries pedicellate; five or six stamens.

Distribution is confined to the Komatic and Olifants Rivers in the Transvaal. It hybridizes with S. woodii (Seem.).

Salix × wimmeriana Gren. & Godr. (S. purpurea L. × S. caprea L.) A large bushy shrub with greyish-brown branches; branchlets brown, finely pubescent, becoming glabrous and glossy; leaves thinly pubescent at first, soon becoming glabrous, oblong, oblanceolate or lanceolate 3.5–5 cm long, 1.5–2 cm wide, apex shortly acuminate or acute, base cuneate, margins entire or unevenly and indistinctly serrulate towards the apex; lamina dark green above, pale and glaucous beneath; axillary buds ovate, acute and yellowish-brown; petioles pubescent, 5–6 mm long; stipules ovate, small and caducous; catkins precocious in March or April, ovate, 2–2.5 cm long, 1–1.5 cm in diameter, subsessile; staminal filaments hairy, connate at the base; anthers red at first, turning bright orange and then yellow; stigma subsessile and oblong.

Occurs sporadically with the parents in Europe and is also cultivated.

One of the most ornamental and undemanding of all large shrubs. The male catkins are very prolific and create a spectacular blaze of colour in the spring.

Salix woodii Seem. A large tropical shrub or small erect tree 3–5 m (10–16 ft) or more high; spring leaves 1.5–2 cm long, 2–3 mm wide, narrowly obovate, apex shortly acuminate, base attenuate-cuneate; summer leaves 8–14 cm long, 7–9 mm wide, narrowly lanceolate or narrowly elliptic, conspicuously and regularly serrate, apex finely tapering acuminate or acute, base cuneate or attenuate-cuneate; stipules small and caducous; ovaries pedicellate; five to eight stamens.

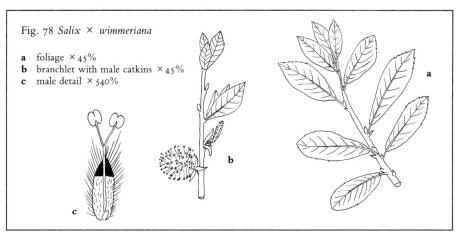

Fig. 78 *Salix × wimmeriana*

a foliage × 45%
b branchlet with male catkins × 45%
c male detail × 540%

Distribution overlaps *S. wilmsii*, with which it hybridizes on the Olifants and Komatic Rivers in the Transvaal; in Natal, along the Tugela, Um-Geni and Um-Lazi river basins; it also occurs in Zimbabwe on the Sabie River. See also *S. wilmsii* footnote for explanation of South African *Salix* leaves.

Salix xerophila Flod.   A medium-sized bushy shrub 2–3 m (6–10 ft) high, with numerous dark grey-brown branches; branchlets pubescent; leaves oblong or oblong–obovate, serrate, lamina sparsely pubescent above and beneath; stipules prominent and persistent; catkins precocious, sessile and elliptic or ovate; two stamens, filaments free with basal hairs; ovary pedicellate and pubescent; style distinct; stigma deeply cleft.

Distribution ranging from Lapland to the Ural Mountains.

Salix yoshinoi Koidz. 'Yoshino-Yanagi'   A small, erect tree 3–6 m (10–20 ft) high; branchlets grey, densely silky pubescent becoming sparsely pubescent or glabrous later; leaves lanceolate, up to 10 cm long, 2.5 cm wide, apex acute or shortly acuminate, base rounded, margins serrulate; lamina sparsely pubescent becoming glabrous above, densely pubescent beneath becoming sparsely pubescent, multiple lateral nerves; petioles sericeously hairy, 5 mm long; catkins coetaneous, female – 1–1.5 cm long, shortly pedunculate, leaf bracts hairy with rounded apex, ovary densely white pubescent, sessile; style long, narrow and glabrous; male catkins 1.5–3 cm long, 6–8 mm diameter, staminal filaments with basal hairs.

An ornamental species, native of Honshu, Japan.

FOOTNOTES TO CHAPTER 4:

*Great difficulty has been experienced in the past with identification of South African *Salix* species because of the dimorphic character of their leaves. Two types of leaf are produced. The earliest, or spring leaves, are usually very small, entire, rather like foliar bracts and are caducous. The much larger summer leaves which follow are often serrate or serrulate, frequently remaining on the branchlets until pushed off by the swelling buds in their axils. Hence these trees are sometimes almost evergreen.

CHAPTER FIVE

Ornamental Trees and Shrubs for Small Gardens

As previously stated, the ultimate size of trees and shrubs is controlled not only by the species, but also by the soil and prevailing local conditions. Some species already recommended for use in large areas are equally suitable for small gardens. The colourful clones of *S. alba* provide a good example. The regular coppicing of *S. alba* var. *vitellina*, *S. alba* 'Britzensis', *S. alba* 'Chermesina' and *S. alba* 'Cardinalis' drastically restricts their height and spread, increasing the number of branchlets and accentuating their vivid, shining winter stem colouring. *S. daphnoides* and *S.* × *rubens* can similarly be pruned back hard to encourage good stem colour and to keep them within the scale of small gardens.

Ornamental trees and shrubs that are equally suitable for small and large gardens, without resort to pruning, detailed in Chapter 4 include: *S. acutifolia*, *S. adenophylla*, *S. amplexicaulis*, *S. canariensis*, *S. caspica*, *S. elaeagnos*, *S. exigua*, *S. gracilistyla*, *S. gracilistyla* var. *melanostachys*, *S. integra* 'Pendula', *S. irrorata*, *S. japonica*, *S. myrsinifolia* (*nigricans*) var. *alpicola*, *S. miyabeana*, *S. pellita*, *S. phylicifolia*, *S.* × *pontederana*, *S. purpurea* 'Richartii', *S. schraderiana* (bicolor), *S.* × *seringeana*, *S.* × *sirakawensis*, *S. triandra* var. *hoffmaniana*, and *S. triandra* 'Semperflorens'.

S. magnifica, *S. fargesii* and *S. moupinensis*, also previously described, do not generally achieve their full potential in cold temperate conditions. Their young foliage is frost-susceptible but can be very attractive in small protected gardens.

Contorted types are interesting. *S. matsudana* 'Tortuosa', *S. matsudana* '(Caradoc)' and *S.* × *alba* 'Snake' do not generally outgrow their station and can be planted in the small garden if space is available.

Ornamental species specially suited to small gardens that have not hitherto been described are:

Salix alaxensis (Anderss.) Cov. var. alaxensis A small erect shrub 0.5 m to exceptionally 3 m (1.5–10 ft) high; branches reddish-brown and persistently grey-lanate; branchlets densely covered with long white hairs; buds villous; mature leaves narrowly ovate or obovate, 5–12 cm long, 2–4 cm wide, apex acute, base narrowly cuneate, margins entire, revolute, undulate and often glandular; lamina bright green, hairy or glabrescent above, densely white lanate beneath; petioles 6–20 mm long, pubescent and frequently with a basal enlargement engulfing the bud; stipules 5–20 mm long, linear, glandular and pubescent. Catkins precocious or subprecocious, sessile on branches of the preceding year. Male catkins 3–5 cm long, two stamens, filaments 5–8 mm long, glabrous, free or connate. Female catkins 5–15 cm long, ovaries pubescent, 1.5 mm long, styles 2–3 mm long;

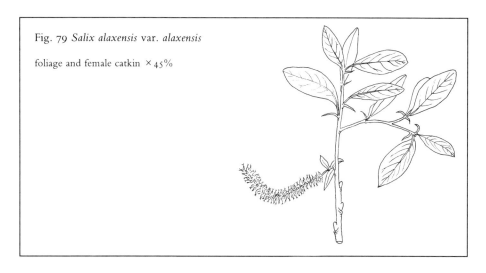

Fig. 79 *Salix alaxensis* var. *alaxensis*

foliage and female catkin × 45%

stigmas 1–2 mm long; ovaries sessile or with pubescent pedicels up to 0.5 mm long; scales ovate, apex acute, 1.5–3 mm long, dark brown or blackish, with long straight hairs on both surfaces twice as long as the scale.

Grows in sand and gravel bars of rivers and along the edges of lakes in the Arctic regions in North America, Canada and in the Chukotsk Peninsula in Asia.

This species is closely related to *S. candida* and is similar in appearance. *S. alaxensis* var. *alaxensis* differs in its large stipules, long styles and very short pedicels.

An attractive small shrub with grey-haired branches, white-haired branchlets, and a strikingly white lanate layer beneath the leaves, which are bright green above.

Salix alaxensis (Anderss.) Cov. var. *longistylis* (Rydb.) Schneid.   Differs from var. *alaxensis* in being tall shrubs or small trees, 2–6 m (6–20 ft) high, with glaucous branches and branchlets, sparsely pubescent, soon becoming glabrous; buds are smaller and the petiolar base is not enlarged; the apex of the flower scale is usually obtuse.

One of the first willows to be found on glacial moraines. Also present in Arctic tundra in central and eastern Alaska and Yukon Territory; south in the Rocky Mountains to northern British Columbia.

Salix arbuscula L. var. *erecta* Anderss. (*S. waldsteiniana* Willd. *S. arbuscula* var. *waldsteiniana* (Willd.) Koch; *S. arbuscula* ssp. *waldsteiniana* (Willd.) Braun-Blanquet.)   A small bushy shrub with glabrous green branchlets. Leaves obovate to elliptic, 2–8 cm long, 2–3 cm wide, base cuneate, margins crenate-serrate or entire. Lamina bright glabrous green with a prominent midrib beneath. Catkins coetaneous in April on peduncles 4–6 mm long with four ovate or lanceolate glabrous leaf bracts. Catkins cylindrical, very erect, dense-flowered, 2–3 cm long, 5–8 mm diameter; flower scales small, apex obtuse, black-tipped and hairy; ovaries sessile and subglabrous with a few scattered hairs in the upper half, style distinct, stigmas bifid.

A native of the eastern Alps, north Balkans and the Carpathians. Found particularly in limestone areas.

An attractive and very hardy small shrub, ideal for the small garden, seldom exceeding 1 m high and 1 m in diameter.

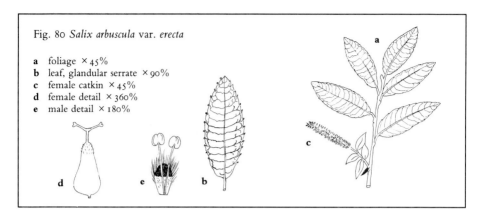

Fig. 80 *Salix arbuscula* var. *erecta*

a　foliage × 45%
b　leaf, glandular serrate × 90%
c　female catkin × 45%
d　female detail × 360%
e　male detail × 180%

Salix arbusculoides Anderss.　Small shrubs 1–4 m (3–13 ft) high; branches with an exfoliating surface, glossy, reddish-brown and slender; branchlets sparsely pubescent. Mature leaves narrowly elliptic or narrowly ovate 5–8 cm long, 1–1.5 cm wide, the apex narrowly acute, base acute; lamina glabrous and glossy above, sericeously pubescent beneath, margins glandular-serrulate; petioles 5–10 mm long; stipules 1–3 mm long with revolute, glandular margins. Catkins coetaneous or subprecocious, subsessile or on short leafy branchlets. Male catkins 2–3 cm long with basal leaf bracts, two stamens with free, glabrous filaments. Female catkins 3–10 cm long, often loosely flowered, pedicels up to 0.5–1 mm long, ovaries pubescent, styles up to 0.5 mm long, stamens four-lobed; one adaxial nectary slightly longer than the pedicel; scales oblong with long hairs on both sides.

An small North American native shrub living along streams and bordering alpine and Arctic tundra. Common in central Alaska and the Yukon, not reaching the Pacific coast. It extends east to Hudson Bay and south in the eastern Rocky Mountains to British Columbia and Alberta.

An ornamental, glossy leafed, arctic species.

Salix argyrocarpa Anderss.　A small twiggy shrub 0.5–1.7 m (2–6 ft) high; branchlets short bearing numerous leaves and bud scars, reddish-brown, pubescent at first, becoming glabrous. Leaves narrowly elliptic to oblanceolate, 3–6 cm long, up to 1 cm wide, apex acute, base acute or obtuse, margins revolute and crenulate, glossy dark green with impressed venation above, glaucous and variably sericeous beneath, veins numerous and parallel. Catkins 1–2.5 cm long, coetaneous in June and July, on leafy peduncles up to 1.5 cm long; scales oblanceolate, rounded or acute, blackish and villous; capsule lanceolate 2–4 mm long, sericeously pubescent; pedicel 1–2 mm, sericeous; style 0.5 mm long; stigmas entire to divided.

A North American species found on mountain slopes and in valleys from the Gaspé Peninsula to Newfoundland and the coast of Labrador.

Salix athabascensis Raup. (S. pedicellaris Pursh var. athabascensis Boivin.)　Small erect shrubs 0.5–1.5 m (1.5–5 ft) high; branches greyish-brown with some surface exfoliation; branchlets reddish-brown pubescent with short curved hairs, becoming glabrous and glossy; immature leaves sericeously pubescent with mixed white and rusty hairs above; mature leaves narrowly elliptic or obovate, 1.5–5 cm long, 1–2 cm wide, coriaceous, apex acuminate or acute, base acute or

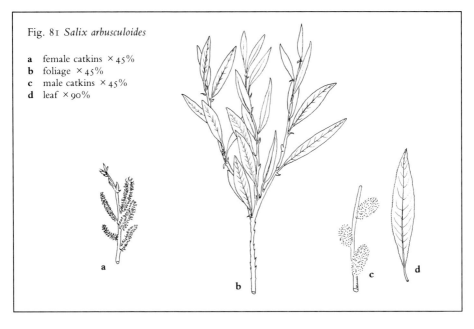

Fig. 81 *Salix arbusculoides*

a female catkins × 45%
b foliage × 45%
c male catkins × 45%
d leaf × 90%

round, often unequal, margins entire or glandular-serrate, flat or slightly revolute; lamina becoming glabrous, glossy and reticulate above with persistent rusty hairs on the midrib, remaining sparsely sericeous or glabrous and glaucous beneath; petioles 3–10 mm long, pubescent; stipules minute; catkins coetaneous on leafy branchlets. Male catkins 5–10 mm long; two stamens, filaments free with basal pubescence, two nectaries. Female catkins 1–3.5 cm long, loose-flowered, pistils 2 mm long, densely grey-pubescent, one adaxial nectary half as long as pedicel, styles 0.5–1 mm long, partially bifid; stigmas 0.5 mm long with four linear lobes; scales ovate, apex rounded, 1–2 mm long, pubescent, yellowish, brown at apex.

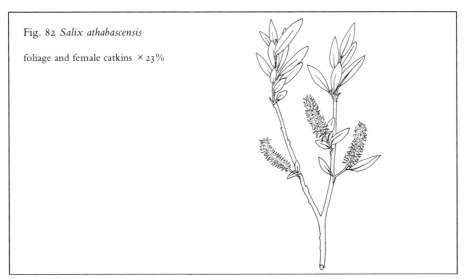

Fig. 82 *Salix athabascensis*

foliage and female catkins × 23%

A small Arctic species living mainly in marshes in Alaska, the North-West Territories, north Yukon, Alberta and northern Saskatchewan.

***Salix barclayii* Anderss.**   A small shrub 1–3 m (3–10 ft) high; branches dark reddish-brown, glabrous or with persistent indumentum for the first two years; branchlets yellowish-green, glossy, densely pubescent becoming sparsely pubescent or glabrous. Leaves obovate or elliptic 3–9 cm long, 1–5 cm wide, the leaf apex broad with an acute or acuminate tip; leaf-base rounded, sometimes sub-cordate or acute and unequal; leaf margins glandular serrulate or subentire; lamina of immature leaves sparsely white pubescent on the upper surface especially along the midrib, glabrous or minutely pubescent beneath. In mature leaves the upper surface is green, slowly becoming glabrous except for the midrib which may remain persistently hairy, the lower surface is soon glabrous and glaucous. Leaves drying dark brown or black; petioles green, up to 20 mm long. Catkins coetaneous on leafy peduncles up to 3 cm long with basal bracts, the rachis and persistent dark-brown or blackish scales densely covered with long hairs; male catkins 3–4 cm long, 1–1.5 cm diameter; two stamens; filaments glabrous, free or connate near the base; female catkins 4–7 cm long; capsules 5–6 mm long, glabrous; pedicel short; style distinct 0.5–1.5 mm long; stigmas short and bilobed. Stipules up to 2 cm long, ovate or narrowly elliptic, apex acuminate, margins glandular serrulate, glaucous and glabrous beneath.

Colonies occur on glacial moraine, on the edges of lakes and river banks in Alaska, southern Yukon and adjacent North-West Territories. Southward in the Rocky Mountains to British Columbia, Washington and Alberta.

A hardy species with attractive male catkins.

***Salix barrattiana* Hook.**   A low alpine shrub up to 1 m high with a wide spread, often up to 2 m in diameter. Branches gnarled, dark brown, glossy and pubescent; branchlets short with short internodes and hairy, very oily buds; the leaves are densely packed towards the ends of the branchlets; mature leaves elliptic to narrowly obovate, 4–10 cm long, 1–3 cm wide, acute at both ends; leaf margins glandular-serrulate or entire; lamina glossy, sparsely pubescent above, sericeously grey-pubescent beneath; petioles 5–10 mm long; stipules ovate, margins glandular and oily. Catkins precocious, sessile on the previous year's branches; male catkins 3–5 cm long, two stamens, filaments 5 mm long, glabrous and free; female catkins 5–12 cm long, ovaries densely sericeous. Scales narrowly oblong, dark brown with long straight hairs.

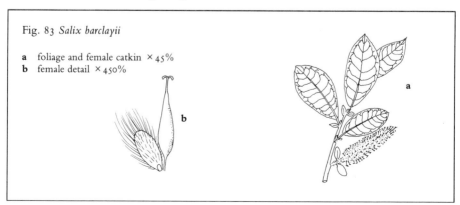

Fig. 83 *Salix barclayii*

a   foliage and female catkin × 45%
b   female detail × 450%

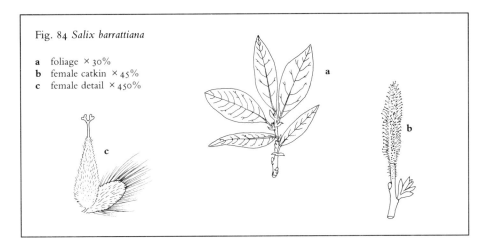

Fig. 84 *Salix barrattiana*

a foliage × 30%
b female catkin × 45%
c female detail × 450%

A native of Arctic North America, forming low thickets along the gravel margins of streams in the mountains of Alaska, Yukon, North-West Territories, southwards to Alberta, British Columbia and north-western Montana.

A distinctive species with its erect branchlets and densely crowded grey leaves. The very oily buds and stipules and densely pubescent ovaries distinguish it from *S. lanata* ssp. *richardsonii*, to which it is closely related.

Salix bockii Seem.   A small shrub 1–3 m (3–10 ft) high; branchlets long and slender, covered with minute grey hairs; leaves typically recurved, fine, oblong to obovate, 6–15 mm long, 3–6 mm wide, dark glossy green above, sericeously hairy and bluish-white beneath, margins entire or sparsely serrate. Catkins serotinous, appearing in the autumn (September to October), on short peduncles arising from the leaf axils of the current year's growth; female catkins 3–4 cm long, 1 cm diameter; male catkins shorter, two stamens, with filaments totally connate; bracts of catkins narrowly lanceolate and acuminate; ovaries sessile and pubescent.

A native of west Szechwan, China, growing in river beds at altitudes up to 2,750 m (9,000 ft). Female cuttings were introduced to Great Britain by Ernest Wilson in 1908. The male form is rare in cultivation, although very attractive.

A unique small species, catkin production being restricted to the autumn. With neat habit and attractive myrtle-like foliage it is an ideal small ornamental shrub.

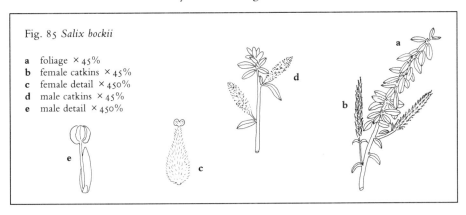

Fig. 85 *Salix bockii*

a foliage × 45%
b female catkins × 45%
c female detail × 450%
d male catkins × 45%
e male detail × 450%

Salix brachycarpa Nutt. ssp. *brachycarpa*   An erect shrub 0.5–2 m high with thick
reddish-brown, variably pubescent branches. Branchlets pubescent or lanate;
leaves broadly or narrowly obovate or elliptic; mature leaves sparsely or densely
pubescent on both sides, glaucous beneath; petioles red-tinged, 1–5 mm long;
stipules broad, up to 1.5 mm long. Catkins coetaneous, densely-flowered on leafy
lateral branchlets; male catkins 5–15 mm long, shortly cylindric to globose, two
stamens with glabrous filaments sometimes connate at the base, each two-lobed;
female catkins 15–20 mm long, shortly cylindric or subglobose; ovaries densely
white-lanate subsessile or sessile and short-beaked, capsules pale brown and
minutely pubescent; styles 0.5–1 mm long; scales broadly elliptic, light brown,
with long straight or curly hairs on both sides.

A montane species inhabiting alpine slopes, unstable limestone scree and stream
margins in south-eastern Yukon, adjacent British Columbia and the North-West
Territories; southwards in the cordillera to Utah and Colorado; eastward in
Canada to Hudson Bay and the Gaspé Peninsula; southern Alberta and Saskatchewan.

An attractive low shrubby species closely related to *S. glauca*, *S. arctica* and to
the Eurasian *S. reptans* Rupr.

Salix brachycarpa Nutt. ssp. *niphoclada* (Rydb.) Argus   A small shrub up to 2 m
(6 ft) high, differs from ssp. *brachycapra* by its tendency to spread laterally;
branches thin and flexible, reddish-brown or yellowish, often persistently
pubescent. Mature leaves 2.5–5 cm long, 7–14 mm wide; apex acute-attenuate;
base cuneate to rounded, margins entire or distantly glandular; lamina sparsely
pubescent above, variably pubescent and glaucous beneath, sometimes with
marginal hairs. Young leaves sericeously pubescent. Petioles reddish or yellowish.
Stipules 2–4 mm long, narrowly ovate, pubescent, with glandular margins. Male
catkins 1.5–4 cm long, narrowly cylindrical with very small anthers; female
catkins 2.5–5 cm long, slender and loosely flowered, styles 0.2–0.5 mm long,
entire or bifid. Scales narrowly elliptic, pubescent on both sides.

An Arctic species present on the edges of streams and in mountains, on unstable
limestone and glacial deposits. Occurs in the mountains of Alaska, throughout
Yukon Territory to adjacent British Columbia; North-West Territories to
Hudson Bay.

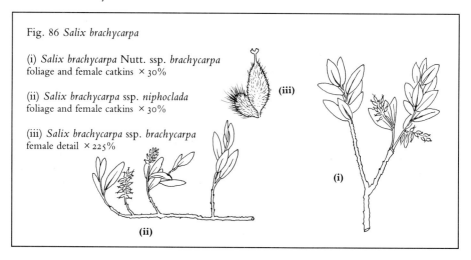

Fig. 86 *Salix brachycarpa*

(i) *Salix brachycarpa* Nutt. ssp. *brachycarpa*
foliage and female catkins × 30%

(ii) *Salix brachycarpa* ssp. *niphoclada*
foliage and female catkins × 30%

(iii) *Salix brachycarpa* ssp. *brachycarpa*
female detail × 225%

(iii)

(i)

(ii)

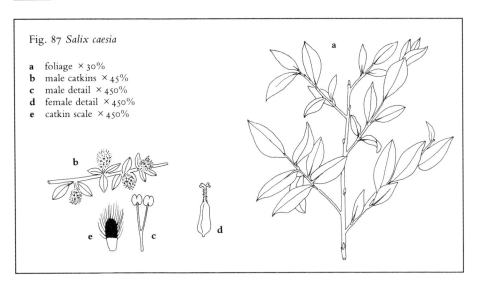

Fig. 87 *Salix caesia*

a foliage × 30%
b male catkins × 45%
c male detail × 450%
d female detail × 450%
e catkin scale × 450%

Salix brachycarpa 'Blue Fox'   A beautiful small clone with blue/green foliage, not generally attaining 0.5 m (1.5 ft) high.

Salix caesia Vill. 'Blue Willow'   A small, many-branched bushy shrub up to 2 m (6 ft) high; branchlets slender, glabrous, glossy, dark brown; buds glabrous, yellow; leaves thick, obovate or oval, apex abruptly pointed, base cuneate, margin entire, 2–3 cm long, 1–2 cm wide, glabrous on both sides, strongly blue/grey above, whitish beneath; petioles very short, 1–2 mm long; stipules minute. Catkins prolific, coetaneous, produced in April or early May, 1–1.5 cm long, 1–1.25 cm diameter, radiating outwards alternately along the branchlets; catkins sessile or with short peduncles up to 3 mm long with three to six ovate or broadly elliptic leaf bracts, glabrous above, sericeous with minute hairs beneath. Male catkins – two stamens, filaments free or united up to half their length, anthers dark purplish-red becoming light golden when mature. Female catkins – ovary sessile or subsessile, pubescent; style half as long as the ovary. Scales narrowly oblong, apex rounded, hairy and blackish.

A native of Siberia, central Asia and to a limited extent in the European Alps.

A very ornamental, extremely hardy, small shrub with spectacular blue mature leaves and very attractively coloured small male catkins.

An excellent shrub for a small garden.

Salix calcicola Fern. and Wieg. 'Lime-Loving Willow'   A spreading small shrub 0.5–2 m (1.5–6 ft) high; branchlets hairy becoming glabrous, thick with many bud scars; buds prominent, ovate, up to 10 mm long; stipules reniform or semi-cordate, glandular-serrulate, and persistent. Petioles thick, 2–4 mm long; leaves ovate or orbicular 2–5 cm long, 1.5–4 cm wide, acute or short-acuminate, subentire to glandular-serrulate, base cordate or rounded, glaucous with prominent venation beneath, catkins thick, precocious or coetaneous, 3–8 cm long, sessile on previous year's branches from July to September; male – two stamens; filaments glabrous, free; female – capsules 8–10 mm long, glabrous; pedicels up to 0.4 mm long; styles 2–3 mm long; stigmas 0.5–1 mm long. Scales obovate, obtuse, blackish, long-hairy.

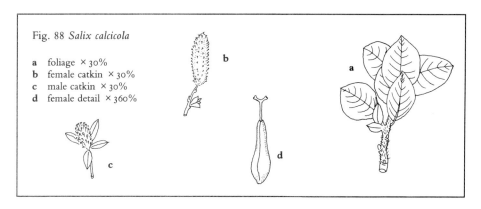

Fig. 88 *Salix calcicola*

a   foliage × 30%
b   female catkin × 30%
c   male catkin × 30%
d   female detail × 360%

A slow-growing shrub from the calcareous cliffs of north west Newfoundland and Gaspé Co., Quebec, north and north-west to Hudson Strait and northern Manitoba.

Salix candida Flugge ex Willd.   A small shrub 0.5–3 m (1.5–10 ft) high, with dark-grey pubescent branches becoming glabrous; branchlets densely white lanate; young leaves downy white above, becoming glabrescent later; mature leaves narrowly elliptic to narrowly ovate, 5–10 cm long, 1–2.5 cm wide; apex and base acute; margins revolute, subentire, glandular; lamina dull green with impressed venation above, densely white lanate with a prominent pale-yellow midrib beneath; petioles 5–8 mm long, pubescent; stipules narrowly ovate, lanate, 2–5 mm long. Catkins coetaneous on short leafy, floriferous branchlets; male catkins 1–2 cm long, subsessile, two stamens, glabrous, 5 mm long, free or connate below; female catkins 2–3 cm long, ovaries densely white lanate; styles 0.5–1 mm long, coloured red; stigmas 0.2–0.3 mm long; pedicels 0.1–1.2 mm long, lanate; scales oblong 1–1.5 mm long, brown and pubescent on both sides.

A widely distributed species in the boreal forest of North America, the northern Canadian prairies, Alaska and the Yukon, preferring a moist alkaline habitat.

A very ornamental shrub with striking white young foliage and branchlets.

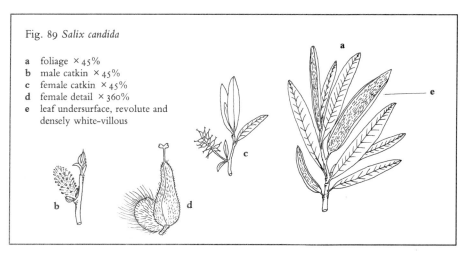

Fig. 89 *Salix candida*

a   foliage × 45%
b   male catkin × 45%
c   female catkin × 45%
d   female detail × 360%
e   leaf undersurface, revolute and
    densely white-villous

***Salix caprea* 'Pendula'** popularly known as the **'Kilmarnock Willow'** The pendulous form of *S. caprea* L. with identical foliage and catkins. It is represented by two clones, one male and one female, each usually grafted onto a straight stock of the required length raised from a cutting. The original Kilmarnock Willow was the male clone with very stiff vertical pendulous branches and prolific golden catkins. The female clone bears the silver catkins, and the branches are more flexible. It is known as 'Weeping Sally' and when left ungrafted is quite effective if grown on a raised mound of earth.

The Kilmarnock Willow is a good pendulous willow for the small garden because being grafted, it does not increase its original height. Any lateral branches, which sometimes arise from the stock or trunk, should be pruned hard back. Sometimes the grafted scion comprising the weeping branches tend to die back. Vigorous pruning of the affected branchlets into healthy tissue usually stimulates the production of vigorous fresh pendulous branchlets.

Salix capussi A small, slow-growing tree of Russian origin, attaining a height of approximately 3 m (10 ft) in ten years. Branchlets numerous, with bushy, feathery, blue/green foliage; leaves lanceolate, serrate, narrowly acuminate and cuneate. Catkins are serotinous, appearing after the leaves are fully developed. Male anthers are very attractive.

Female cuttings have been successfully raised in Great Britain from plant material recently collected from the Frunze Botanic Gardens, in the foothills of the Tien Shan Mountains.

When this species becomes generally available it will prove ideal for small gardens because of its small size, relatively slow growth and attractively coloured feathery foliage.

***Salix chlorolepis* Fern.** A small erect shrub 0.5–1 m (1.5–3 ft) high with short dark-brown glabrous branchlets bearing many bud scars; internodes short, with crowded leaves; buds stout and blunt; petioles thick, 1–3 mm long; leaves elliptic, oblanceolate to narrowly obovate, 1–3 cm long, 5–10 mm wide, entire or minutely serrulate, glabrous, flat and bright green above, glabrous and glaucous beneath, with raised reticulate venation. Catkins few; 6–12 mm long, on short leafy peduncles; scales narrowly obovate, 1.5–2.5 mm long, green and glabrous; two stamens with free, glabrous filaments; ovaries glabrous, subsessile; styles distinct; stigmas subsessile.

A rare North American species restricted to Mount Albert, Gaspé Peninsula, Quebec. It has been suggested that it is a hybrid of *S. uva-ursi* and *S. pedicellaris.*

***Salix commutata* Bebb.** A low shrub up to 1 m (3 ft) and occasionally 2 m (6 ft) high; branches dark grey, stiff and spreading, producing a flattened crown; branchlets densely or sparsely villous. Leaves oblong-elliptic, 5–8 cm long, 2–3.5 cm wide, apex acute, base round or cordate; margins entire to partially or wholly glandular serrulate. Immature leaves densely villous on both sides; mature leaves yellowish-green, villous with long adpressed hairs above, villous and non-glaucous green beneath; both surfaces often become sparsely hairy. Petioles short, 2–6 mm long, villous; stipules 2–6 mm long, glandular serrulate and villous. Catkins coetaneous on leafy branchlets; male – 2–4 cm long, two stamens, filaments free or connate below. Female catkins 5–7 cm long; ovaries glabrous 2–5 mm long, reddish or green; styles 0.5–1 mm long; stigmas bifid 2 mm long. Scales narrowly oblong, light brown, darker towards the apex, with long hairs.

A North American montane pioneer species on glacial moraines, screes and silt

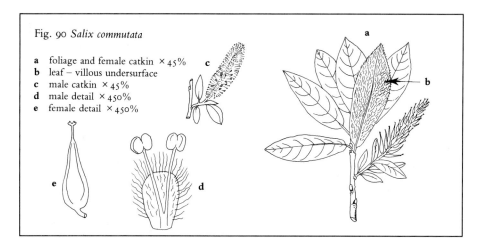

Fig. 90 *Salix commutata*

a foliage and female catkin × 45%
b leaf – villous undersurface
c male catkin × 45%
d male detail × 450%
e female detail × 450%

along river margins, ranging from mountains in Alaska and the Yukon, the North-West Territories, British Columbia; southward in the Cordilleras to California, Utah, Montana and Wyoming.

A slow-growing distinctive small shrub with attractive sparsely silvery-hairy leaves.

Salix cordifolia Pursh.   An erect or semi-erect small shrub 0.5–2 m (1.5–6 ft) high; branchlets thick, pale brown, densely hairy when young, becoming glabrous dark brown later; leaves oval or obovate, 2–8 cm long, 2–5 cm wide, apex obtuse or acute, leaf margins entire or crenulate, base cordate or rounded; lamina sericeously villous above and below, becoming subglabrous dark green above and glaucous beneath; petioles 5–10 mm long, pubescent to glabrous. Catkins coetaneous, 2–6 cm long, 1.5–2 cm diameter when in fruit, on leafy peduncles up to 3 cm long. Scales oblanceolate, pale brown, long-haired, rounded to acute. Two stamens, filaments glabrous and free; ovaries densely grey-pubescent; pedicels up to 1 mm long, pubescent; styles 0.5–1 mm long, entire or divided at the apex; stigmas 0.5 mm long, usually bifid.

A North American native inhabiting shores and boggy ground from New-foundland and south-eastern Quebec to Greenland and Hudson Bay.

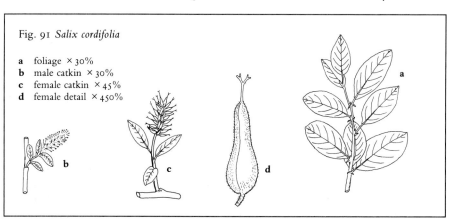

Fig. 91 *Salix cordifolia*

a foliage × 30%
b male catkin × 30%
c female catkin × 45%
d female detail × 450%

***Salix crataegifolia* Bertol.**   A depressed or erect small shrub up to 1 m high; branchlets densely coated with long hairs, becoming glabrous and dark purple later. Leaves 6–12 cm long, 3–5 cm wide, elliptical, bright glabrous green above, sericeously hairy glabrescent beneath; lateral veins numerous up to 20 pairs. Female catkins 5–12 cm long, approximately 1 cm in diameter; rachis subglabrous. Scales reddish-brown with long sericeous white apical hairs; ovary glabrous, 5 mm long; pedicel short; style 1.5–2 mm long.

A native of northern Italy.

A good species with ornamental foliage, suitable for small gardens.

***Salix* × *dichroa* Kern. (*S. purpurea* L. × *S. aurita* L.)**   A small to medium-sized bushy shrub; branchlets glabrous or slightly pubescent, becoming glabrous; leaves oblanceolate, oblong or obovate, glabrous bright green above, glaucous and pubescent beneath, apex acute or slightly cuspidate; catkins precocious in March and April, two stamens, filaments connate in their lower half and with basal hairs, pedicel almost half as long as the ovary; stigmas subsessile.

A very hardy and ornamental shrub displaying the typical qualities of both parents.

***Salix* × *doniana* Sm. (*S. purpurea* L. × *S. repens* L.)**   A many-branched ascending shrub 1.5–2.5 m (5–8 ft) high; branchlets shining reddish-brown; leaves very sericeous beneath at first, soon becoming glabrous and glaucous, the upper surface bright glossy green. Like *S. purpurea*, some of the leaves are opposite or subopposite. The lamina is oblanceolate, 2–5 cm long, 0.5–1.5 cm wide, with an abruptly acute or sub-cuspidate apex, margins subentire or remotely serrulate, slightly recurved. Petioles very short; stipules very small or absent; catkins precocious, in March or early April, sessile or shortly pedunculate with sericeous basal leaf bracts; male catkins are shortly cylindrical 1–2 cm long, 0.6 cm wide, scales yellowish at the base, reddish above, with a black apex; two stamens, either free, partially or totally connate; anthers dark purple; female catkins very compact, cylindrical, less than 1.5 cm long and 0.5 cm wide, scales black-tipped and densely hairy; ovaries white pubescent, 2 mm long; styles and stigmas very short.

Although an uncommon hybrid, two distinct forms of *S. doniana* exist in Great Britain. The typical, more slender form first originated from Scotland. More recently, in 1947, a distinctly more robust broader-leafed form was identified in south Lancashire. It is probable that the Lancashire form is a hybrid between *S. purpurea* and *S. repens* var. *argentea*.

An extremely hardy, small shrub willow thriving in the poorest soils, with a very ornamental compact bushy habit. Strongly recommended for small gardens.

***Salix farriae* Ball.**   A branching shrub 0.5–1 m (1.5–3 ft) high, branchlets sparsely pubescent, soon becoming glabrous; leaves 3–5 cm long, 1–2 cm wide, elliptic or elliptic-ovate, slightly pubescent at first, mature leaves glabrous on both surfaces, glaucous beneath, margins entire or minutely serrulate; petioles short, 2–8 mm long; stipules small and deciduous; catkins coetaneous or serotinous, borne on short, leafy peduncles; scales yellowish with a brown apex, with long hairs from within, glabrous outside; male catkins slender, 1–2 cm long; two stamens, with glabrous, free filaments; female catkins 1.5–3 cm long when ripe; ovary and capsule glabrous; capsule 4–6 mm long; pedicel short, up to 1 mm long; style short but distinct, 0.5–0.8 mm long, exceeding the length of the short bifid stigmas.

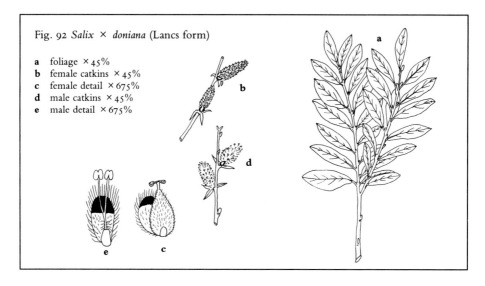

Fig. 92 *Salix* × *doniana* (Lancs form)

a   foliage × 45%
b   female catkins × 45%
c   female detail × 675%
d   male catkins × 45%
e   male detail × 675%

A North American mountain species growing on lake shores and stream banks, in the mountains extending from Alaska and Yukon to Manitoba, south-east in British Columbia and west Montana and Wyoming.

Salix foetida Schleich. (Salix arbuscula L. ssp. foetida (Schleich.) Salix arbuscula L. var. humilis (Anderss.))   A small, bushy, shortly branching shrub 0.5–2 m (1.5–6 ft) high; branchlets light brown and glabrous; leaves elliptic-lanceolate, up to 5 cm long, sharply and regularly serrate; the teeth bearing prominent yellow glands; lamina dark green, glabrous and glossy above, glabrous and paler green beneath. Catkins coetaneous, thicker than those of *S. arbuscula*, twice as long as wide on bracted peduncles 3–5 mm long.

A native of the European Alps, from France to the High Tauern, thriving best in acid soil.

A neat, relatively compact little shrub, with dark glossy leaves, well-suited to small gardens.

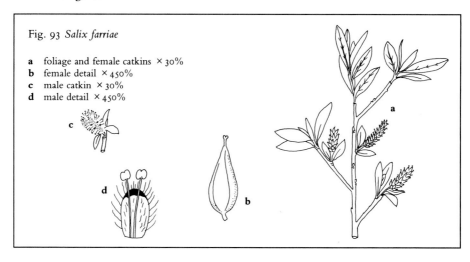

Fig. 93 *Salix farriae*

a   foliage and female catkins × 30%
b   female detail × 450%
c   male catkin × 30%
d   male detail × 450%

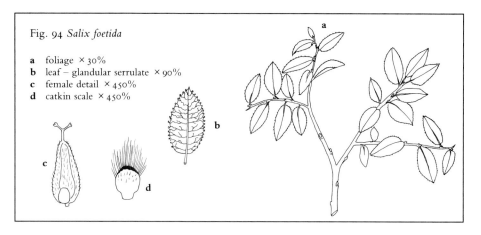

Fig. 94 *Salix foetida*

a foliage × 30%
b leaf – glandular serrulate × 90%
c female detail × 450%
d catkin scale × 450%

Salix × ***friesiana*** **Anderss. (*S. viminalis* L.** × ***S. repens* L.)** A slender, erect, branching shrub 0.5–2 m (1.5–6 ft) high with dark-brown glabrous branches; branchlets densely pubescent throughout their first year; leaves crowded, lanceolate, 4–8 cm long, 0.5–1.5 cm wide, lamina sparsely pubescent and dull green above, densely sericeously pubescent beneath, apex acuminate, margins entire, often undulate and recurved; petioles short, 2–4 mm long; stipules lanceolate 4–6 mm long, 1–2 mm wide, minutely glandular-serrulate, caducous; catkins precocious in March or April, oblong-ovoid 1–3 cm long, 0.5–0.8 cm in diameter, with two or three small basal leaf bracts, lanceolate and sericeous beneath; scales oblong densely hairy, 2–3 mm long, brown, the apex darker and acute or rounded; male flowers, two stamens with glabrous, free filaments 3–5 mm long; anthers 1 mm long; female flowers, ovaries densely pubescent, 2–3 mm long, styles short, stigmas linear, undivided or bifid.

A rare hybrid originally found in Sutherland, Scotland and more recently on Southport sandhills in south Lancashire. In Europe it has been recorded in isolated localities in Scandinavia, Austria, Germany, Yugoslavia and Russia.

A beautiful and very hardy small shrub, ideal for the small garden. Male catkins produced on bare stems are prolific and very striking in the early spring.

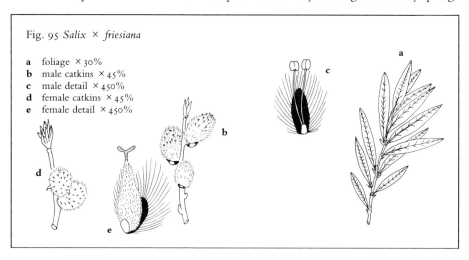

Fig. 95 *Salix* × *friesiana*

a foliage × 30%
b male catkins × 45%
c male detail × 450%
d female catkins × 45%
e female detail × 450%

***Salix glabra* Scop.**   A shrub 1–1.5 m (3–5 ft) high with a rounded crown; branches stout and dark glabrous brown; branchlets glabrous, glossy, chestnut-brown; mature leaves thick broadly elliptic or obovate, 5–6 cm long, 2.5–4 cm wide, glabrous on both sides, very glossy and dark green above, paler green beneath, apex acuminate, base cuneate, leaf margins distinctly and regularly glandular-serrate. Stipules absent or very small. Catkins coetaneous in April, erect on short leafy stalks 1–2 cm long; male catkins – stamens much longer than the scales, anthers purple becoming pale yellow later. Female catkins 3–6 cm long, 1–1.5 cm in diameter; ovary narrowly conical, 5–7 mm long, glabrous and pedicellate, styles short, 1–2 mm long, stigmas bifid. Scales dark brown, narrowly ovate, apex rounded with some straight hairs.

A native of the eastern European Alps. One of the best small species; very hardy, with outstandingly ornamental dark glossy green foliage.

***Salix glauca* L. 'Arctic Grey Willow'**   Erect shrubs up to 1 m (3 ft) high, sometimes taller; branchlets reddish-brown to grey, pubescent, becoming yellowish, glabrous and glossy; leaves obovate, narrowly obovate or elliptic, 3–10 cm long, 1–3 cm wide, apex and base acute or obtuse, margins entire, often glandular towards the base and sometimes revolute; lamina finely pubescent above turning dark glossy green when mature, white pubescent beneath at first becoming glabrous later; petioles up to 1.5 cm long; stipules prominent 1–1.5 cm long, narrowly elliptic, margins glandular; catkins coetaneous on leafy branchlets in June or July; male catkins 1.5–2.5 cm long, two stamens, filaments free or united at the base, glabrous or with basal hairs, anthers red at first turning brown when mature, two nectaries – adaxial and abaxial. Female catkins 2–8 cm long, cylindrical, ovaries densely white lanate; styles 0.5–1 mm long, entire or bifid; stigmas with four linear lobes as long as style; one adaxial nectary; scales dark brown, pubescent.

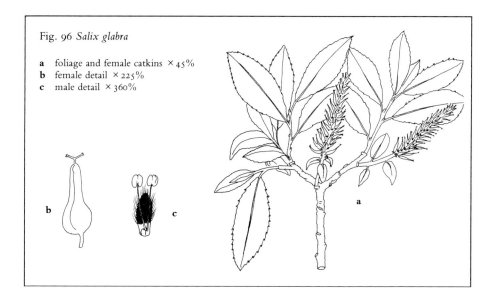

Fig. 96 *Salix glabra*

a foliage and female catkins ×45%
b female detail ×225%
c male detail ×360%

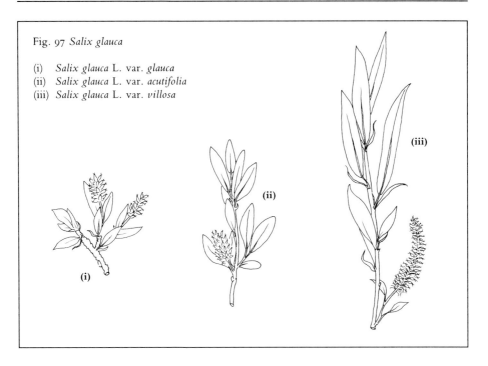

Fig. 97 *Salix glauca*

(i)   *Salix glauca* L. var. *glauca*
(ii) *Salix glauca* L. var. *acutifolia*
(iii) *Salix glauca* L. var. *villosa*

A circumpolar species occurring in Alaska, Yukon, north British Columbia, and in Eurasia from Arctic Scandinavia to the Chukotsk and Kamchatka Peninsula in the former USSR.

An extremely hardy dwarf willow with attractive foliage.

Three well-defined varieties of *S. glauca* exist in Arctic North America: (G. W. Argus, 'Genus *Salix* in Alaska and the Yukon Pub', de Bot., No 2, 1973).

i *S. glauca* L. var. *glauca* (the Beringea phase)
Very similar to the Scandinavian *S. glauca*, with villous branchlets and short internodes; leaves villous to pubescent on both sides; petioles short, stipules longer than the petioles; ovaries lanate; pedicels short.

Confined to the western coastline of Alaska.

ii *S. glauca* L. var, *acutifolia* (the Western phase)
Leaves long, lanate beneath, glabrous to sparsely pubescent above; petioles long; stipules narrowly elliptic and long; pedicels long.

Occurs in central Alaska, Yukon Territory and in northern British Columbia.

iii *S. glauca* L. var. *villosa* (the Rocky Mountain phase)
Leaves more glabrescent, stipules less prominent and catkins are smaller than var. *acutifolia*.

Distributed in the Rocky Mountains from northern British Columbia and adjacent Yukon Territory to Utah and New Mexico, extending east to Hudson Bay.

In arctic Russia (Skvortsov 1966) forms of *S. glauca* also vary, depending upon their location. In some regions the leaves are small, sparsely pubescent, stipules absent, catkins and branchlets are short. In other areas of Arctic Russia a large-leafed form occurs with long stipules and catkins similar to the Alaskan var. *acutifolia*.

Salix glaucosericea Flod. '**Alpine Grey Willow**' A slow-growing shrub 1–1.5 m (3–5 ft) high, with widely angled and ascending thick, stiff, greyish branches. Branchlets densely grey-pubescent, short and thick, becoming glabrous, glossy and light brown. Young leaves densely white-lanate beneath with a very prominent midrib, darker and hairy above. Mature leaves oblanceolate, oblong-elliptic or slightly obovate, 6–8 cm long, 2–3 cm wide, apex obtuse or rounded, base cuneate or rounded, margins entire, lamina pale green above, bluish-green beneath, with silky grey hairs on both surfaces; petioles 4–6 mm long, pubescent; stipules small or absent; catkins 3–5 cm long, 1–1.5 cm diameter, coetaneous, erect, lanate on short leafy, densely hairy peduncles about 1 cm long with three to four narrowly elliptic leaf bracts densely sericeous beneath and adpressed hairs above. Male catkins, flowers with two stamens considerably longer than the scales, filaments free with basal hairs, anthers pale yellow; scales with a broadly rounded dark brown apex and dense long curly hairs sprouting from the apical half. Female catkins – ovary shortly pedicellate, narrowly conical, pubescent; style one sixth as long as the ovary, divided at the apex; stigmas wide-spreading, slender and bifid.

A native of the French Alps, mostly at altitudes above 1,800 m (6,000 ft) in acid soil.

A strikingly ornamental alpine species with particularly beautiful foliage and catkins. Suitable for small gardens. Thriving best in an exposed situation.

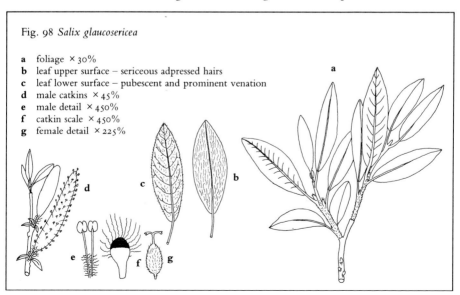

Fig. 98 *Salix glaucosericea*

a foliage × 30%
b leaf upper surface – sericeous adpressed hairs
c leaf lower surface – pubescent and prominent venation
d male catkins × 45%
e male detail × 450%
f catkin scale × 450%
g female detail × 225%

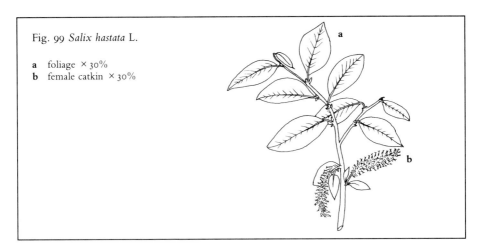

Fig. 99 *Salix hastata* L.

a foliage × 30%
b female catkin × 30%

Salix hastata L. **'Halberd-Leaved Willow'**   A many-branched low-spreading
shrub 1–1.5 m (3–5 ft) or occasionally up to 3 m (10 ft) high, with brown
glabrescent branches, with indumentum persisting for the first two years,
sometimes becoming purplish. Branchlets reddish-brown, densely white-pubescent, sparsely pubescent or glabrous. Immature leaves sparsely white to rusty-
pubescent above and beneath. Leaves not drying black. Mature leaves very
variable, elliptic, ovate to obovate, 2–8 cm long, 1–4 cm wide, apex acute, base
acute, rounded or cordate, margins entire or minutely, irregularly glandular-
serrulate and revolute. Lamina firm-textured glabrous and glossy above with a
few persistent rust-coloured hairs on the midrib, pale green and glabrous (non-
glaucous) beneath. Petioles 3–6 mm long, red-tinged and pubescent; stipules
large, ovate, margins glandular-dotted. Catkins coetaneous on short leafy
floriferous branchlets. Male catkins 1.5–4 cm long, two stamens – filaments
3–5 mm long, glabrous and free. Female catkins 3–7 cm long, loosely flowered;
ovaries green, red-tinged at the base, glabrous; capsules 4–8 mm long; styles
sometimes bifid and slightly longer than the two- to four-lobed stigmas; pedicels
pubescent, very short, up to 1 mm long; one nectary, adaxial, broad, narrowing
towards the apex, half as long as the pedicel; scales oblong, apex acute, 1–2 mm
long, pale brown and sparsely pubescent.

　　Widely distributed in the mountains of northern Alaska, the Yukon and the
North West Territories in North America. It is also present in mountainous parts
of central and southern Europe, extending to north-east Asia and Kashmir.

Salix hastata L. var. *farrae* **Hult.**   Differs from the species with only sparsely
pubescent yellowish branchlets; leaves smaller, narrower and strongly glaucous
beneath; catkins shorter.

　　S. hastata var. *farrae* has a scattered distribution in south-east British Columbia,
Alberta, Idaho, Montana and Wyoming.

In Europe (Rechinger 1964, Flora Europea) three subspecies occur:

1 *S. hastata* ssp. *hastata*
Leaves obovate or broadly elliptical with serrulate margins. Present in the
mountains throughout northern and central Europe, occuring sporadically in the
mountains of southern Europe.

2 *S. hastata* ssp. *vegeta*
Leaves orbicular, petioles 2–3 mm long. A lowland willow in Scandinavia and central Europe.

3 *S. hastata* ssp. *subintegrifolia*
Leaves lanceolate, margins entire. A northern Scandinavian subspecies.

Salix hastata L. 'Wehrhahnii'   A relatively slow-growing cultivar with an ultimate height of 2 m (6 ft) under ideal conditions. Branches stout, stiff, greyish-brown, ascending and branching laterally. Branchlets dark reddish-brown and glabrous. Young leaves sericeously white pubescent beneath and minutely, sparsely pubescent above. Lamina bright green above, paler green beneath. Mature leaves dark green glabrescent above, sparsely pubescent beneath. Leaf buds dark red. Catkins precocious in March, very erect and lanate, 4–7 cm long, 1–1.5 cm diameter, on pubescent peduncles 1 cm long, with three to five ovate leaf bracts glabrous bright green above and villous paler green beneath. Rachis pubescent; scales 1–1.5 mm long, obovate with a rounded apex, black, covered with long, dense curly hairs, Two stamens – long, glabrous and free, projecting beyond the lanate layer formed from the curly hairs on the catkin scales. Anthers golden-yellow.

A very ornamental male cultivar with vertical pure-white woolly catkins and golden anthers when mature.

If space permits, three or more plants placed in close proximity produce a spectacular display of catkins in the early spring.

Salix hegetschweileri Heer. (S. rhaetica Kern.)   A medium-sized, erect, many-branched, glabrous shrub; leaves elliptic to obovate glabrous and glossy dark green above, paler green and glabrous beneath, leaf margins widely glandular-serrate; petioles 3–5 mm long; catkins precocious, elliptic, sessile and erect 3–5 cm long; staminal filaments with basal hairs.

An ornamental Swiss alpine native species.

Salix helvetica Vill. (S. nivea Ser.) 'Swiss Willow'   A low shrub, branching radially from a central caudex to form a circular compact mound from ground

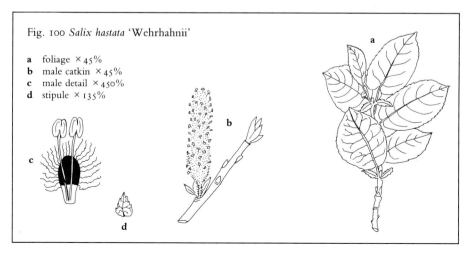

Fig. 100 *Salix hastata* 'Wehrhahnii'

a   foliage × 45%
b   male catkin × 45%
c   male detail × 450%
d   stipule × 135%

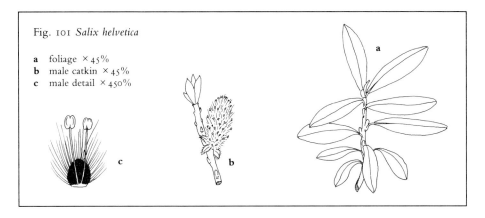

Fig. 101 *Salix helvetica*

a foliage × 45%
b male catkin × 45%
c male detail × 450%

a
c
b

level, approximately 1 m (3 ft) in diameter and 0.5 m (18 in.) high. Branches thick; branchlets twiggy, thick with short internodes, pubescent at first, densely sericeously white, becoming glabrous and glossy dark brown; leaves obovate or elliptic-lanceolate, entire, apex rounded or acute, base cuneate or acute; lamina of young leaves pubescent above and beneath, mature leaves 4–6 cm long, 2–2.5 cm wide, densely white lanate beneath, greyish green sparsely pubescent above. Catkins relatively large, 3–5 cm long, 1–1.5 cm diameter, precocious or coetaneous in March and April, erect, subsessile or with a sericeously pubescent peduncle up to 5 mm long. Immature catkins densely silver-hairy with three small elliptic leaf bracts, sericeous beneath and glabrous above; rachis pubescent; male catkins densely pubescent, two filaments, glabrous with dark-red anthers becoming golden when mature; female catkins densely pubescent, ovary with a very long style; stigma bifid and forked. Scales black, short, widely ovate, apex obtuse, covered with long, straight, sericeous hairs.

A native of the Swiss Alps and the Tatry Mountains.

A superb compact grey-leafed alpine shrub with extremely beautiful male anthers. Requires an exposed position.

Salix hibernica Rech. f. 'Irish Willow' A small or medium-sized strongly branched, upright shrub 1.5–2.5 m (5–7 ft) high; branchlets glabrous and yellowish-green with short internodes; axillary buds yellow; leaves broadly elliptic or broadly lanceolate-elliptic, 4–8 cm long, 3–4.5 cm wide, upper surface glabrous and very glossy bright green, glabrous and glaucous beneath, apex rounded, obtuse or shortly cuspidate, margins entire or irregularly crenate; petioles pale yellow, 1–1.5 cm long; stipules small or absent; catkins precocious in March and April, 2–3 cm long, erect dense-flowered, very shortly pedunculate with three small sericeous basal leaf bracts. The catkins are oval and lanate; ovaries narrowly conical, sericeously pubescent; styles distinct, stigma almost sessile, partially divided; scales lanceolate, black, densely long-hairy.

An attractive species, native of north-west Ireland, with unusually glossy bright-green foliage.

Salix integra Thunb. 'Alba Maculata' (*S. i. fuiri-kuroyanagi*; *S. i.* 'Hakuro Nishiki')
A small slender-branched shrub 1–1.5 m (3–5 ft) high; branchlets thin, glabrous, shining bright pink; unfolding leaves glabrous, translucent, white, suffused with pale pink; mature leaves generally paired, subsessile, oblong or oval, thin,

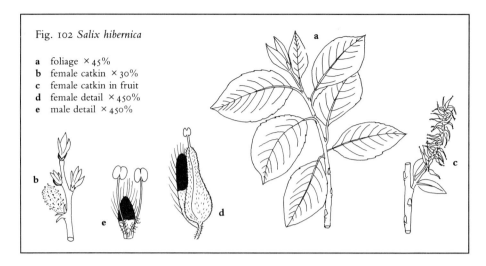

Fig. 102 *Salix hibernica*

a   foliage × 45%
b   female catkin × 30%
c   female catkin in fruit
d   female detail × 450%
e   male detail × 450%

glabrous, apex obtuse or rounded, base obtuse or cordate, margins entire or partially and indistinctly serrate towards the apex; lamina strongly mottled with bright green-and-white variegation, with considerable differences between individual leaves, some being almost entirely white.

A very strikingly variegated ornamental Japanese cultivar occupying very little space within the small garden. In view of the lack of chlorophyll in the white leaves, annual autumn pruning is advisable to encourage the production of new shoots for the following season.

Salix integra Thunb. 'Pendula'   An excellent pendulous cultivar that can be left as a vigorous arching shrub with pendulous branches. Alternatively, it can be trained upwards or grafted to produce a small weeping tree. Treated in this way its translucent tinted foliage clearly surpasses that of the Kilmarnock Willow (*S. caprea* 'Pendula'), which is dull by comparison. Beautiful effects can also be obtained by planting the ungrafted shrub behind a retaining wall or within a large raised urn. Previously mentioned in Chapter 4 for large gardens, it is equally effective and suitable for the small garden.

Salix kazbekensis Skv.   A small or medium-sized shrub with slender, spreading branches; branchlets glabrous, pale brownish-green, with purplish stems supporting the immature leaves; leaves 2–4 cm long, 1–1.5 cm wide, narrowly elliptic to narrowly obovate, apex acute or obtuse, base cuneate, margins glandular-serrate; lamina glabrous, glossy dark green above, glabrous and paler green beneath with a prominent midrib, 8–10 pairs of primary lateral veins reticulate venation visible beneath. Petioles purplish 2–3 mm long. Catkins, coetaneous in April and May, erect on glabrous peduncles up to 1.5 cm long bearing three to four narrowly elliptic leaf bracts minutely sericeous beneath. Catkins narrowly cylindric, 2–4 cm long and 3–6 mm in diameter; ovaries minutely pubescent and subsessile, with a very short pedicel; style distinct; stigmas bifid and slender; scales oblong, apex rounded, blackish towards the apex with short straight hairs restricted to the apical third.

A Russian species in mountainous regions of the Caucasus, Armenia and Georgia. Recently introduced into Great Britain.

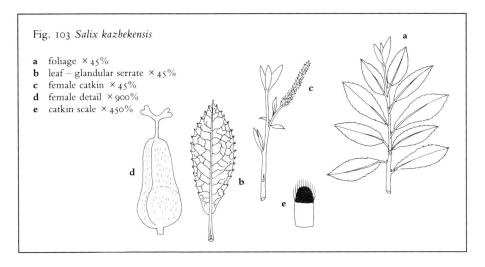

Fig. 103 *Salix kazbekensis*

a foliage × 45%
b leaf – glandular serrate × 45%
c female catkin × 45%
d female detail × 900%
e catkin scale × 450%

Salix kochiana **Traut.** A loosely branched small shrub up to 2 m (6 ft) high; branches pale grey and glabrous, widely spreading; branchlets glabrous, shining dark reddish-brown or purplish; leaves show considerable variation in relative position along the branchlets, some being opposite or subopposite and others alternate; young leaves are translucent, thin, brown-tinged; mature leaves sessile or subsessile, 1–3 cm long, 5–12 mm wide, oblong, elliptic, or oblong-obovate, the apex typically mucronate, base rounded, margins entire; lamina glabrous on both sides, bright green above, becoming blue/green with age, paler green beneath. Catkins coetaneous in April and May, numerous, alternating along the branchlets at regular intervals on peduncles 0.5–1 cm long bearing 6–7 small leaf bracts, minutely pubescent beneath. Catkins 1–1.5 cm long, 4–6 mm in diameter; ovaries minutely sericeously pubescent, sessile or subsessile; styles distinct; stigmas reddish, almost connate; scales oval with a rounded apex, glabrous yellowish-green.

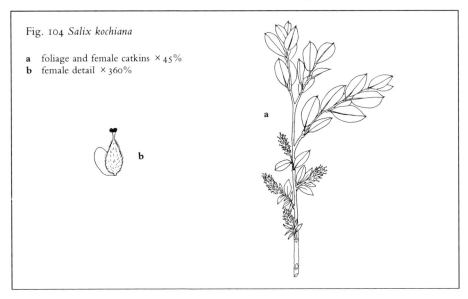

Fig. 104 *Salix kochiana*

a foliage and female catkins × 45%
b female detail × 360%

An interesting and ornamental species with attractive leaves. Extremely hardy, tolerating dry exposed situations.

Salix lanata L. 'Woolly Willow'   A tough, bushy, stiffly branched shrub 1–1.5 m (3–5 ft) high, branches thick and somewhat gnarled; branchlets and buds densely white lanate; leaves elliptic, rounded to obovate, 2–6 cm long, 1.5–3 cm wide, apex acute, base rounded or cordate, lamina thick and tough, both sides densely white lanate when young, later becoming glabrous and dull green above, blue/grey and reticulate beneath; petioles 5–10 mm long; stipules large, 6–8 mm long, ovate, entire with prominent venation; catkins coetaneous in May, densely yellowish lanate, male catkins 4–6 cm long, female catkins up to 8 cm long in fruit; two stamens, glabrous and free, anthers golden; ovaries glabrous and subsessile; styles long.

A native of Scandinavia, northern Europe, Arctic Russia and Scotland.

An ornamental, slow-growing, very hardy species with white lanate young foliage, and erect yellowish catkins at the tips of the branches.

Salix lanata L. ssp. richardsonii   A sturdy shrub 0.5–3 m (1.5–10 ft) high, distinguishable from *S. lanata* L. by its glabrous to glabrescent, smaller leaves, and by its catkins which are white lanate rather than yellowish lanate.

The North American Arctic form, present on mountain slopes and moraines throughout central Alaska and Yukon, British Columbia, Hudson Bay and Baffin Island.

SALIX LANATA CLONES:

S. lanata L. 'Drake's hybrid'   A slow-growing, stiffly branched dwarf shrub rarely exceeding 0.3 m (1 ft) high, spreading from a stout, gnarled, central caudex. Branches stout, glabrous greenish-brown; branchlets short, light green, glabrous with short internodes and numerous bud scars; leaves concentrated towards the tips of the branchlets, cordate or suborbicular, 2–4 cm long, 1.5–3 cm wide, young leaves with adpressed hairs on both surfaces overlapping the margins;

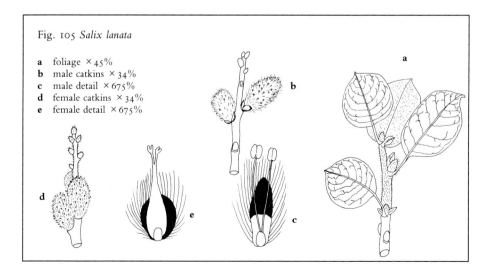

Fig. 105 *Salix lanata*

a   foliage   × 45%
b   male catkins   × 34%
c   male detail   × 675%
d   female catkins   × 34%
e   female detail   × 675%

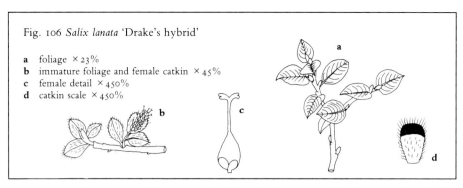

Fig. 106 *Salix lanata* 'Drake's hybrid'

a   foliage × 23%
b   immature foliage and female catkin × 45%
c   female detail × 450%
d   catkin scale × 450%

mature leaves remaining sparsely hairy dark green with impressed reticulate venation above, pale green with hairs restricted to the prominent midrib below. Catkins coetaneous in March and April. Ovary glabrous, subsessile and dark brown; style elongate, equal to the length of the ovary; stigmas dark brown and bifid.

An ornamental dwarf female clone ideal for a small rock garden.

S. *lanata* L. 'Mark Postill'   A female clone 0.5–1 m (1.5–3 ft) high with leaves similar in shape and texture to *S. lanata* L. It differs from *S. lanata* in the following respects:

The stipules are prominent, persistent, broadly cordate and glandular serrate. The leaves are very densely crowded, with shorter internodes. Leaf pubescence with long adpressed hairs is mainly confined to the upper surface, the lower surface being sparsely puberulent with long hairs confined to the midrib. Catkins precocious in April, pure white lanate (not yellowish), very erect, and 8–12 cm long when in fruit; ovary slender, glabrous and twice as long as style; scales triangular, apex and margin black, densely lanate with curly white hairs 3–5 mm long on both surfaces.

A very ornamental small, slow-growing female clone with strikingly prominent white lanate catkins and closely packed white-pubescent leaves.

S. *lanata* L. 'Mrs Mac'   A male clone slowly growing to reach 1.5 m (5 ft) high. Buds yellow and glabrous; young leaves densely covered on both sides with long silky

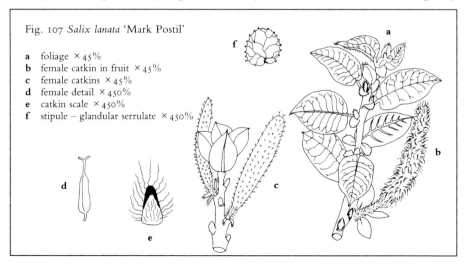

Fig. 107 *Salix lanata* 'Mark Postil'

a   foliage × 45%
b   female catkin in fruit × 45%
c   female catkins × 45%
d   female detail × 450%
e   catkin scale × 450%
f   stipule – glandular serrulate × 450%

silver hairs. Mature leaves dark green and glabrous above, remaining sericeously hairy beneath; leaf texture thinner than *S. lanata*; leaf shape variable but tending to be less rounded, more narrowly elliptic and less reticulate beneath than the species. The male catkins large and globose up to 4 cm long and 3 cm wide. Two stamens, filaments 1–1.5 cm long; anthers large and golden-yellow.

A beautiful willow with outstandingly good golden male catkins.

***Salix lapponum* L. 'Lapland Willow'**   An erect, densely branched small shrub 0.5–1.5 m (1.5–5 ft) high; branchlets sericeously pubescent, becoming glabrous and dark brown later; leaves oval, lanceolate or narrowly elliptic, apex acute or slightly rounded, base acute or rounded, 2.5–6 cm long, 1–2.5 cm wide, entire, downy pubescent above, thickly and persistently lanate beneath, silvery white at first becoming grey; petioles 0.5–1 cm long; stipules small or absent; catkins precocious, strikingly silvery sericeous on bare stems in April and May; male catkins sessile 2–2.5 cm long; female catkins 3–4 cm long on short peduncles; two stamens, glabrous and free, anthers red becoming pale yellow; ovaries densely pubescent and subsessile; scales densely long pubescent.

The species is distributed in the mountains of Scandinavia, Lapland, Poland, north-west Russia and in some mountains of central and south-eastern Europe, but is not present in the Alps. In Great Britain it exists at altitudes above 300 m (1,000 ft) in Scotland and the Lake District.

A very decorative silver/grey-leafed species, ideal for an exposed situation in a small garden.

***Salix lapponum* L. var. *daphneola* Tausch.**   A smaller, more bushy and spreading shrub than the species; branchlets glabrous; leaves glabrous, bright glossy green above, light green beneath.

Natural distribution restricted to the highest mountains.

Readily grows in gardens at low levels but is less decorative than the species.

***Salix lapponum* L. 'Grayii'**   A small, smoothly-rounded, clump-forming dwarf willow less than 1 m (3 ft) high and up to 1 m (3 ft) in diameter, densely branching

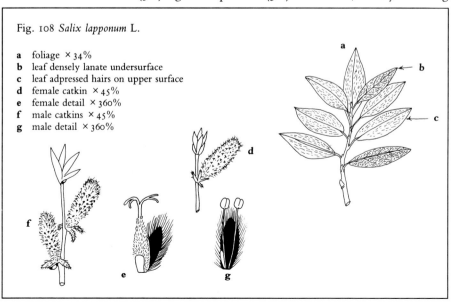

Fig. 108 *Salix lapponum* L.

a   foliage × 34%
b   leaf densely lanate undersurface
c   leaf adpressed hairs on upper surface
d   female catkin × 45%
e   female detail × 360%
f   male catkins × 45%
g   male detail × 360%

from ground level; branches grey and glabrous; branchlets greyish-brown puberulent becoming glossy dark brown; immature leaves white pubescent above and beneath; mature leaves densely crowded, smaller than those of pure *S. lapponum*, very densely silver-lanate beneath, downy with appressed hairs, reticulate and blue/green above; buds bright red; female catkins precocious in April, sessile or subsessile, up to 5 cm long, sericeously silver with three densely sericeous basal leaf bracts; ovary densely pubescent; scales pubescent long-hairy, base yellow, apex black.

An extremely beautiful female clone with conspicuous silvery/white foliage forming a shapely compact mound, the branches becoming invisible beneath the leaves.

Salix medwedewii Dode.   A small shrub with glabrous branchlets; leaves linear-lanceolate or narrowly elliptic, 6–12 cm long, 4–6 mm wide, glandular serrate; lamina glabrous above, glabrous and glaucous beneath; female catkins dense-flowered.

A native of Asia Minor.

Salix melanostachys Mak.   Previously described in Chapter 4 under *S. gracilistyla* var. *melanostachys*. Suitable also for small gardens, this is not a widely arching species, occupying little space, and has very spectacular catkins.

Salix 'Micrugosa'   A small, compact, erect and many-branched shrub up to 2 m (6 ft) high; branchlets slender, glabrous, light brown with numerous bud scars. Leaves small 1–3 cm long, 0.5–1.5 cm wide, elliptic, acute at both ends, margins entire; lamina glabrous fresh bright green somewhat rugose with impressed venation above, glabrous and paler green with reticulate venation and a prominent midrib beneath; stipules very small or absent; petioles 2–3 mm long; catkins ovoid, precocious in April towards the ends of the branchlets; male catkins up to 1 cm long and 3–5 mm wide on very short peduncles 1–2 mm long bearing three to four minute lanceolate leaf bracts sericeous beneath; two stamens, glabrous; anthers bright orange at first, pale yellow later; scales reddish, pubescent.

A very neat ornamental little shrub of obscure origin with conspicuous fiery-coloured catkins.

Salix muscina Dode.   A medium-sized shrub or small tree with a neatly branching habit. Branches light brown, glabrous and shining; branchlets purple, downy-pubescent becoming glabrous; immature leaves pubescent on both sides and red-tinged; buds small, triangular and red; mature leaves 5–8 cm long, 2–3.5 cm wide, lanceolate-elliptic, apex generally rounded, sometimes acute, base rounded and frequently unequal, margins subentire or sparsely glandular-serrate or crenate and sometimes undulate; lamina bright glabrous, glossy green with impressed venation above, pale green and sparsely pubescent with prominent reticulate venation beneath; petioles purplish 2–4 mm long; stipules minute, ovate, serrate and caducous.

A hardy European species with attractive foliage and branchlets.

Salix myrtillifolia Anderss.   A low-growing, decumbent shrub less than 1 m (3 ft) high; branches glabrescent, greyish-brown, the lowest trailing at ground level; branchlets brown, sparsely pubescent and glossy; closely related to *S. novae-angliae*, with identical glandular crenate or crenate-serrulate leaf margins, but

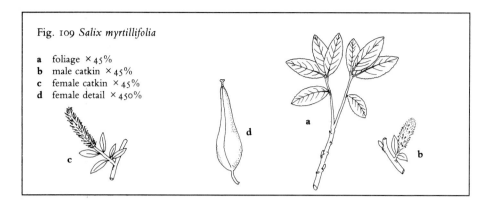

Fig. 109 *Salix myrtillifolia*

a foliage × 45%
b male catkin × 45%
c female catkin × 45%
d female detail × 450%

with smaller leaves glossy and glabrous on both sides and with a more rounded apex; young leaves reddish, glabrous and translucent; stipules minute; styles very short (0.3–0.5 mm long), almost half as long as *S. novae-angliae*; scales sparsely pubescent, shorter than the pedicels.

A North American dwarf growing on the margins of lakes and rivers in central Alaska; Mackenzie River delta; in southern Yukon Territory; eastwards across Canada to Newfoundland; south in the Rocky Mountains to British Columbia and Alberta.

A hardy species thriving best in relatively exposed moist situations.

Salix novae-angliae Anderss.   An erect shrub 0.5–3 m (1.5–10 ft) high; branches dark brown, persistently pubescent or becoming glabrous; branchlets densely villous becoming sparsely pubescent; young leaves red-tinged, pubescent; mature leaves narrowly elliptic to narrowly obovate, 3–7 cm long, 1–3 cm wide, apex acute or obtuse, base rounded, margins glandular crenate or crenate-serrulate; lamina becoming glabrous above with white or rusty hairs along the midrib, glabrescent, glossy and non-glaucous beneath; petioles 3–5 mm long, pubescent and pale yellow; stipules small, 2–5 mm long, semi-ovate with glandular-crenate margins; catkins coetaneous on leafy branchlets; male catkins up to 2 cm long, filaments glabrous and free; female catkins 2–5 cm long; ovaries glabrous; styles

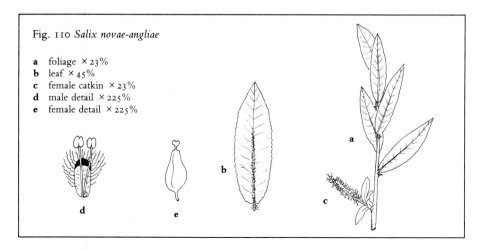

Fig. 110 *Salix novae-angliae*

a foliage × 23%
b leaf × 45%
c female catkin × 23%
d male detail × 225%
e female detail × 225%

0.5–1 mm long; pedicels 1–1.5 mm long; scales oblong, apex dark brown, paler below, pubescent with wavy hairs.

A North American species, native of central Alaska, southern Yukon and adjacent North West Territories; southward in the Cordilleras to California and eastward to Saskatchewan.

Salix 'Onusta'   A distinctive low, widely branching, small shrub up to 1 m (3 ft) high with slender dark-brown glabrous branches; branchlets purplish-red, glabrous; buds red and glabrous; leaves small, youngest leaves minutely pubescent, mature leaves 1–2 cm long, 2–5 mm wide, narrowly elliptic, oblong or narrowly obovate, apex obtuse, base rounded, margins entire; lamina dark green, glabrous, shining with deeply impressed venation above, glaucous and reticulate beneath; catkins precocious in April, sessile, short-cylindric or ovoid becoming spherical when mature, 1.5–2 cm in diameter surmounting three to five linear-lanceolate glabrous leaf bracts; two stamens, 4–5 mm long, free and glabrous; anthers brilliant orange becoming golden-yellow; scales narrowly oblong, apex rounded, reddish and glabrous.

A hardy and very ornamental, little spreading male clone of uncertain origin with striking catkin colours. Ideal for the small garden.

Salix pantosericea Goerz.   A small erect strongly branched shrub 1.5–3 m (5–10 ft) high; branchlets pubescent at first, becoming yellowish-green glabrous and glossy; leaves narrowly elliptic, lanceolate or oblanceolate, 6–12 cm long, 2–3.5 cm wide, and thick textured; lamina glabrous, glossy, bright green above, paler green and sericeously puberulent beneath, margins entire, apex shortly acuminate or cuspidate, base rounded or acute; buds light brown, glabrous; petioles 1 cm long; stipules small or absent. Catkins coetaneous.

A native of Japan, Korea, Manchuria and Mongolia.

A very hardy, attractive small shrub with brilliant shining golden-green stems in winter.

Salix × patula Ser. (S. elaeagnos Scop. × S. aurita L.)   A small bushy, many-branched shrub 1.5–2.5 m (5–8 ft) high; branchlets grey-pubescent; leaves oblong, oblanceolate or lanceolate, apex acuminate or acute, base acute; lamina of young leaves densely pubescent on both sides; mature leaves sparsely pubescent above, densely grey-pubescent beneath; catkins cylindrical on bracted peduncles; staminal filaments totally connate with basal hairs; pedicel about half as long as the ovary; stigmas oblong, shorter than the style.

A very hardy relatively slow-growing European cultivar, mainly of botanical interest.

Salix pedicellaris Pursh.   A small shrub very similar to S. athabascensis (for a detailed comparison see also under S. athabascensis Raup.) with erect branches 0.2–1.5 m (8 in–5 ft) high, rarely exceeding 1 m (3 ft); leaves coriaceous, reticulate and typically waxy glaucescent above, glaucous on both sides with a somewhat rounded apex; catkins loose-flowered. It differs from S. athabascensis in having entirely glabrous leaves, branchlets with minute straight hairs, pistils glabrous and reddish, pedicels 2–3 mm long, styles 0.1–0.2 mm long.

A North American Arctic species inhabiting wet fens in Watson Lake, south-eastern Yukon, adjacent British Columbia and southern North West Territories; southward in the Rocky Mountains to Washington; eastward to Newfoundland; northern United States from Minnesota to New England.

Salix pedunculata Fern.　A small erect shrub 0.5–2 m (1.5–6 ft) high; branchlets widely angled, light brown, downy puberulent or reddish, shining and sometimes distinctly pruinose; leaves narrowly elliptic, oblong or narrowly obovate 3–8 cm long, 2–4 cm wide, apex acute or rounded, base cuneate, margins variable from entire to minutely crenate-serrulate; lamina glabrous and glossy above, glaucous, somewhat sericeous and reticulate beneath; primary veins numerous and parallel; petioles 5–8 mm long; catkins coetaneous in June and July, up to 8 cm long; male catkins subsessile, female catkins on short bracted peduncles; scales narrowly oblong, 2–4 mm long, apex acute or slightly rounded, blackish with long hairs; pedicels puberulent, 1–2 mm long, ovaries sericeously pubescent; styles 1–2 mm long, entire; stigmas partially or totally bifid.

A North American species mainly confined to stream banks and lake margins in the Gaspé Peninsula and Newfoundland, northwards along the Labrador coast.

A hardy willow with attractive branchlets and glossy foliage.

Salix planifolia Pursh. ssp. *pulchra* (Cham.) Argus var. *pulchra*　A shrub up to 2 m (6 ft) high with procumbent or ascending, purple-tinged, glossy brown branchlets; leaves narrowly elliptic, lanceolate, subentire, glandular, serrulate or crenate, 3–6 cm long, 1–2.6 cm wide, acuminate or acute, base acute or cuneate; lamina glabrous and dark green above, paler glabrous green beneath; petioles short; stipules prominent, 5–12 mm long, linear, glandular-serrulate, acute, longer than the petioles and often persistent up to four years. Catkins subsessile, rachis elongate, leaf bracts brown; anthers 0.4–0.8 mm long. Female catkins 1–2.5 cm long in flower, extending up to 8 cm long in fruit; pedicels 0.2–0.6 mm long; nectaries red-tinged, approximately twice as long as pedicel.

A small native of the Arctic tundra, widespread throughout Alaska, rare in Yukon Territory. Widely distributed in Asia from Novaya Zemlya to the Chukosk Peninsula.

A beautiful small willow with glossy shoots and shining dark-green leaves.

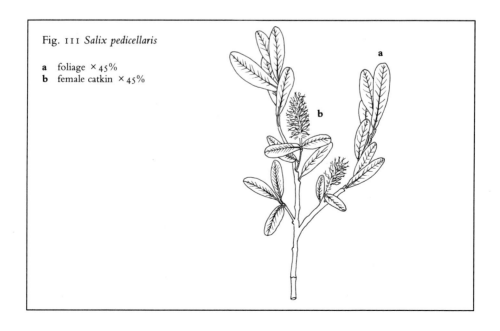

Fig. 111 *Salix pedicellaris*

a　foliage × 45%
b　female catkin × 45%

Fig. 112 *Salix purpurea* 'Pendula'

a foliage × 30%
b female catkins × 45%
c female detail × 450%
d catkin scale × 450%

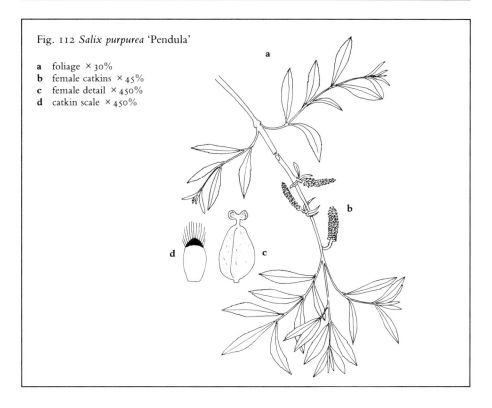

Salix planifolia **Pursh. ssp.** *pulchra* **var.** *yukonensis* **(Schneid.) Argus**   Taller than var. *pulchra*, 0.5–3 m (1.5–10 ft) high; branches sometimes persistently pubescent; branchlets pale brown, densely white or rusty pubescent; mature leaves with pubescent midrib and petiole; stipules glabrous or pubescent.

Inhabits stream banks and alpine tundra in the Yukon and British Columbia. Also present in northern Asia.

Salix purpurea **L. var.** *gracilis* **(nana)**   A small erect shrub seldom exceeding 1 m (3 ft) high; branches and branchlets numerous, ascending to form a dense compact little bush with a somewhat rounded crown; branchlets very slender, glabrous, dark red or green; leaves alternate, narrowly or linear-lanceolate, 1.5–3.5 cm long, 2–5 mm wide, apex acuminate, base cuneate or acute, margins entire or partially serrulate, lamina dull glabrous green above, glaucous blue beneath; petioles pale green, glabrous, 1–3 mm long; exstipulate; bud scales dark red; catkins small and cylindrical.

A neat, compact little willow thriving in poor soils. Pruning every two years stimulates fresh shoots, maintaining a good crown.

Salix purpurea **L. 'Pendula'**   A small shrub with whitish-grey, glabrous arching branches; branchlets pendulous slender, very flexible, dark purplish-red, glabrous and glossy; the youngest shoots coloured maroon at first; leaves subsessile, opposite or subopposite narrowly obovate or oblanceolate, 2–6 cm long, 2–8 mm wide, some minutely and regularly serrulate, others subentire, apex shortly acuminate or acute, base rounded or cuneate; lamina glabrous blue/green above, glabrous and glaucous beneath. Catkins coetaneous in April and May, cylindrical 1.5–2.5 cm long on short peduncles 2–3 mm long, at right angles on horizontal branchlets and strongly recurved on pendulous branchlets; two or three small, narrow leaf-like bracts below each catkin; peduncle and rachis minutely sericeously pubescent; scales very small, ovate, apex blackish-tipped and bearded with a few hairs; ovary somewhat ovoid and sericeously puberulent; style very short and indistinct; stigmas bifid and subsessile.

Generally represented in cultivation as a female clone. It can either be left to grow as an attractive arching shrub or trained as a small weeping tree by removing the lower lateral buds. To achieve quick results it can be grafted onto a vertical rootstock 2–2.5 m (6–8 ft) high. *S. purpurea* 'Pendula' is the ideal miniature weeping willow for the very small garden. It is also extremely hardy, withstanding prolonged drought.

Salix purpurea L. 'Nancy Saunders'   A very ornamental small female clone with numerous slender, glossy, dark-red branchlets and narrowly oblanceolate leaves, blue/green above, glaucous beneath.

Salix purpurea L. 'Rana'   A small, rather broad-leafed male clone with greyish-yellow shining branchlets and pale-brown buds. Leaves bright lime-green.

Salix purpurea L. 'Richartii'   A very beautiful female clone with blue mature leaves and translucent young leaves delicately tinted with pale pink and orange; winter branchlets glossy dark brown; previously recommended for large gardens, it is equally suitable for small gardens. Hard pruning every third year stimulates new shoots and maintains its shape.

Salix pyrenaica Gouan.   A low shrub 0.5 m to (occasionally) 1 m (1.5–3 ft) high, with ascending and some procumbent reddish-brown, densely-leafed, glabrescent branchlets; leaves up to 3.5 cm long ovate-elliptic or obovate, densely pubescent above and beneath at first; later becoming glabrous and green with prominent reticulate venation beneath, margins entire with some persistent marginal hairs, apex obtuse, base rounded; catkins loosely flowered, ovate, 1–2 cm long in July and August at the tips of the branchlets; flower scales 2 mm long, obovate, apex obtuse, brown, lanate on both surfaces, staminal filaments glabrous, anthers yellow; capsules ovoid, densely pubescent; ovary subsessile with pedicel 0.5 mm long; style and stigma bifid.

A native of the Pyrenees, Cordillera Cantabrica. Only the female plant under cultivation. An attractive little shrub best grown in a rocky situation.

Salix repens L. var. fusca Wimm. et Grab.   A vertically ascending densely compact shrub 1.5–2.5 m (5–8 ft) high, possessing the botanical characteristics of *S. repens* L. var. *ericetorum* Wimm. et Grab. described in Chapter 6, differing only in its vertical mode of growth.

A somewhat unusual form of *S. repens* L. creating a striking contrast when placed behind small bushy shrubs.

Salix rosmarinifolia L.   A small, erect, very flexible, densely branching shrub 1–2 m (3–6 ft) high; the previous year's branchlets dark brown, sparsely pubescent and steeply ascending; the current year's branchlets reddish, pubescent and slender; leaves numerous, narrowly lanceolate, sericeously pubescent on both surfaces when young, apex acute, base rounded, margins entire, very slightly revolute;

lamina dark green and glabrous above when mature, remaining sericeously pubescent beneath with a prominent midrib and eight to ten pairs of lateral veins; petioles 1–2 mm long; stipules absent; catkins prolific, coetaneous in April, globose, arising from short shoots up to 1 cm long with two or three leaf bracts sericeously pubescent beneath; scales small, narrow–oblong extending to the base of the ovary, pubescent, apex rounded, blackish; staminal filaments free and glabrous; ovary sericeously hairy; style very short; stigmas distinct and widespread; pedicel 2–3 mm long, pubescent.

A native of central and eastern Europe extending to Belgium, northern Italy and Sweden.

A beautiful slender shrub with attractive leaves and erect habit. Extremely hardy. This species is often confused with *S. elaeagnos* 'Angustifolia' (*S. lavandulifolia* Koch. var. *rosmarinifolia* Hort. non L.)

***Salix* × *sadleri* Syme (*S. lanata* L. × *S. herbacea* L.)**   A small, slow-growing, thick-branched shrub up to 0.5–1 m (1.5–3 ft) high; branches rough dark brown, glabrous; branchlets trailing, light green, sparsely pubescent; leaves broadly ovate or suborbicular 2.5–6 cm long, 1.5–4 cm wide; young leaves puberulent above and beneath; mature leaves broadly ovate, margins subentire or glandular-serrate, apex shortly acuminate or cuspidate, base cordate or rounded and unequal; lamina glabrous, glossy, dark green above with impressed venation, whitish glaucous with prominent reticulate venation beneath; petioles pale green, puberulent, 0.5–1 cm long; buds reddish-brown, puberulent; stipules prominent, cordate, glandular serrate; catkins coetaneous and shortly cylindrical in April, 2–3 cm long, 1–1.5 cm diameter, erect on a hairy peduncle 0.5–1 cm long with four leaf bracts sericeous beneath; peduncle and rachis pubescent; scales obovate, black and hairy in the apical half; staminal filaments long, free and glabrous; immature anthers orange becoming dark golden-yellow later. Female catkins – ovaries broadly flask shaped and glabrous; styles long; stigmas shortly oblong, entire or bifid.

An attractive small hybrid with broad glossy leaves and conspicuous erect catkins.

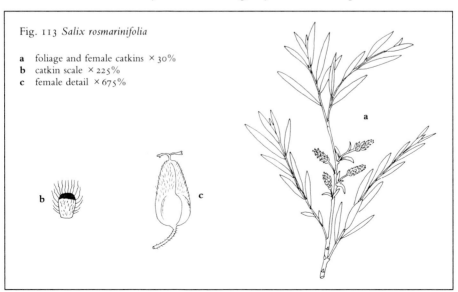

Fig. 113 *Salix rosmarinifolia*

a foliage and female catkins × 30%
b catkin scale × 225%
c female detail × 675%

Occurs with the parents on rocky ground at high altitudes in Russia, Scandinavia and in the Highlands of Scotland.

Salix × seringeana Gaud. (S. caprea L. × S. elaeagnos Scop.)   (See also Chapter 4.) Suitable for large or small gardens, with very ornamental greyish-white pubescent foliage.

Salix sikkimensis Anderss.   A shrub or small tree with widely spreading glabrous, glossy branchlets; leaves lanceolate, sericeously pubescent and copper-coloured beneath; catkins precocious and subsessile in May, curved and silver-haired; male catkins 2.5–5 cm long; female catkins up to 10 cm long with obovate notched scales; capsules densely pubescent.

A native of eastern Nepal and south-west China found on stream banks at high altitudes.

Salix sitchensis Sanson.   A small shrub 0.5–2 m or occasionally 3 m (1.5–10 ft) high, branches dark brown with grey pubescence persisting for two years; branchlets brittle, densely sericeous becoming sparsely pubescent. Leaves narrowly elliptic or obovate, 4–10 cm long, 1.5–4 cm wide, apex rounded or with an obtuse tip, base cuneate; leaf margins glandular serrulate or irregularly glandular crenate, revolute; lamina sparsely pubescent above becoming glabrous bright green and darkening later, lower surface glossy and densely white with matted straight silky hairs; petioles 5–10 mm long, pubescent, pale yellow; stipules semi-ovate, pubescent, very small 0.5–1.5 mm long; catkins coetaneous, on leafy, floriferous branchlets. Male catkins 2–3 cm long; one stamen, entirely connate, staminal filaments 5 mm long, glabrous; female catkins 3–8 cm long, ovaries pubescent, styles 0.5–1 mm long, stigmas very short; pedicels pubescent 1–1.5 mm long; scales narrowly oblong, brown with darker apex, hairy on both surfaces.

A North American species growing on sand and gravel bars of rivers and glacial moraines in Alaska and adjacent British Columbia; southward to Washington and California.

It is a pioneer species, surviving extreme conditions.

An interesting and very distinctive shrub.

Salix starkeana Willd. (S. livida Wahl.)   A small, erect shrub up to 1 m (3 ft) high with slender, glabrous branches; branchlets sparsely pubescent yellowish or brown becoming glabrous; buds yellow and appressed; leaves broadly lanceolate to broadly obovate, apex shortly acuminate with the tip laterally deflected, 5–6 cm long and 2–2.5 cm wide; lamina sparsely pubescent or glabrous and reticulate above, blue/green and glabrous beneath with prominent venation, margins glandular-serrate; petioles 2–3 mm long; stipules broadly elliptic, coarsely serrate and persistent. Catkins lax, up to 3 cm long, precocious, on short leafy peduncles; scales yellowish, lanceolate, sparsely pubescent with marginal hairs. Staminal filaments glabrous and green; ovary densely pubescent supported on a long pedicel, long-beaked when in fruit; style indistinct; stigmas ovoid and erect.

A native of north-eastern Europe extending southwards but not ascending into the Alps.

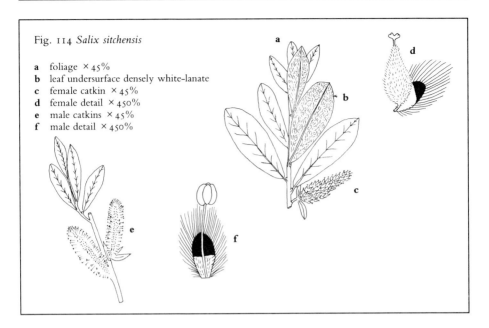

Fig. 114 *Salix sitchensis*

a foliage × 45%
b leaf undersurface densely white-lanate
c female catkin × 45%
d female detail × 450%
e male catkins × 45%
f male detail × 450%

Salix 'Stuartii' (*S. lanata* L. × *S. lapponum* L.)   A shorter and more spreading shrub than *S. lanata* L., attaining not more than 1 m (3 ft) high. Leaves are more oblong and densely white lanate. Catkins darker yellow, with pubescent ovaries and pedicels as in *S. lapponum* L.

A probable hybrid between *S. lanata* L. and *S. lapponum* L., first discovered by Dr Charles Stuart in Berwickshire, Scotland in 1902. Only female forms are in cultivation.

A good ornamental willow for the small garden.

Salix subalpina Forbes (*S. elaeagnos* Scop. × *S. repens* L.)   A small erect shrub up to 0.5 m (1.5 ft) high with ascending branches, pubescent until the second year; leaves oblanceolate or elliptic-lanceolate, apex acuminate, base cuneate, 2.5–6 cm long, 0.5–2 cm wide, margins entire or slightly serrate towards the apex; lamina puberulent becoming glabrous bright green above, persistently grey-lanate beneath. Catkins 2.5–3 cm long, cylindrical, stamens with bright-yellow anthers.

An ornamental cultivar originally introduced from Switzerland.

Salix subcoerulea Piper.   A shrub up to 2 m (6 ft) high; branchlets pubescent becoming glabrous, purple and often pruinose later; leaves lanceolate to oblanceolate, 3–8 cm long, apex short-acuminate or acute, base rounded or cuneate, margins slightly crenate or entire, lamina glabrous blue/green above, glossy sericeously white, densely tomentose beneath with a prominent yellow midrib; petioles 3–8 mm long; catkins subsessile, male catkins 2–4 cm long, female catkins up to 5 cm long; pedicel half the length of the nectary; capsule 5 mm long.

A North American species from Washington to Wyoming, Colorado, New Mexico, Utah and California.

A beautiful little willow with conspicuously white pruinose branchlets.

Salix × subsericea Doell. (*S. repens* L. × *S. cinerea* L.)   A low, many-branched shrub up to 1 m (3 ft) high; branchlets slender, dark brown, pubescent, becoming

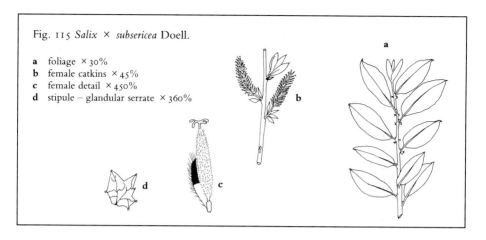

Fig. 115 *Salix* × *subsericea* Doell.

a   foliage × 30%
b   female catkins × 45%
c   female detail × 450%
d   stipule – glandular serrate × 360%

glabrous later; leaves narrowly oblong or elliptic, 2–5 cm long, 1–2.5 cm wide, apex acute, margins narrowly recurved; lamina bright green and sparsely hairy above, sericeously grey-pubescent or glabrous beneath; petioles up to 5 mm long; stipules small and caducous. Catkins precocious in April or May, subsessile with small sericeous leaf bracts, 2–3 cm long, 0.5–1 cm diameter, scales oblong, hairy, obtuse and brown; ovaries subsessile, narrow and pubescent, 2–3 mm long, styles short, stigmas bifid or subentire.

Widely distributed in Europe; only female plants recorded in Great Britain from isolated areas in Wales and Scotland, *cinerea* var. *oleifolia* being involved.

Salix × **subsericea** (Anderss.) Schneid. (*S. sericea* × *S. petiolaris* Rydb.) 'False Silky Willow'   An erect, thin-branched, very flexible, diffuse little shrub 1–2.5 m (3–8 ft) high; branchlets very slender, orange to brown, puberulent, glabrescent. Leaves narrow-lanceolate or oblanceolate, 3–8 cm long, 1–1.5 cm wide, apex shortly acuminate or acute, base obtuse, margins partially or totally serrulate; lamina pubescent above, densely sericeously pubescent and glaucous beneath; petioles glabrous and slender 0.5–1 cm long; stipules small, lanceolate and caducous.

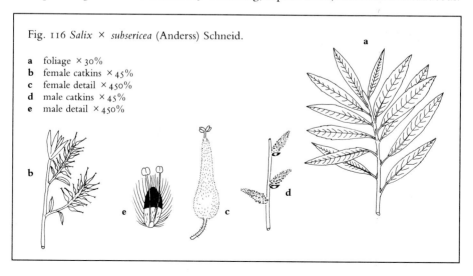

Fig. 116 *Salix* × *subsericea* (Anderss) Schneid.

a   foliage × 30%
b   female catkins × 45%
c   female detail × 450%
d   male catkins × 45%
e   male detail × 450%

Catkins, precocious in April or early May, 2–4 cm long, 1–1.5 cm diameter, becoming lax, on sericeously hairy peduncles 0.5–1.5 cm long with narrow, pointed puberulent, basal leaf bracts; scales narrowly oblong, apex rounded or acute, black and villous; male catkins – stamens at the base usually mature before those at the apex giving rise to an overall elongated conical shape initially, two stamens, filaments glabrous and free; ovaries narrow, 5–8 mm long, minutely sericeous; pedicels 2–3 mm long, puberulent; styles up to 0.2 mm long, entire; stigmas 0.2–0.5 mm long, entire to bifid.

A North American willow widely distributed in water-meadows on stream banks from Quebec to Alberta and south Saskatchewan; southwards to Massachusetts and northern parts of Indiana, Illinois and Nebraska.

An extremely graceful little willow with ornamental foliage and beautiful male catkins. A very good shrub for small gardens.

Salix syrticola Fern.   (See Chapter 4.) Also suitable for small gardens, contrasting well with darker-leafed shrubs.

Salix tatrae Wol. (S. alpina Scop. × S. silesiaca Willd.)   A small shrub forming a rounded mound rising up to 1 m (3 ft) high and extending 1–1.5 m (3–5 ft) in diameter; branches slender, shining, dark brown, horizontal to ascending; youngest branchlets green, puberulent; immature leaves glabrous light green above, sericeously puberulent beneath; mature leaves obovate or narrowly elliptic, 4–8 cm long, 1–2.5 cm wide, apex acute or obtuse, base acute or cuneate, margins crenulate; lamina glabrous dark green with impressed venation above, paler glabrous green beneath with a few hairs on the prominent midrib, eight to ten pairs of primary nerves; stipules ovate, serrulate. Catkins coetaneous in April or May, 4–8 cm long, erect, slender, cylindrical, 5–8 mm in diameter on leafy peduncles 1–3 cm long; ovaries glabrous, flask shaped with a conspicuously bulbous base; pedicels 1–2 mm long, pedicels and rachis sericeously puberulent; styles short and indistinct; stigmas dark red, bifid; scales narrowly oblong, apex acute or round, black tipped and bearded with long hairs.

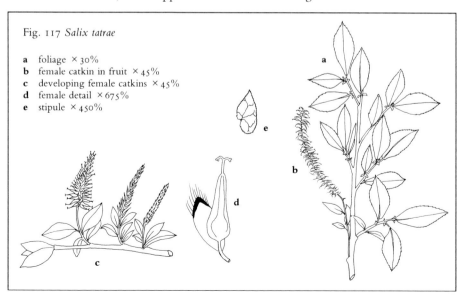

Fig. 117 *Salix tatrae*

a   foliage × 30%
b   female catkin in fruit × 45%
c   developing female catkins × 45%
d   female detail × 675%
e   stipule × 450%

A native of the Tatry Mountains, Czechoslovakia.

A very hardy, relatively compact and ornamental willow, very suitable for the small garden.

Salix tristis Ait. (*S. humilis* var. *microphylla* Anderss. Fern.) 'Dwarf Upland Willow'   A small, many-branched shrub 0.5–1 m (1.5–3 ft) high, very similar to *S. humilis* on a much smaller scale; branchlets slender, brown-tinged, pubescent; leaves concentrated towards the tips of the branchlets, narrowly oblanceolate, 2–5 cm long, 0.5–1 cm wide, apex acute, base cuneate, margins entire; lamina dark green pubescent becoming glabrous above, densely grey-pubescent and glaucescent beneath; petioles very short. Catkins precocious between February and April, prolific, sessile, without leaf bracts, 1–2 cm long, oval; scales oblanceolate, apex obtuse, 1–2 mm long, blackish and villous. Two stamens, filaments glabrous and free; ovaries narrowly lanceolate, densely pubescent; pedicels 1–2 mm long, pubescent; styles short 0.2–0.3 mm long, equal to bifid stigmas.

An attractive, extremely hardy North American species; isolated specimens occurring in exposed dry, sandy situations on mountain slopes or road sides from Massachusetts to North Dakota, southwards to Tennessee and centrally to Nebraska.

Salix tweedyi (Bebb.) Ball. (*S. barrattiana* var. *tweedyi* Bebb.)   A slow-growing shrub up to 3 m (10 ft) high; branchlets thick, densely villous persisting into their second year; immature leaves with sparse long hairs on both sides; mature leaves glabrous dark green above, paler green (non-glaucous) and glabrous beneath, 5–10 cm long, 2–6 cm wide, elliptic to elliptic-obovate, obtuse or acute at both ends, margins glandular serrulate to entire; catkins precocious to coetaneous, sessile on the previous year's branchlets; scales persistent, densely long-hairy and blackish; male catkins 6–8 mm long, dense-flowered; ovaries subsessile, glabrous or with a few distal long hairs; style distinct, 1.5–3 mm long.

A montane North American shrub living on stream banks and moist ground in the mountains of north Wyoming, west and north-west across west Montana and Idaho, to Washington and south British Columbia (Falkland). Common in the Big Horn Mountains.

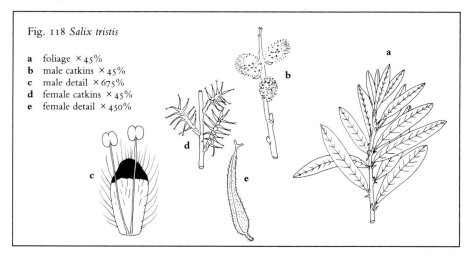

Fig. 118 *Salix tristis*

a   foliage × 45%
b   male catkins × 45%
c   male detail × 675%
d   female catkins × 45%
e   female detail × 450%

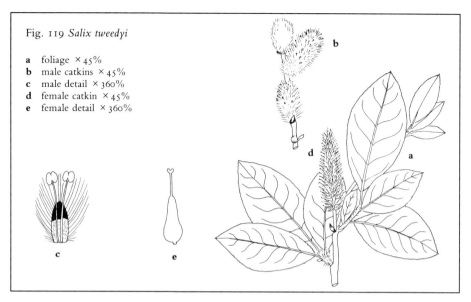

Fig. 119 *Salix tweedyi*

a foliage × 45%
b male catkins × 45%
c male detail × 360%
d female catkin × 45%
e female detail × 360%

S. tweedyi possesses certain features similar to *S. barrattiana* and *S. barclayii* but has longer styles than these two species.

Salix vulpina Anderss. (S. miquelii Anderss. S. miquelii var. vulpina Anderss. S. diaseniensis Seem.) 'Kitsune-Yanagi' A small to medium shrub with glabrous, glossy, dark-brown branches; branchlets whitish and brown pubescent; leaves oblong to elliptic, 3–10 cm long, 2–3.5 cm wide, acute to obtuse at both ends, margins irregularly serrate, lamina glabrous dull green above, glaucous and brownish-yellow pubescent beneath particularly along the midrib; petioles 5–10 mm long; male catkins dense-flowered, on short peduncles, 2.5–4 cm long, 5–6 mm in diameter; scales small, reddish-brown, villous; staminal filaments free or slightly connate with basal hairs; ovaries pedicellate, glabrous; style distinct, slender; stigmas short.

A Japanese species, native of Hokkaido, Honshu, Shikoku and Kyushu.

An ornamental willow, rarer in the West than the female clonal hybrid *S. tsugaluensis* 'Ginme' described in Chapter 4. The name '*vulpina*', meaning 'foxy', is probably derived from the reddish-brown colouring of the hairs of the catkin scales.

Salix wallichiana Anderss. (S. disperma Roxb. ex D. Don.) A shrub or small tree up to 3 m (10 ft) or occasionally 5 m (16 ft) high; branches greenish-grey; branchlets and immature leaves sericeously pubescent; mature leaves 5–10 cm long, oblong to ovate-lanceolate, apex narrowly acuminate, base cuneate to broad cuneate, margins entire or glandular-serrulate, lamina glabrous above, glabrous and glaucous beneath or remaining sericeously pubescent; petioles 1–1.5 cm long, glabrous. Catkins very villous, precocious in May or June; male catkins up to 4 cm long, subsessile or with sericeous peduncles and leaf bracts; female catkins to 6 cm long; ovaries pubescent and rostrate; style short; stigmas emarginate; scales oblong, dark brown, sericeously hairy; fruiting catkins up to 10 cm long, capsules 6–8 mm long and densely pubescent.

A very hardy species living on stream banks at high altitudes, ranging from Afghanistan to south-west China.

CHAPTER SIX

Dwarf and Ground-hugging Alpine Species for Rock Gardens

An understanding of the natural conditions in which wild alpine *Salix* species live is essential for their successful cultivation. These small shrubs are specifically adapted to high altitudes, fully exposed to the elements and provided only with their basic requirements. They thrive in small pockets of leaf mould with their roots in the gritty mineral products of rock erosion. They can be killed by kindness if subjected to the excessive use of fertilizers and rich living at low altitudes. Under these abnormal conditions the survivors tend to be sappy and overgrown, often becoming totally unrepresentative of their true species.

Ideally, these small mountain species should be planted in an exposed alpine bed or rockery using a moisture-retentive but well-drained medium specially prepared for this purpose. (See Chapter 3 'Planting Dwarf Alpine Willows'.)

Salix alpina Scop. (S. jacquinii Host.)   A small shrub rarely exceeding 30 cm (1 ft) high with branches appressed at ground level; branchlets dense, ascending, slender, dark reddish-brown and glabrous; leaves 1–2 cm long, elliptic or obovate, apex obtuse or acute, base cuneate or rounded, leaf margins subentire and variably ciliate; lamina of immature leaves brown-tinged, puberulous beneath; mature leaves glabrous and glossy above, glabrous beneath. Catkins coetaneous, slender on short peduncles along the branchlets, some terminal with two or three ovate leaf bracts brownish towards their apex and sericeous beneath. Female catkins loose-flowered; ovaries glabrous, reddish; style distinct; stigmas very clearly divided. Male catkins – two filaments, glabrous and free; anthers

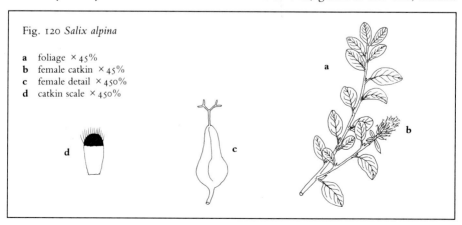

Fig. 120 *Salix alpina*

a foliage × 45%
b female catkin × 45%
c female detail × 450%
d catkin scale × 450%

dark purple at first. Catkin scales spathulate, apex red, truncate or rounded with short straight hairs.

A native of the eastern Alps and Carpathian Mountains.

An extremely hardy alpine species with attractive glossy foliage, ideally situated among rocks.

Salix × ambigua Ehrh. (S. aurita L. × S. repens L.)   A low, spreading small shrub with densely pubescent branchlets, becoming glabrous reddish-brown later, with longitudinal striae; leaves narrowly oblong or obovate, sericeously pubescent above and beneath, later becoming dark green above and remaining sericeously pubescent beneath; stipules prominent, ovate-acute and persistent; catkins precocious in April and May, erect, sessile or shortly pedunculate, ovoid or shortly cylindrical, 6–12 mm long, up to 5 mm in diameter; leaf bracts ovate, sericeously hairy; catkin scales oblong, pale brown with a dark tip, densely pubescent, 1 mm long, with a rounded apex; male catkins – two filaments, glabrous, free and much longer than the catkin scales; anthers yellow; female catkins – ovaries narrowly flask shaped, pedicellate and densely tomentose; style short but distinct; stigmas oblong, erect or spreading, usually entire, occasionally bifid. Confusion with small undernourished specimens of the hybrid S. aurita × S. cinerea (S. multinervis Doell.) is usually resolved by the presence of the conspicuous sericeous hairs on the undersurface of the leaves of S. × ambigua.

Widely distributed on moorland throughout Great Britain, Europe and Russia.

A very hardy hybrid, thriving in an exposed site.

Salix apoda Traut.   A ground-hugging species; branchlets horizontal, stout, stiff, glabrous and light green with short internodes. Leaves 2–5 cm long, 1–2.5 cm wide, obovate, ovate or elliptic, minutely glandular serrulate, apex acute, base rounded or cordate; lamina glabrous light green above, glabrous whitish glaucous below; stipules prominent, rounded, cordate, serrulate and persistent; catkins erect coetaneous or precocious in March or April, subsessile with a finely pubescent peduncle 1–2 mm long and three or four elliptic glabrous leaf bracts. Male catkins 2.5–5 cm long, 6–10 mm in diameter; two filaments, glabrous and free; anthers dark orange at first, becoming pale yellow at maturity. Female catkins up to 10 cm long in fruit; ovary subsessile and glabrous; style distinct; stigmas linear and entire. Catkin scales narrowly lanceolate, covered with long, straight sericeous hairs, apex acute or rounded and black-tipped.

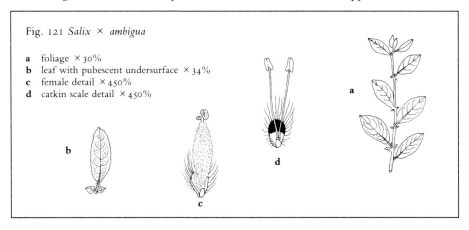

Fig. 121 *Salix × ambigua*

a   foliage × 30%
b   leaf with pubescent undersurface × 34%
c   female detail × 450%
d   catkin scale detail × 450%

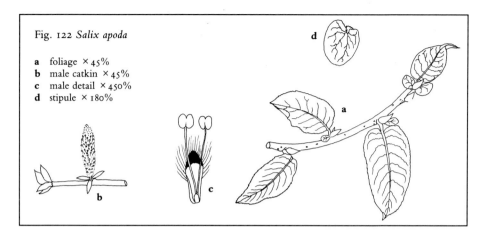

Fig. 122 *Salix apoda*

a foliage × 45%
b male catkin × 45%
c male detail × 450%
d stipule × 180%

The male clone, introduced into Great Britain from the Caucasus by Walter Ingwersen, is one of the most ornamental ground-hugging dwarf willows. Although relatively slow-growing it will ultimately cover a large area.

Salix arbuscula L. (S. formosa Willd.) 'Mountain Willow'   A dwarf shrub with spreading or ascending branches, rarely more than 60 cm (2 ft) high. Mature branchlets glabrous, glossy, dark brown; young shoots sometimes pubescent; leaves ovate or elliptic, 1–2 cm long, 1–1.5 cm wide, apex acute or obtuse, base cuneate or rounded, margins narrowly recurved, glandular serrate or subentire; lamina glabrous, lustrous and sometimes reticulate above, green or glaucous and sometimes appressed-hairy beneath; petioles up to 3 mm long; stipules minute, caducous or lacking; catkins coetaneous in May or June, up to 1–2 cm long, narrowly cylindrical, 4–5 mm diameter, erect or suberect on short leafy peduncles; catkin scales broadly obtuse, up to 1.5 mm long, brownish, densely covered with white hairs; male catkins – two filaments, glabrous and free, anthers dark red or purple, female catkins – ovary sessile or shortly pedicellate, densely pubescent; style distinct, with two short, slender, notched or entire stigmas.

In Great Britain *S. arbuscula* occurs locally in mid-Perthshire and adjacent Argyll, usually on damp mountain slopes at altitudes of over 600 m (2,000 ft). Its

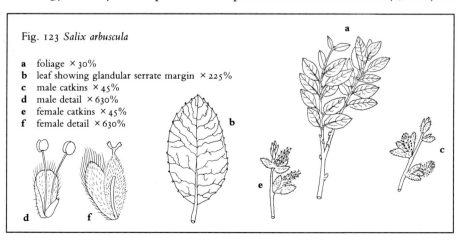

Fig. 123 *Salix arbuscula*

a foliage × 30%
b leaf showing glandular serrate margin × 225%
c male catkins × 45%
d male detail × 630%
e female catkins × 45%
f female detail × 630%

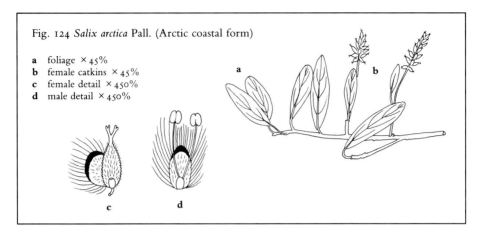

Fig. 124 *Salix arctica* Pall. (Arctic coastal form)

a foliage × 45%
b female catkins × 45%
c female detail × 450%
d male detail × 450%

distribution also extends from north Scandinavia eastwards to Siberia.

An excellent spreading dwarf species, ideal in a rock garden.

**Salix arctica Pall., (*S. anglorum* Cham., *S. arctica* var. *torulosa* Raup.,
S. arctica ssp. *crassijulis* Skv., *S. anglorum* var. *araiclada* Schneid.,
S. arctica var. *araiclada* Raup., *S. anglorum* var. *antiplasta* Schneid.,
S. arctica var. *antiplasta* Fern.)**   A very polymorphic dwarf species. Usually
prostrate or trailing, with appressed branches which sometimes root or are
partially buried and dark brown. Branchlets forming a loose mat, yellowish-
green to reddish-brown, variably pubescent or densely villous becoming glabrous. Leaves show marked variation in different populations according to their
geographical distribution. In Alaska the Arctic Ocean population has narrowly
obovate to narrowly elliptic leaves. In Bering Sea populations, leaves are almost
circular to broadly elliptic. Pacific coastal forms possess broadly elliptic or
obovate leaves. Young leaves are sparsely pubescent above; mature leaves
glabrescent and glossy above with persistent marginal and midrib hairs, the
undersurface glabrescent and glaucous with some persistent long hairs producing
a bearded apex. Petioles of very variable length, from 5–35 mm long, correlated
with the leaf length; stipules absent or minute and linear.

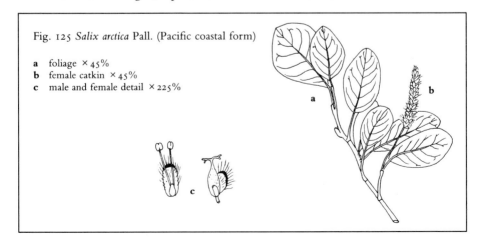

Fig. 125 *Salix arctica* Pall. (Pacific coastal form)

a foliage × 45%
b female catkin × 45%
c male and female detail × 225%

Catkins coetaneous; male catkins 2–5 cm long borne on floriferous branchlets 1–5 cm long, two stamens, filaments 4–5 mm long, glabrous and free, one adaxial nectary and rarely a second abaxial nectary. Female catkins 5–12 cm long (1.5–5 cm in Arctic Ocean populations) on floriferous branchlets 3–8 cm long; ovaries reddish-brown, densely pubescent; capsules 5–10 mm long, reddish pubescent; styles red 0.5–2 mm long, entire or bifid up to one-third of their length; stigmas 1 mm long with four linear or two broad lobes; pedicels 0.2–1.6 mm long, pubescent; single adaxial nectary up to four times as long as the pedicel. Catkin scales broadly oblong, brown with a dark-brown or black apex, pubescent on both sides. Scales of the Pacific coastal form are light brown.

A prostrate Arctic alpine and subalpine species with a circumpolar distribution occurring in Arctic tundra or glacial moraine; present throughout Arctic and alpine Alaska and Yukon Territory, extending eastward to Greenland, Arctic Europe and Arctic Asia.

Salix arctica Pall. var. petraea Anderss., (S. petrophylla Rydb.)   A dwarf shrub with creeping branches, sometimes partially buried, with long suberect spreading yellowish glabrous branchlets, producing mats up to 10 cm or more deep; leaves elliptic to broadly oblanceolate 2.5–5 cm long, 1–2 cm wide, apex acute or rounded, base broadly cuneate or rounded, margins entire or partially denticulate, lamina puberulous at first becoming glabrous bright green above, glabrous and glaucous beneath; petioles 4–6 mm long; catkins 2–5 cm long, densely flowered, erect, very hairy on leafy lateral shoots; catkin scales obovate, blackish sparsely covered with long sericeous hairs; ovaries subsessile, pubescent; style distinct, 0.5 mm long; stigmas long, narrow and bifid; two stamens, glabrous and sometimes connate at the base.

Closely related to *S. arctica* Pall., but more southern in distribution and more generally in cultivation. A native of the mountains of western North America, ranging from British Columbia and Alberta to California, Wyoming, Colorado and New Mexico.

An attractive and very hardy dwarf willow adapted to rocky situations, highly recommended for the alpine bed or large rockery.

Salix arctophila Cock. ex Heller   A dwarf decumbent trailing shrub; branches long, slender, chestnut-brown; branchlets slender, yellowish, glabrous; leaves broadly or narrowly elliptic or obovate, 2–4 cm long, 0.5–1.5 cm wide; apex obtuse or acute; base obtuse, acute or cuneate; leaf margins glandular serrulate or entire with minute glands; young leaves puberulous beneath; mature leaves glabrous, glossy, yellowish-green above, glabrous and glaucous beneath; petioles

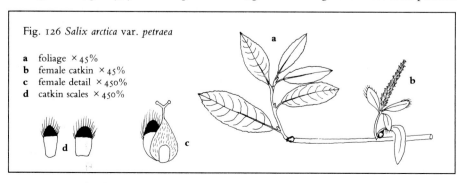

Fig. 126 *Salix arctica* var. *petraea*

a   foliage × 45%
b   female catkin × 45%
c   female detail × 450%
d   catkin scales × 450%

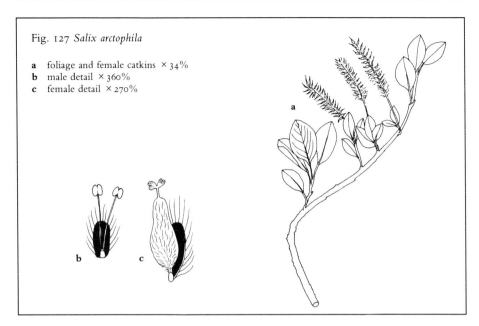

Fig. 127 *Salix arctophila*

a foliage and female catkins × 34%
b male detail × 360%
c female detail × 270%

3–12 mm long; stipules absent or up to 4 mm long, glabrous with glandular margins. Catkins coetaneous on erect, leafy branchlets; male catkins 2–5 cm long, two stamens, filaments 6–8 mm long, glabrous and purple; female catkins 2–6 cm long; pistils 2–5 mm long, sparsely pubescent with short, crinkled, refractive hairs, maroon coloured; capsules 5–8 mm long, glossy; styles 0.5–1 mm long, occasionally bifid and red; stigmas 0.2–0.5 mm long, bifid; pedicels pubescent, 1 mm long; one adaxial nectary half as long as the pedicel; catkin scales oblong, 1–1.5 mm long, purple or black, pubescent with long straight hairs.

An eastern Canadian Arctic species, also in eastern Alaska, extending westwards to Bullen on the Arctic Coast and to Jago Lake in the Brooks Range.

A similar species to *S. arctica* Pall., but with more slender, glabrous branchlets, glandular-serrate leaf margins and glabrous laminae. The nectary length of *S. arctica* Pall. is one-and-a-half to four times the pedicel, but only half as long as the pedicel in *S. arctophila*.

Salix arenaria L., (*S. argentea* Sm., *S. repens* L. var. *argentea* (Sm.) Wimm. and Grab.; *S. repens* var. *nitida* Wenderoth 'Nitida') A small shrub, larger, more erect and stoutly branched, with larger leaves than *S. repens* L.; creeping habit, stems steeply ascending and arching; the previous year's branchlets thick, dark-brown or grey, pubescent; leaves broadly obovate or suborbicular, those on strong shoots up to 4 cm long and 2.5 cm wide, lamina remaining silky pubescent on both sides, margins frequently glandular serrate and revolute; stipules ovate, acute, pubescent; catkins precocious in April and May, erect, sessile or subsessile, and ovoid, 2–3 cm long, 0.5–1 cm diameter, female catkins smaller than the males; catkin scales narrowly oblong, apex truncate, sericeously hairy, up to 2 mm long, reddish-brown towards the apex. Male catkins – two stamens, filaments free, glabrous or with basal hairs, 5–8 mm long; anthers golden-yellow, oblong; female catkins, pedicels sericeously pubescent; 1–1.5 mm long ovaries densely pubescent 2–2.5 mm long; style about 0.5 mm long, glabrous and distinct; two stigmas, shortly bifid or entire.

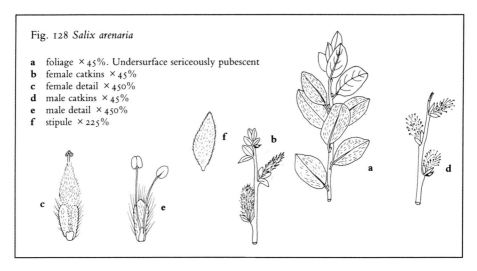

Fig. 128 *Salix arenaria*

a   foliage × 45%. Undersurface sericeously pubescent
b   female catkins × 45%
c   female detail × 450%
d   male catkins × 45%
e   male detail × 450%
f   stipule × 225%

A very ornamental and hardy willow with bright-golden male catkins along bare stems and, later, with beautiful silky-silver leaves.

The distribution is chiefly coastal, growing on sand dunes from the European Atlantic coasts to the North Sea and the Baltic. It also occurs among rocks in moorland in north Scotland.

Salix × ausserdorferi Hut. (*S. glaucosericea* Flod. × *S. retusa* L.)   A low, spreading, slow-growing dwarf shrub usually under 6 cm (2¼ in.) high with branches radiating from a central caudex. Branches thick, somewhat gnarled, and closely appressed to the ground; branchlets stout, brown, glabrous with short internodes; leaves, covering the soil, are narrowly elliptic 4–8 cm long, 1–2 cm wide, apex acute or rounded, base acute or obtuse, margins entire, lamina glabrous and glossy dark green above, paler green and minutely pubescent beneath; venation impressed above, prominent beneath, the veins running nearly parallel with the midrib. Catkins coetaneous in April and May arising from leafy peduncles along the branchlets. Female catkins 2–3 cm long, loose flowered; pedicel short, pubescent; ovary sericeously hairy; style very short; stigmas very distinct, bifid,

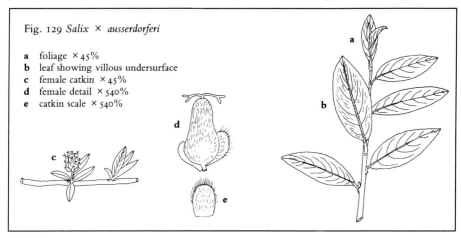

Fig. 129 *Salix × ausserdorferi*

a   foliage × 45%
b   leaf showing villous undersurface
c   female catkin × 45%
d   female detail × 540%
e   catkin scale × 540%

linear and outspread; catkin scales small; covered with short hairs, apex truncate; a single adaxial nectary.

An attractive hybrid growing flush against the soil. Does not spread excessively and is very hardy.

***Salix* × *boydii* E. F. Linton (*S. reticulata* L. × *S. lapponum* L.)** An erect, rigid small shrub up to 90 cm (3 ft) high; branches gnarled, thick and stiff; branchlets sparsely pubescent at first; buds subspherical puberulous becoming glabrous; leaves coriaceous, broadly obovate or almost orbicular, up to 3 cm long, base cordate, lamina downy above becoming glabrous blue/grey with deeply impressed venation, the lower surface permanently lanate with prominent midrib and veins; petioles very short. Catkins female, dark grey, up to 2 cm long and appear shortly before the leaves; catkin scales obovate, sericeously hairy, with a rounded apex; ovary-ovoid, sessile and pubescent.

An excellent small erect dwarf female clone, ideal among boulders in an exposed situation in an alpine bed or in a trough. A very slow-growing dwarf willow.

Originally discovered in the mountains of Angus in Scotland by William Boyd. It is considered possible that a third species, *S. herbacea*, may have originally also been a parent because of the short petioles and subspherical glabrescent buds.

***Salix brevipens* Flod.** A small erect shrub rarely exceeding 30 cm (1 ft) high; branches gnarled, stiff and spreading; branchlets dark brown and glabrous with short internodes; leaves narrowly elliptic, glabrous dark green above, glabrous paler green below, leaf margins entire or minutely serrate. Catkins, precocious in March, are borne on short pubescent peduncles 3–5 mm long with three or four basal leaf bracts, narrowly elliptic, pubescent beneath, glabrous above. Male catkins globose up to 2 cm long and 1.5 cm in diameter. Two stamens, with glabrous, free, filaments; anthers crimson, turning golden-yellow when mature. Catkin scales lanceolate, the apical half black, the basal half red, covered with long, dense, straight, sericeous hairs.

A very ornamental slow-growing small male clone thriving best in an exposed rocky situation.

***Salix breviserrata* Flod.** A low shrub with branches appressed to ground level and exfoliating bark; branchlets ascending, dark brown; leaves small, ovate or elliptic, leaf margins glandular serrate, lamina dark green glabrous above, densely pubescent and bright green beneath; leaves turning yellow in the autumn and persisting for some time; catkins precocious in March or April, stoutly cylindrical, on lateral peduncles; male catkins, with two stamens, filaments maroon-coloured glabrous and free; anthers violet at first; female catkins – ovary pedicellate, style distinct, stigma purple; catkin scales pink.

A good dwarf willow for a rock garden, a native of the European Alps and Pyrenees.

***Salix calyculata* Hook. ex Anderss.** A mat-forming, creeping small shrub with ascending sericeously pubescent branchlets up to 30 cm (1 ft) high; young leaves sericeously pubescent; mature leaves 1–3 cm long, narrowly elliptic, apex acute, base cuneate, leaf margins serrate, lamina glabrous and glossy above, sparsely pubescent beneath; petioles short; catkins coetaneous in June and July borne on short leafy lateral stems; male catkins up to 2 cm long, ovoid and hairless; female catkins 1.5–2 cm long, ovoid; capsules 7–9 mm long.

A native of Nepal, living on damp alpine slopes at high altitudes.

Salix × cernua Lint. (*S. herbacea* L. × *S. repens* L.)   A dwarf, prostrate, trailing or ascending shrub under 10 cm high with a thick network of tough, rooting branches; branchlets appressed, pubescent becoming glabrous dark reddish-brown later; leaves oblong, obovate or ovate, 0.5–1.5 cm long, 0.3–1 cm wide, sparsely pubescent or glabrous and dark lustrous green above, dull glabrous green or grey-pubescent beneath, apex acute, obtuse or rounded, base rounded, leaf margins serrulate or subentire; laminae with prominent venation; petioles very short, 2–3 mm long; stipules absent or minute; catkins coetaneous in May and June, shortly pedunculate at the tips of the leafy lateral shoots, catkins up to 2 cm long and 5 mm in diameter; male catkins with two stamens; filaments glabrous and free, up to 5 mm long; anthers yellow, dark orange or red-tinged; two nectaries, the adaxial broadly oblong, the abaxial longer, narrower and sometimes divided nearly to the base; female catkins with a shortly pedicellate ovary, glabrous or pubescent, 2–3 mm long, 1 mm wide; style short and distinct; two stigmas, double-cleft into four short narrow lobes. Capsules 3–5 mm long, reddish.

A native of rocky heaths in Scotland. It has also been recorded from Norway. A good hardy slow-growing shrublet meriting a pocket in the rock garden.

Salix chamissonis Anderss.   A prostrate dwarf shrub with long reddish-brown branches trailing along the ground; catkins and vegetative branchlets arising at right angles to a branch; branchlets yellowish, pubescent, becoming glabrous; leaves obovate to elliptic-obovate, 3–5 cm long, 2–3 cm wide, apex obtuse, rounded or retuse, base cuneate, margins uniformly glandular-serrulate; lamina of mature leaves glabrous and glossy above, pubescent becoming glabrous and glaucous beneath; petioles 5–10 mm long; stipules narrowly elliptic, 3–10 mm long and glandular-serrulate; catkins coetaneous on leafy, floriferous branchlets; male catkins 2–3 cm long; two stamens, filaments glabrous, to 8 mm long with red anthers; one adaxial nectary – 1 mm long. Female catkins 4–6 cm long, rachis pubescent, pistils reddish, 2.5–5 mm long, densely covered with crinkled, refractive hairs; pedicels 0.2–0.4 mm, pubescent; styles 1 mm long, reddish, bifid; stigmas 0.5 mm long; capsules 4–10 mm long, copper-coloured, becoming glabrous, the beak remaining slightly pubescent; one nectary – adaxial, 0.3–0.6 mm long, dark red, equal to or fractionally longer than the pedicel; catkin scales ovate 1–3 mm long, dark brown or blackish, with hairs on both sides double the length of the scales.

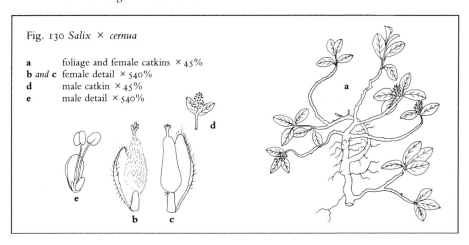

Fig. 130 *Salix × cernua*

a   foliage and female catkins × 45%
b *and* **c** female detail × 540%
d   male catkin × 45%
e   male detail × 540%

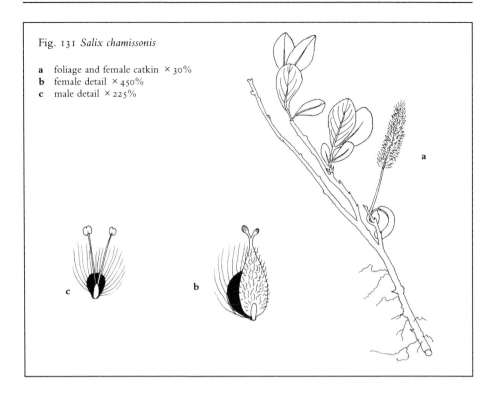

Fig. 131 *Salix chamissonis*

a foliage and female catkin × 30%
b female detail × 450%
c male detail × 225%

A small Arctic alpine North American species in the mountains of Alaska, northern Yukon and adjacent North West Territories. A wide-ranging species it also occurs in Asia, eastern Siberia, Kamchatka Peninsula, and the Chukotsk Peninsula.

S. chamissonis is related to *S. myrsinites* L., *S. saxatilis* Turcz. and *S. arctophila* Cock. These four species all exhibit the same crinkled, refractive hairs covering the pistils and glandular-serrulate leaf margins. *S. chamissonis* differs from *myrsinites* in possessing obovate leaves, glaucous beneath and with shorter petioles. It has more prominently and uniformly glandular-serrulate leaf and stipule margins than *S. arctophila*.

Salix × *cottetii* Kern. (*S. retusa* L. × *S. myrsinifolia* Salisb.)   A small prostrate shrub with glabrous spreading, rooting branches; branchlets dense, ascending or horizontal, pubescent, becoming glabrous and yellowish-brown; leaves elliptic to obovate, 2–4 cm long, 1–2 cm wide, acute or obtuse, leaf margins serrulate, lamina pubescent on both sides at first, glabrous bright green above when mature and remaining pubescent on the midrib and veins beneath. Catkins shortly cylindrical, 1–1.5 cm long on short, pubescent, leafy peduncles; ovary glabrous, style distinct and elongate; two stamens, filaments glabrous and free; anthers yellow; catkin scales oblong with a dark brown, retuse, pubescent apex.

Originated from the European Alps. Only a male clone in cultivation.

An ornamental and relatively fast-growing clone producing attractive fresh green foliage and effective ground cover in the rock garden.

Salix *dodgeana* Rydb.   (see *S. rotundifolia* ssp. *dodgeana* (Rydb.) Argus)

Salix × ***felina*** **Buser. ex G. and A. Camus (*S. myrsinifolia* Salisb.** × ***S. repens*** **L.)**   A sprawling dwarf shrub with densely pubescent branchlets becoming glabrous, glossy dark brown; leaves lanceolate, sparsely pubescent above, persistently grey-pubescent beneath; catkins coetaneous, erect and cylindrical; female catkins – ovaries pedicellate and densely pubescent; styles distinct and short; stigmas linear and divided into two narrow lobes; the catkin scales are oblong and narrowly spathulate and brown. Male catkins have not been recorded. A small hybrid occurring in rocky situations on mountain slopes in Scotland and the European Alps.

Salix × ***finnmarchica*** **Willd. (*S. myrtilloides* L.** × ***S. repens*** **L.)**   A low dwarf much-branched shrub up to 30 cm (1 ft) high with relatively long, glabrous, very slender, arching and spreading branchlets; leaves broadly elliptic or obovate, up to 2 cm long, leaf margins finely serrulate, lamina glabrous dark green above, pubescent becoming glabrous bluish-green beneath later; catkins precocious, very prolific on bare stems in March and April, cylindrical 1–1.5 cm long, 3–5 mm in diameter, arising from short peduncles 2–5 mm long; peduncles and rachis hairy; the mature catkins are subsessile at first, becoming pedunculate as they mature; three or four basal pointed leaf bracts are sericeously pubescent beneath; catkin scales narrowly oblong with a black tipped, rounded and hairy apex. Two stamens, filaments glabrous and free; anthers golden-yellow.

A native of Norway and Sweden.

An excellent little willow with an attractive habit, very hardy, thriving in rock gardens, with a remarkable display of male catkins in the early spring.

Salix flabellaris **Anderss.**   A small dwarf creeping shrub; branches thick, spreading and occasionally erect up to 60 cm (2 ft) high; leaves 2 cm long, elliptic to obovate, glabrous and glossy above, glabrous and glaucous beneath; leaf margins subentire or serrate. Male catkins 2 cm long, yellowish, glabrous and slightly pedunculate, two stamens with filaments glabrous and free. Female catkins 2–3 cm long with entire stigmas; fruiting catkins lax; capsules to 3.5 mm, reddish and glabrous; catkin scales obovate, glabrous and brown.

A native of western Himalaya, covering rocky alpine slopes at high altitudes.

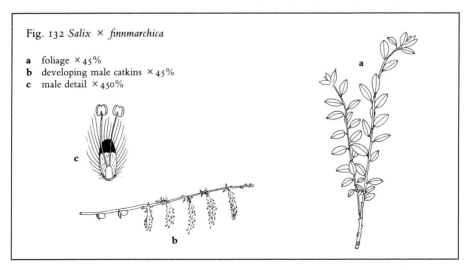

Fig. 132 *Salix* × *finnmarchica*

a   foliage × 45%
b   developing male catkins × 45%
c   male detail × 450%

Salix formosa **Willd.:**   (see *S. arbuscula*)

Salix furcata **Anderss. (*S. hylematica* Schneid. *S. nepalensis* Hort. *S. fruticu-
losa* Anderss.)**   A lax, spreading, carpeting small shrub or sometimes erect;
branchlets glabrous with short internodes; leaves elliptic-lanceolate or spathulate
5–8 mm long, entire or minutely serrate towards the apex, glabrous and glossy
with a deeply impressed midrib above, glabrous and whitish glaucous beneath;
catkins very prolific ovoid with hairless broadly ovate reddish–purple catkin
scales, borne on short lateral peduncles or sessile and often clustered with two to
five bracts sericeously hairy beneath; rachis densely and minutely pubescent;
peduncles 1–1.5 cm long, maroon, puberulous; male catkins up to 1.5 cm long,
two stamens, filaments purple, free with long basal hairs, mature anthers pale
yellow; female catkins up to 2.5 cm long, ovaries glabrous; styles deeply cleft;
fruiting catkins red, pedunculate, cylindrical 2–5 cm long; capsules 2–3 mm long,
glabrous.

   A native of the Himalayas from Uttar Pradesh to Bhutan, common on moist
rocky slopes at high altitudes.

   An extremely beautiful little spreading shrub with tiny glossy leaves, very
ornamental purple catkins and young shoots. Ideal in a gritty, well drained and
exposed situation in the rock garden.

   Often confused with *S. lindleyana* – see under *S. lindleyana* Wallich. ex Anderss.

Salix fuscescens **Anderss.**   A low, trailing shrub spreading from a central caudex;
branches brown and rooting; branchlets glabrous yellowish-brown, becoming
reddish-brown later with catkins arising at right angles; leaves obovate to elliptic,
usually narrowed towards the base 1.5–3.5 cm long, 1–2 cm wide, apex round or
obtuse, margins glandular serrate in the lower half, glabrous and glossy bright
green with prominent venation above, glaucous beneath; petioles 2.5–5 mm
long, reddish; stipules absent; catkins coetaneous on long, leafy branchlets; male
catkins up to 1.5 cm long, rachis pubescent, two stamens, filaments glabrous, one
nectary, adaxial; female catkins 1.5–6 cm long, sparsely flowered, pistils 4–5 mm
long, long-beaked, dark reddish-brown, pubescent with short rusty hairs; styles
entire or bifid; stigmas four lobed; pedicels 1–2.5 mm long, pubescent; one
nectary, adaxial 0.4–0.6 mm long, half as long as pedicel; catkin scales oblong,
with long hairs on both sides, apex dark brown.

   Distributed in wet Arctic tundra trailing in moss, occurring throughout Alaska
apart from the south-eastern coast, also in the north of Yukon Territory and the
North West Territories from the Mackenzie Delta; southward to northern
Manitoba. It also occurs in eastern Asia in the Chukosk Peninsula and Kamchatka.

   S. fuscescens is closely related to *S. myrtilloides* and *S. pedicellaris*, but differs with
its wider leaves and pubescent pistils. The name *S. arbutifolia* wrongly used in
certain literature is now correctly replaced by *S. fuscescens*.

Salix × *gillotii* **G. and A. Camus (*S. lapponum* L. × *S. phylicifolia* L.)**   A
low, spreading small shrub with sparsely hairy-pubescent branchlets later becoming glabrous and shining reddish-brown; leaves lanceolate or narrowly oblong,
apex acute, leaf margins serrulate, lamina sparsely hairy becoming glabrous and
lustrous green above, glaucous and persistently villous beneath. Catkins precocious,
erect and cylindrical; catkin scales oblong with a rounded apex; ovaries densely
pubescent, narrow, with short pedicels; style elongate; stigmas linear and entire or
divided into two very narrow lobes. Male catkins have not been recorded.

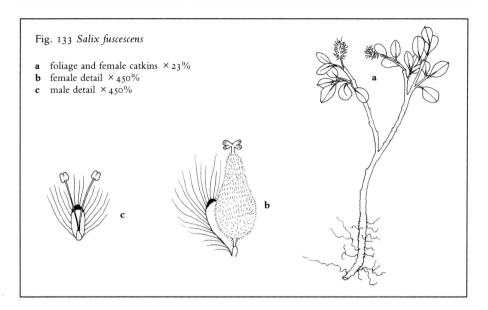

Fig. 133 *Salix fuscescens*

a foliage and female catkins × 23%
b female detail × 450%
c male detail × 450%

A small bushy hybrid occurring in mountainous regions of Scandinavia. Its natural presence in Britain is doubtful.

***Salix* × *grahamii* Borrer. ex Baker (*S. aurita* L. × *S. herbacea* L. × *S. repens* L.)** A low, prostrate or trailing shrub up to 30 cm (1 ft) high; branchlets greyish-brown pubescent becoming glabrous and glossy. Leaves broadly ovate to elliptic, 1.5–4 cm long, 1–3 cm wide, pubescent soon becoming glabrous and dark glossy green above, paler and sparsely pubescent along the prominent midrib beneath, apex obtuse or shortly acute, base rounded, margins coarsely crenate-serrate; petioles 5–7 mm long, red-tinged, puberulous; stipules up to 8 mm long, ovate, glandular serrulate and caducous; catkins cylindrical up to 1.5 cm long, 3–4 mm diameter, coetaneous in April or early May, on the tips of short lateral shoots bearing leaf bracts. Catkin scales oblong, 2–3 mm long, 1–2 mm wide, obtuse, light brown with a reddish apex and sparsely hairy; nectary narrowly tapered at the apex; ovary glabrous with a short pubescent pedicel; style distinct, reddish; stigmas deeply double cleft into linear recurved lobes.

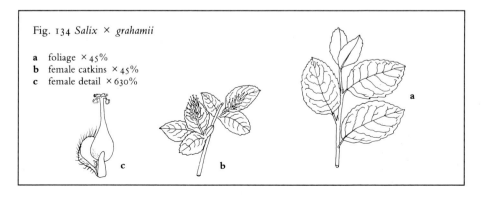

Fig. 134 *Salix* × *grahamii*

a foliage × 45%
b female catkins × 45%
c female detail × 630%

A very hardy dwarf hybrid with characteristic dark glossy green leaves. A good willow for the rock garden. Only the female forms are known, originating from Sutherland in Scotland.

Salix 'Hastata Lanata' (*S. hastata* L. × *S. lanata* L.)   A very erect, columnar dwarf hybrid up to 60 cm (2 ft) high; branches short, dark brown, and glabrous; branchlets erect, stout, with prominent leaf scars, sparsely pubescent; leaves broadly hastate or obovate, apex obtuse, base broadly cuneate or rounded, lamina dark green with minute hairs and impressed venation above, glabrous pale green with prominent, somewhat reticulate venation beneath. Catkins coetaneous in May, white-lanate, 1.5–3 cm long, 7–10 mm diameter, very erect, elongate-ovate on pubescent peduncles 5–8 mm long with three or four hairy leaf bracts. Ovary glabrous, subsessile; style distinct; stigmas bifid and outspread. Catkin scales narrowly lanceolate, black, covered with dense curly hairs through which the stigma, style and apex of the ovary protrude.

An ornamental erect female clone contrasting with trailing dwarf species in a rock garden.

Salix hidakamontana Hara. 'Hidaka-Mine-Yanagi'   A low shrub 10–20 cm (4–8 in.) high with decumbent branches; branchlets sericeously pubescent, becoming glabrous later; leaves suborbicular to elliptic 2–4 cm long, 1.5–3.5 cm wide, apex retuse or obtuse, base cordate or rounded, leaf margins entire, subentire, or undulate-serrate, lamina glabrous with impressed venation above, glabrous and glaucous with raised reticulate venation beneath; petioles 1–2.5 cm long; catkins at the tips of leafy branchlets, densely flowered 2–6 cm long in fruit; capsules narrowly ovoid, 4–5 mm long, subsessile, glabrous; catkin scales ovate or oblong, obtuse, sericeously hairy.

A dwarf alpine species growing in the Hidaka mountain range in Hokkaido, Japan.

Salix hylematica Schneid.:   (see *S. furcata* Anderss.)

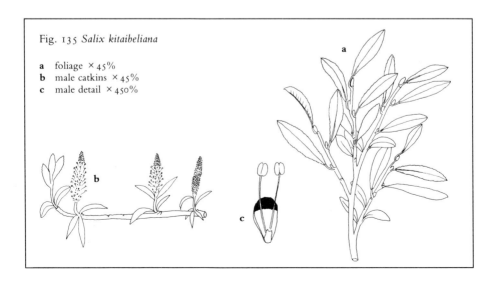

Fig. 135 *Salix kitaibeliana*

a foliage × 45%
b male catkins × 45%
c male detail × 450%

***Salix kitaibeliana* Willd.** A procumbent dwarf shrub with long, straight, stiff, light-brown glabrous branches radiating from a central caudex and closely appressed to the ground without peripheral rooting; branchlets purplish or reddish-brown, glabrous and glossy, decumbent or shortly ascending; leaves narrowly elliptic or narrowly obovate, apex acute, subacute or rounded, base cuneate, 2–3.5 cm long, 0.5–1.3 cm wide, margins serrate or subentire, lamina glabrous and glossy dark green with impressed venation above, pale glabrous green with a prominent yellowish-green midrib and six to eight pairs of prominent primary lateral veins beneath; catkins coetaneous, 2–4 cm long, 1 cm diameter, erect or suberect; female catkins, ovaries glabrous, styles one-sixth to one-eighth as long as the ovary; male catkins, two stamens, filaments glabrous and free; anthers red at first, becoming pale yellow at maturity.

A beautiful dwarf species with branches closely hugging rock surfaces.

***Salix × laestadiana* Hartm. (*S. lapponum* L. × *S. caprea* L.)** A sprawling shrub or occasionally a small tree; branchlets densely grey-pubescent at first, becoming sparsely pubescent and dark brown later; leaves elliptic or obovate-elliptic, densely grey-tomentose beneath, margins entire; catkins coetaneous, catkin scales oblong, dark brown and densely hairy; ovaries pedicellate, narrowly flask-shaped; style short but distinct; stigmas short and entire. Male catkins have not been recorded.

An alpine hybrid occurring among rocks at high altitudes in Scotland, Scandinavia and Russia.

***Salix* 'Lanata Repens' (*S. lanata* L. × *S. repens* L. (Linton)** A slow-growing dwarf female clone rarely exceeding 60 cm (2 ft) high, morphologically similar to *S. lanata* but with smaller leaves. Nearer to *S. repens* in its more decumbent habit. Branches short, stout, rigid, wrinkled and brown; branchlets pale yellowish-green, pubescent; leaves 2–4 cm long, 1.5–2 cm wide, broadly elliptic or obovate, apex acute or obtuse, base broadly cuneate or rounded, margins entire and hairy at first; lamina dark green, sparsely pubescent with scattered adpressed hairs and impressed reticulate venation above, white lanate beneath at first, becoming shortly pubescent later with long hairs restricted to the midrib; petioles 2–3 mm long, yellowish, pubescent; buds stout, yellow, pubescent; stipules ovate, apex acute, pubescent; catkins up to 3 cm long, elongating in fruit, coetaneous in May with sericeous basal leaf bracts; ovaries glabrous, narrowly flask shaped; styles long and very distinct.

An ornamental dwarf alpine with silver-grey young foliage. A very compact little shrub and an excellent subject for a small rock garden. Originally raised and distributed by Rev. E. F. Linton, and listed as Linton No: 99.

***Salix × laschiana* Zahn. (*S. repens* L. × *Salix caprea* L.)** A small, spreading shrub with dense, slender branchlets, sparsely pubescent at first, soon becoming glabrous dark reddish-brown; leaves obovate sparsely grey-pubescent becoming dark green and glabrous above, densely sericeously pubescent at first beneath, becoming sparsely pubescent later; the apex acute or often obliquely deflected at the tip. Catkins precocious or coetaneous; catkin scales subacute, blackish and densely hairy; ovaries densely grey-pubescent; style distinct; stigmas entire; two stamens, glabrous and free.

A small hybrid growing on mountain slopes and rocky heathland in Scotland, Scandinavia, Austria, Germany and Czechoslovakia. The British specimens all resemble *S. repens*, with sprawling branches and small leaves; whereas the shrubs growing elsewhere in Europe are larger and more like *S. caprea*.

***Salix lindleyana* Wallich. ex Anderss.**   A small, creeping, tight mat-forming shrub very similar to *S. hylematica* Schneid. (*S. furcata* Anderss.) but differing in the catkins, which are shorter, 6–10 mm in the male and under 1.5 cm long in the female, terminating leafy branchlets as long as the sterile shoots. The rachis is only sparsely hairy and the staminal filaments are entirely glabrous, the anthers dark brown. *S. lindleyana* is smaller, more compact than *S. furcata* and entirely creeping in habit. *S. furcata* is more lax with branchlets up to 20 cm or more long and is sometimes erect.

S. *lindleyana* is a Himalayan native occurring on rocky, alpine slopes at high altitudes, from Pakistan to south-west China.

An ideal species for the small rock garden or in a sink garden. It should be totally exposed and never crowded or overhung by other species.

***Salix* × *lintonii* G. and A. Camus (*S.* × *scotica* Druce)**   A small low-spreading shrub with puberulous branchlets, becoming glabrous dark brown later; leaves obovate or broadly obovate, sparsely pubescent above, densely and persistently grey-pubescent beneath with prominent venation. Catkins coetaneous, erect and cylindrical; ovaries pedicellate, much longer than the catkin-scales, densely pubescent with iridescent hairs; the styles short but distinct; the stigmas very short, entire or bifid.

A dwarf hybrid endemic to rocky mountain slopes in Scotland. Only the female has been recovered from the wild, but male plants have been distributed by E. F. Linton from artificially grown hybrids bearing large cylindrical catkins with subacute, long-hairy, reddish catkin scales and two stamens with glabrous, free filaments and red anthers.

***Salix* × *margarita* White (*S. aurita* L. × *S. herbacea* L.)**   A low, decumbent or ascending dwarf shrub, under 30 cm (1 ft) high; branchlets sparsely pubescent becoming glabrous, glossy, reddish-brown; leaves suborbicular, 1–3 cm in diameter, dark green glabrous above, paler green and pubescent beneath or hairy along the midrib and primary nerves; leaf margins coarsely blunt-serrate; petioles up to 1.5 cm long; stipules auricular, denticulate, prominent and caducous; catkins 1–1.5 cm long, coetaneous in April or May, shortly pedunculate with ovate, hairy leaf bracts. Catkin scales oblong, apex obtuse, brownish, sparsely hairy, up to 2 mm long and under 1 mm wide; nectary narrowly oblong; ovary densely pubescent, ovoid, shortly pedicellate; style short; stigmas distinct, double cleft.

A rare dwarf hybrid occurring on rock ledges in the Scottish Highlands and also in Norway.

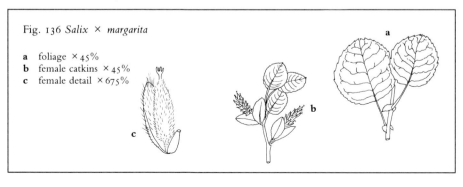

Fig. 136 *Salix* × *margarita*

a   foliage × 45%
b   female catkins × 45%
c   female detail × 675%

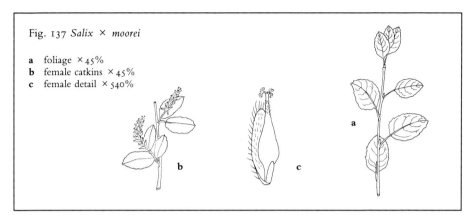

Fig. 137 *Salix* × *moorei*

a foliage × 45%
b female catkins × 45%
c female detail × 540%

***Salix* × *moorei* White (*S. aurita* L. × *S. herbacea* L. × *S. repens* L.)** A low, prostrate shrub, very similar to *S.* × *grahamii* with the same parentage, differing only in the longer, narrower catkin scales and sparsely or densely hairy ovaries with glabrous pedicels.

Originally discovered on Muckish Mountain, County Donegal in Ireland.

A very hardy and quite fast-spreading dwarf shrub. (See also under *S.* × *grahamii*.)

***Salix mummularia* Anderss. (*S. tundricola* Schljak.)** A trailing dwarf shrub; branches slender, radiating from a stout central caudex, lustrous chestnut-brown, sometimes glaucous. Branchlets yellowish-brown, sparsely pubescent with long spreading hairs. Leaves subcircular, the largest mature leaves 10–15 mm long, 8–12 mm wide, apex round to obtuse, base subcordate to round, lamina conspicuously reticulate with several glandular teeth on the margins of the lower half. Catkins produced by lateral buds and long, trailing vegetative shoots; female flowers with only four or five flowers, ovaries glabrous.

A native of Arctic tundra in Alaska and northern Russia.

Similar to *S. rotundifolia* which occurs in wet tundra, has non-reticulate, entire leaves and with catkins arising from subterminal buds and short vegetative shoots.

***Salix myrsinites* L. 'Whortle-leaved Willow'** A low, spreading or closely compact bush, up to 30 cm (1 ft) high, with rooting underground branches; branchlets sparsely pubescent becoming glabrous, glossy dark reddish-brown; leaves frequently persistent for some time after withering, extremely variable in shape and size, ovate, obovate, oblong or occasionally lanceolate, 1.5–5 cm long, 0.5–3 cm wide, glossy dark green above, sparsely pubescent becoming glossy paler green beneath with reticulate venation; leaf margins uniformly finely glandular-serrulate; apex acute or obtuse, base rounded or cuneate; petioles short and thick; stipules ovate or oblong, up to 5 mm long, 4 mm wide, serrulate and generally persistent but sometimes lacking or caducous. Catkins few, coetaneous in May and June, erect and terminal on short lateral shoots, peduncles up to 2 cm long, sparsely pubescent; leaf bracts lanceolate, pubescent and serrulate; catkin scales brown or reddish, oblong or obovate, up to 2 mm long and 1 mm wide, sericeously long-hairy. Male catkins, two stamens, filaments maroon-coloured, free, glabrous or with basal hairs; anthers purple before dehiscence; nectary oblong, up to 0.5 mm long. Female catkins bigger than the male, cylindrical

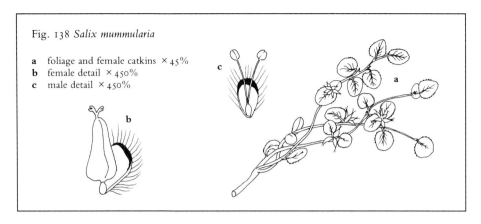

Fig. 138 *Salix mummularia*

a foliage and female catkins × 45%
b female detail × 450%
c male detail × 450%

3–6 cm long, 1–2 cm wide; ovary 4–5 mm long, densely pubescent with iridescent hairs; style distinct, up to 2.5 mm long; stigmas erect or spreading, up to
1 mm long, usually deeply divided.

S. myrsinites grows on rock ledges at high altitudes sparsely occurring in many
areas in Scotland. It also occurs widely in Scandinavia and eastwards to the Ural
Mountains. It often hybridizes with *S. myrsinifolia* (*nigricans*) and *S. glauca*, the
resulting hybrids exhibiting the purple flowers and glossy undersurface of the
leaves of *S. myrsinites*.

A very ornamental dwarf willow perfectly adapted to an exposed situation in
the rock garden.

Salix myrsinites var. jacquiniana (Willd.) Koch.   Similar to *S. myrsinites* L. with
entire or subentire leaves. (*See* Chap 7).

**Salix × myrsinitoides Druce. (*S. myrsinifolia* Salisb. × *S. phylicifolia*
L.)**   An erect shrub with sparsely pubescent branchlets, soon becoming glabrous
and glossy dark brown. Leaves obovate, apex acute, lamina dark green glabrous
and glossy above, pubescent at first becoming glabrous and glaucous beneath, the

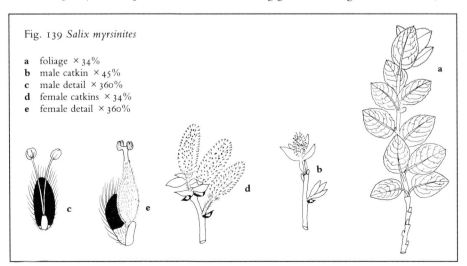

Fig. 139 *Salix myrsinites*

a foliage × 34%
b male catkin × 45%
c male detail × 360%
d female catkins × 34%
e female detail × 360%

midrib remaining sparsely pubescent; stipules broadly ovate; catkins coetaneous, large cylindrical and erect; ovaries densely villous with short pedicels; styles long; stigmas divided into four linear lobes. Male catkins have not been recorded.

This hybrid occurs in moist rocky situations in mountainous areas in Scotland and Scandinavia.

***Salix myrtilloides* L. 'Swamp Willow'**   An erect dwarf shrub up to 60 cm (2 ft) high with creeping underground stems, branches stout, rigid brown and glabrous; branchlets, leaves and buds sparsely pubescent at first, becoming glabrous later; mature leaves 1.5–4 cm long, 0.5–2 cm wide, obovate, ovate or elliptic, apex obtuse and abruptly acuminate, base rounded or broadly cuneate, margins entire or sparsely serrate and variably decurved, lamina dark glossy green with impressed venation above, paler green to bluish-green and reticulate beneath; catkins coetaneous in April or May; male catkins 1.5–2 cm long, narrowly cylindrical, sparsely flowered on short leafy peduncles, anthers red, becoming yellow at maturity; female catkins lax on leafy peduncles up to 3 cm long. Ovaries glabrous on long pedicels; styles very short; stigmas purplish and short.

A native of swamps and heaths in northern Europe and Asia from Scandinavia to the Pacific Ocean. It also occurs in bogs in scattered areas in central Europe.

An ornamental slow-growing dwarf willow, adapting well to the rock garden.

***Salix myrtilloides* L. × *S. aurita* L. (*S. rugulosa* N. J. Andersson)**   An erect dwarf shrub differing from *S. myrtilloides* in possessing distinctly crenate, rugose, prominently reticulate leaves, pubescent ovaries and persistent narrowly ovate, serrate stipules.

***Salix myrtilloides* L. × *S. repens* L.:**   (see *S. finnmarchica*)

***Salix myrtilloides* 'Pink Tassels'**   A very ornamental male clone with long maroon staminal filaments and purple anthers.

***Salix nakamurana* Koidz. 'Renge-Iwa-Yanagi', 'Takani-Iwa-Yanagi'**   A small entirely prostrate shrub with rooting branches; branchlets diffusely silky-pubescent at first, becoming glabrous brown and purple-tinged with age; leaves elliptic, obovate or oblong, 2–4 cm long, 1–3 cm wide, apex rounded or obtuse, base obtuse to acute, margins entire or subentire with a few scattered teeth, lamina glabrous with prominent lateral nerves above, glaucous beneath; catkins 3–4 cm long on short lateral shoots in July; catkin scales narrowly oblong, dark brown, hairy on both sides, apex rounded; staminal filaments shortly-connate below; ovaries glabrous, pedicels short; styles distinct; stigmas short-linear and bifid.

A rare dwarf species occurring on mountain slopes in Honshu, Japan.

***Salix nakamurana* Koidz. var. *ericarpa* Kimura**   Ovaries pubescent, otherwise identical and occurring with *S. nakamurana* Koidz.

***Salix nakamurana* var. *yezo-alpina* (Koidz.) Kimura; (*S. yezo-alpina* Koidz.; *S. cyclophylla* Seem., non Rydb. Koidz. 'Maruba-Yanagi')**   A low, widely spreading, prostrate shrub; branches stout and tightly appressed to the ground, with claw-like roots; branchlets pubescent at first becoming glabrous and purplish-brown later; petioles glabrous, 5–20 mm long; leaves thick-textured, varying from broadly obovate, broadly oblong-elliptic, to orbicular up to 5 cm long and 2–5 cm wide, apex rounded, retuse or slightly mucronate, base cordate or broadly cuneate, margins subentire and silky-hairy while young; lamina glabrous with deeply impressed venation above, glaucous with raised reticulate venation beneath; male catkins 1.5–3 cm long, densely flowered, two stamens – filaments glabrous and free; female catkins 2–5 cm long; ovaries subsessile, glabrous; styles slender; stigmas slender and bifid; catkin scales elliptic, nearly half as long as the ovary, apex rounded, densely long-haired.

An alpine willow, totally adherent to mountain slopes in Hokkaido, Japan.

An outstandingly ornamental species totally adapted to clinging to steep rocky terrain.

There is a much more vigorous male clone in cultivation (see Fig. 151, Colour Plates 63–65), with considerably larger leaves, up to 8 cm long, 7 cm wide, with marginal glands, very glossy dark green above, petioles thick, 2–4 cm long, long sericeous marginal hairs when young and prolific, erect, lanate male catkins up to 8 cm. This clone spreads rapidly, the leaves turning bright golden-yellow in the autumn.

Salix nakamurana Koidz. var. neoreticulata (Nak.) Kim. S. neoreticulata Nak. 'Inu-Maruba-Yanagi'   Distinguished by the leaves, glossy above, very prominent reticulate secondary veins beneath and sericeously pubescent ovaries.

Salix nepalensis Hort.:   (see S. furcata Anderss. hylematica Schneid.)

Salix 'Nitida':   (see S. arenaria L.)

Salix × notha Anderss. (S. myrsinites L. × S. phylicifolia L.)   A low, spreading, dwarf shrub; branchlets glabrous, glossy dark brown; leaves obovate, apex acute, margins uniformly serrulate, puberulous beneath at first, later glabrous bright green above and beneath. Catkins coetaneous, ovaries pedicellate, narrowly flask shaped, densely covered with iridescent hairs; styles elongate; stigmas linear and bifid; anthers red.

An ornamental shining little shrub inhabiting moist rocky situations in mountainous areas of Scotland and Scandinavia.

Salix × obtusifolia Willd. (S. aurita L. × S. lapponum L.)   A small, spreading shrub with puberulous branchlets, becoming dark lustrous brown. Leaves oblong or narrowly obovate, dark green above, densely grey-pubescent beneath, margins entire or subentire. Catkins coetaneous, erect and large; ovaries subsessile and densely pubescent; styles long; slender linear, entire or sometimes divided to the base.

An extremely hardy hybrid occurring on rock ledges in the mountains of Scotland, Scandinavia and Russia.

Salix ovalifolia Trautv. var. ovalifolia., (S. ovalifolia var. camdensis Schneid.)   A dwarf trailing shrub with long thin branches up to 45 cm (1.5 ft) long arising from a central stout caudex; branchlets trailing, long and slender, yellowish or brown-tinged, glabrous; the most distal buds are vegetative, the others reproductive; bud scales persist at the base of the shoots. Leaves obovate, elliptic or broadly elliptic, the largest being 1.5–3 cm long, 1–2 cm wide; apex acute, obtuse or rounded; base round, cordate or acute and unequal; margins entire, sometimes revolute, reddish and often hairy; young leaves sparsely long-hairy becoming glabrous; mature leaves glabrous and glossy with conspicuous reticulate venation above, sparsely hairy becoming glabrous, glaucous, sometimes purplish beneath; petioles 2–8 mm long; stipules minute glandular lobes; catkins coetaneous on leafy branchlets 1–2.5 cm long; male catkins up to 2 cm long, two stamens, with filaments free and glabrous (rarely slightly pubescent) and glaucous; capsules 5–6.5 mm long, glabrous and glaucous; styles 0.2–0.8 mm long, stigmas 0.3–0.6 mm long, four lobed. Pedicels glabrous or pubescent. Usually one nectary, adaxial, 0.5–1.5 mm long with two linear or several irregular lobes, reddish, up to three times as long as the pedicel; catkin scales oblong, apex rounded, 1–2 mm long, blackish, sparsely pubescent with straight or curly hairs.

Usually at sea level on beaches and sand spits or salt marshes. Arctic distribution in Yukon Territory, westwards along the coast to the Alaska Peninsula and the Aleutian Islands. It also occurs in the Chukosk Peninsula in Asia.

Salix ovalifolia Trautr. var. *arctolitoralis* (Hult.) Argus   A robust form of the species, differing from var. *ovalifolia* in its leaves, which are sometimes narrowly elliptic, the largest leaves 2.5–5 cm long, 1–2 cm wide (1.5–3.5 times as long as wide), petioles 4–16 mm long, female catkins large – 2–5 cm long, pistils large – 5–10 mm long.

Habitat the same as var. *ovalifolia*, occurring in the Arctic along the north-eastern Alaskan coast, in northern Yukon and the Mackenzie Delta.

Salix ovalifolia Trautr. var. *cyclophylla* (Rydb.) Ball.   Differs from var. *ovalifolia* in having subcircular leaves, apex round or retuse, the largest leaves one to one-and-a-half times as long as wide, very prominently reticulate above; branches stout and less trailing.

Occurs from sea level to 30 m (100 ft) up on shores of lakes, in moss and on beach ridges on the Bering Sea Islands, the Aleutian Islands and the Alaska Peninsula.

Salix ovalifolia Trautr. var. *glacialis* (Anderss.) Argus   Differs from S. var. *ovalifolia* in leaves, sometimes small, ovate; the largest mature leaf 8–14 mm long,

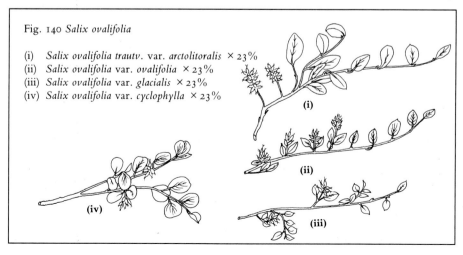

Fig. 140 *Salix ovalifolia*

(i)   *Salix ovalifolia trautv. var. arctolitoralis* × 23%
(ii) *Salix ovalifolia var. ovalifolia* × 23%
(iii) *Salix ovalifolia var. glacialis* × 23%
(iv) *Salix ovalifolia var. cyclophylla* × 23%

4.5–9 mm wide; mature leaves sparsely pubescent to glabrescent above and below; leaf margins remain hairy; petioles 1–3 mm long; male catkins 4–9 mm long and globose on short leafy branchlets 2–3 mm long. Female catkins 0.7–1.3 cm long, globose, pistils pubescent, capsules 4–5 mm long, non-glaucous, pubescent; pedicels 0.2–0.8 mm long.

Occurs on coastal sandy-gravel spits, limited to the Arctic coast of Alaska.

***Salix paludicola* Koidz. 'Miyama-Yachi-Yanagi'**   A dwarf procumbent shrub about 5 cm high with slender rooting branches; branchlets yellowish-brown, glabrous and glossy; leaves obovate, 1–3 cm long, 0.5–2 cm wide, glabrous and glossy above, glabrous and glaucous beneath, apex obtuse or rounded, base broadly cuneate, margins entire or undulate-serrulate; petioles glabrous, 2–5 mm long; male catkins dense-flowered, up to 3 cm long, 1 cm diameter; female catkins terminal on short leafy lateral branchlets, dense-flowered, up to 4 cm long in fruit, the rachis hairy, the catkin scales broadly ovate, yellowish-brown, apex rounded, densely hairy; ovary densely pubescent and shortly pedicellate; styles short; stigmas short, bifid; capsules lanceolate, 7–8 mm long, pubescent.

A rare Japanese alpine species occurring on Mount Daisetsu, Hokkaido.

***Salix pauciflora* Koidz. 'Ezo-Mame-Yanagi'**   A prostrate dwarf shrub with pubescent slender branchlets becoming reddish-brown; leaves obovate to elliptic 6–12 mm long, 3–10 mm wide, obtuse or rounded base, margins entire and sometimes pubescent, lamina coriaceous, glabrous and shining above, pale green and sparsely long-pubescent on midrib beneath; petioles pubescent, 1–4 mm long; male catkins globose, 5–30 flowered, terminal on short lateral branchlets, 3–10 mm long; catkin scales obovate, apex rounded, upper half reddish, margin and inner side hairy, glabrous outside, 1–2 mm long; two staminal filaments, free and glabrous; female catkins 5–30 flowered, 1–2 cm long in fruit; capsules 5 mm long, glabrous and pedicellate; style short; stigmas short and bifid.

A Japanese species inhabiting rocky slopes on Mount Daisetsu, Hokkaido.

***Salix petrophylla* (Rydb.):**   (see *S. arctica* Pall. var. *petraea* Anderss.)

***Salix phlebophylla* Anderss. (*S. anglorum* Cham. *S. paloneura* Rydb.)**   A dwarf shrub producing compact mats up to 2 m (6 ft) in diameter with some rooting

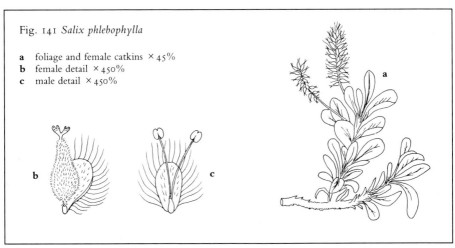

Fig. 141 *Salix phlebophylla*

a foliage and female catkins × 45%
b female detail × 450%
c male detail × 450%

stems partly underground, most aerial and covered with persistent, skeletonized leaves; branches glabrous, glossy and reddish-brown; branchlets glabrous, non-glaucous. Leaves narrowly to broadly obovate or broadly elliptic, 7–15 mm long, 3–12 mm wide, apex acute or retuse, base cuneate, margins entire, reddish and hairy; lamina glabrous and glossy above, sparsely pubescent with long straight hairs becoming glossy and non-glaucous beneath, venation prominent above and beneath. Petioles 1–5 mm long, brown and pubescent; stipules minute glandular lobes. Catkins coetaneous on leafy floriferous branchlets. Male catkins 1.5–2.5 cm long, two stamens, filaments 2.5–4 mm long, glabrous and free, one nectary adaxial, or two adaxial and abaxial 0.4–0.6 mm long. Female catkins 1.5–2.5 cm long, rachis pubescent, with more than 25 flowers. Pistils pubescent and nectaries shorter than the pedicels.

A very hardy alpine species living in Arctic tundra in northern Alaska, northern Yukon, the Alaska Peninsula, the mountains of central Alaska and extending to south-eastern Yukon.

The skeletonized persistent leaves, female catkins bearing over 25 flowers, pubescent pistils and nectaries shorter than the pedicels distinguish it from *S. rotundifolia*, which it otherwise closely resembles.

***Salix × pithoensis* Rouy. (*S. lapponum* L. × *S. repens* L.)**   A low, decumbent shrub with branchlets finely pubescent, becoming glabrous and reddish-brown; leaves lanceolate or ovate-elliptic, dark green above, whitish-grey and densely pubescent beneath, with prominent venation. Catkins precocious; ovaries sparsely pubescent, broadly flask shaped; the style distinct and short; stigmas linear and entire. Male catkins have not been recorded.

A dwarf hybrid found originally among rocks on the Scottish Mountains. It also occurs at high altitudes in Scandinavia.

***Salix × pseudospuria* Rouy. (*S. arbuscula* L. × *S. lapponum* L.)**   An erect or spreading dwarf shrub with sparsely pubescent branches becoming glabrous, glossy, dark brown. Leaves oblong or oblong-ovate, apex acute, lamina sparsely pubescent or dark green and glossy above, glaucous or grey and persistently pubescent beneath wth obscure venation. Catkins coetaneous or sometimes precocious; ovaries densely tomentose and shortly flask shaped; the style distinct and short; stigmas oblong, entire or divided to the base into linear lobes.

S. × pseudospuria occurs on rock ledges on mountains in Scotland, Scandinavia and Russia.

***Salix × punctata* Wahlenb. (*S. myrsinites* L. × *S. myrsinifolia* Salisb.)**   A low, spreading dwarf shrub with finely pubescent branchlets, later becoming glabrous, glossy or dull, dark brown. Leaves pubescent at first, becoming dark green and glabrous above, glabrous or subglabrous paler green beneath, margins conspicuously and uniformly serrate, venation prominent; stipules conspicuous. Catkins coetaneous, erect, thick and cylindrical; ovaries narrowly flask-shaped, variably pubescent with distinctly iridescent hairs; pedicels short; styles long; stigmas long and divided to the base into four linear lobes. The anthers are dark red.

Recorded from rocky alpine slopes in Scotland and Scandinavia.

***Salix repens* L. 'Creeping Willow'**   A very polymorphic plant, represented in the British Isles by a remarkably wide range of variants from slender, prostrate shrubs to robust, erect or ascending, sericeous-leaved forms, frequently comprising distinct local populations. C. E. Moss divides *S. repens* into three varieties:

1 *S. repens* L. var. *argentea* (Sm.) Wimm. et Grab.: (see *S. arenaria* L. described in detail earlier in this chapter)

2 *S. repens* L. var. *fusca* Wimm. et Grab.: (see Chapter 5: the erect ascending form)

3 *S. repens* L. var. *ericetorum* Wimm. et Grab. (could be more appropriately named *S. repens* L. var. *repens*)

A prostrate, decumbent small shrub; branchlets slender, reddish or yellowish-brown, glabrous, pubescent or densely sericeous; leaves very variable in shape, 1–3.5 cm long, 0.5–2.5 cm wide, lanceolate, oblong, ovate-oblong or elliptic, margins usually distinctly recurved, entire or glandular-serrulate, apex acute, obtuse or shortly mucronate and sericeous on both sides, or glabrous and bright green above and sericeously pubescent beneath; nervation indistinct; petioles short, less than 4 mm long; stipules sometimes persistent, prominent, narrowly lanceolate, acute 2–3 mm long, 1–1.5 mm wide, entire or serrulate. Catkins usually precocious on bare stems in April and May, erect or suberect, sessile or subsessile, ovoid, obovoid or shortly cylindrical, 1–3 cm long, 0.5–1 cm diameter; male catkins usually larger than the females; leaf bracts small and sericeous; catkin scales obovate-lingulate, approximately 2 mm long, reddish-brown at the apex or pale yellowish, sparsely or densely sericeously hairy. Male catkins two stamens, filaments 5 mm or more long; free and glabrous or sometimes with basal hairs; anthers yellow; nectary oblong, 0.6 mm long, apex truncate; female catkins, ovaries subsessile or shortly pedicellate, glabrous, pubescent or densely sericeous, 2–2.5 mm long, 1 mm diameter; pedicel pubescent, about 0.5 mm long; style 0.4 mm long, distinct and glabrous; two stigmas, bifid or entire. Capsules up to 8 mm long.

S. repens occurs throughout the British Isles on heaths and moorland wherever the soil is acid. It has a wide distribution throughout Europe, gradually intergrading with *S. rosmarinifolia* L. north of the Mediterranean.

A selection of the numerous variants of *S. repens*, showing differing leaf shapes and pubescence, can be very effective when planted between boulders in a large rock garden. The catkins are prolific and the golden-yellow anthers of the male plants are very colourful in the early spring.

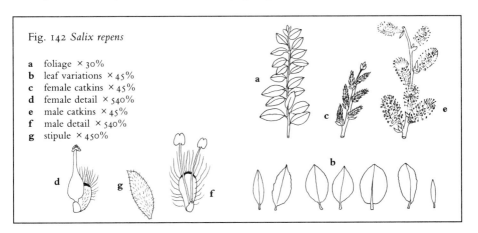

Fig. 142 *Salix repens*

a foliage × 30%
b leaf variations × 45%
c female catkins × 45%
d female detail × 540%
e male catkins × 45%
f male detail × 540%
g stipule × 450%

Some examples of variants from populations in different regions are:

S. repens 'Boyd's Pendulous'
A male clone with long trailing slender branches and branchlets with broadly ovate-oblong leaves, sericeous beneath; most effective when planted above boulders in the rock garden.

S. repens 'Exmoor'
A male clone. Leaves narrowly oblong, dark green, glabrous and glossy above, finely sericeous beneath, margins flat, apex acute or shortly mucronate.

S. repens 'Iona'
An extremely beautiful small male clone, very compact and flattened, forming a circle of gold when in flower. Leaves ovate-oblong, dark green, glabrous above, sericeous beneath, margins recurved, apex obtuse, some shortly mucronate. A very good dwarf for the small rock garden.

S. repens 'Lundy'
A female clone. Leaves broadly ovate-oblong, glabrous bright green above, thinly sericeous beneath, margins slightly recurved, apex obtuse.

S. repens 'Voorthuizen'
A small, attractive female Dutch clone with a flattened neat habit; leaves ovate-oblong or elliptic, dark green and minutely pubescent above, silver-sericeous beneath, apex obtuse, base rounded, margins slightly retuse.

Salix repens L. var. *subopposita* (Miq.) Seem.; (*S. suopposita* Miq.; *S. sibirica* var. *suboppposita* (Miq.) C. K. Schn.) 'No-Yanagi', 'Hime-Yanagi' A small, compact, hebe-like, low shrub, with opposite or subopposite leaves. Branchlets slender, erect, dark brown and densely grey-pubescent at first, becoming glabrous later; leaves broadly lanceolate, broadly oblong-lanceolate or narrowly oblong, 2–5 cm long, 5–15 mm wide, acute at both ends, margins entire, lamina glabrous or subglabrous above, glaucous and sparsely pubescent beneath, densely pubescent when young; petioles 1–5 mm long; male catkins

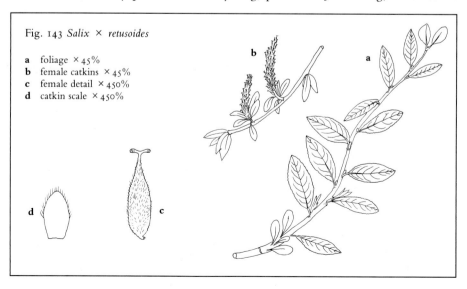

Fig. 143 *Salix* × *retusoides*

a foliage × 45%
b female catkins × 45%
c female detail × 450%
d catkin scale × 450%

precocious, up to 3 cm long and 1 cm diameter, numerous crowding the ends of the branchlets, densely flowered; female catkins shortly cylindrical, short-pedunculate, 1–2 cm long, 8–10 mm diameter in fruit, densely flowered; capsules densely grey pubescent, up to 4 mm long; style very short and indistinct; stigma short, bifid; catkin scales oblong, sericeously pubescent, apex rounded.

A Japanese native from Honshu and Kyushu. It also occurs in South Korea.

An ornamental small shrub with a very neat, densely-leaved and rounded habit, closely appressed to the ground. The male catkins with bright-golden anthers are very prolific and spectacularly colourful on bare stems in March and April.

An excellent shrub for the rock garden.

Salix reptans Rupr. 'Arctic Creeping Willow' A dwarf shrub with reddish-brown procumbent branchlets, pubescent at first becoming glabrous later; leaves ovate to lanceolate, entire, 1.5–3.5 cm long, apex acute or rounded, base broadly cuneate or cordate, lamina persistently dense long hairs on both surfaces, dull green and rugose above, glaucous and reticulate beneath; catkins ovate or cylindrical, densely flowered, 2–4 cm long on leafy branchlets; catkin scales ovate, black in the apical half and long-hairy; capsules sessile, densely pubescent; styles very short; stigmas brown with filiform lobes.

A native of north Russia and Arctic Asia.

Salix retusa L. A low prostrate shrub rising only a few centimetres above ground level; branches long, stout, light brown and glabrous, creeping and taking root; branchlets short, glabrous glossy and green or tinged reddish-brown with short internodes; leaves crowded, obovate or spathulate, 0.5–2.5 cm long, 4–6 mm wide, apex blunt, rounded or retuse, base rounded or cuneate, margins entire, subentire or occasionally minutely serrulate; lamina glabrous on both sides, glossy dark green above, paler green beneath; three to six pairs of primary lateral veins; petioles up to 4 mm long; catkins prolific, erect, pedunculate, shortly cylindrical, about 15 mm long, terminating short leafy shoots in May and June; male catkins – two stamens with filaments glabrous and free, anthers bright golden-yellow; female catkins – ovaries glabrous, shortly pedicellate, styles and stigmas short. Catkin scales obovate, apex rounded or obtuse, yellow or pale brown, glabrous except for a few long marginal hairs.

A native of European mountains, occurring in the Alps, Pyrenees and the Apennines.

A rigid, densely leaved, very effective ground cover eventually spreading over a wide area. The glossy leaves and attractive male catkins combine to form an ornamental alpine shrub.

Two dwarf species superficially resembling *S. retusa* are *S. ovata* and *S. cashmiriana*. They do not form the densely spreading ground cover typical of *S. retusa*. *S. ovata* is a slow-growing shrublet rarely exceeding 15 cm (6 in.) high with short, stiff, glabrous, light brown branches, and small, shining, bright green, ovate leaves. *S. cashmiriana* is a slow-growing, tightly ground-hugging species with long, stiff, glabrous, non-rooting branches, and small, glabrous, glossy, dark green, ovate or obovate leaves. *S. ovata* and *S. cashmiriana* are both ideally suited to the rock garden.

Salix × retusoides Kern. (S. alpina Scop. × S. retusa L.) A totally prostrate dwarf shrub spreading from a single central caudex; branches short, stout, yellowish-brown, glabrous, closely appressed to the surface of the soil without rooting; branchlets long, slender, very flexible and loosely trailing, glabrous and greyish or yellowish-green; leaves evenly spaced along the branchlets with longer internodes than *S. retusa*, obovate, 2.5–4 cm long, 1–2 cm wide, apex obtuse, acute, blunt or occasionally shortly mucronate, base cuneate, margins glandular serrate; lamina glabrous glossy dark green with impressed venation above, glabrous pale green with a prominent midrib and six to eight pairs of primary lateral veins beneath; petioles pale brown or pink, up to 7 mm long; catkins sparse on short lateral branchlets, cylindrical, 2–2.5 cm long, 5–6 mm diameter in April, ovaries 3–4 mm long, narrow and sericeously pubescent; styles very short, stigmas dark brown, distinct and bifid; scales oblong, apex acute, the apical half pale brown, base yellowish, short marginal hairs.

A native of the European Alps. A distinctive glossy-leaved ornamental dwarf alpine hybrid with long slender branchlets loosely radiating from the centre.

Salix rotundifolia Trautv. ssp. rotundifolia   A dwarf shrub 2–5 cm high with many slender branches, mainly underground, arising from a tap-rooted caudex. Branchlets yellowish-brown, sometimes glaucous, bearing two or three leaves; leaves circular, elliptic or narrow-elliptic, 5–15 mm long, 5–10 mm wide, one or two times as long as wide; apex rounded or retuse, base rounded or narrowly cuneate in narrow leaves; margins entire, revolute, reddish and sometimes hairy; lamina glabrous and glossy with primary veins prominent above; glabrous, glossy, green and not glaucous beneath, with three or four secondary veins raised prominently beneath; some leaves often persist for several years but do not become skeletonized; petioles 1.5–2.5 mm long, glabrous, brown; stipules tiny glandular, reddish lobes. Catkins coetaneous or serotinous, borne at the ends of the preceding year's shoots on floriferous, two-leaved, branchlets. Male catkins up to 1 cm long with 7–15 flowers; two stamens with filaments 2–5 mm long, glabrous and free; nectaries long and narrow. Female catkins 1–2 cm long, with 4–12 flowers, rachis pubescent; pistils 1.5–2.5 mm long, glabrous or sparsely pubescent, reddish-brown; capsules 4–8 mm long; styles 0.5–1 mm long, entire or partially bifid; four stigmas, linear lobes 0.5 mm long; pedicels 0.5–10 mm long; a single adaxial nectary 1–1.5 mm long, up to three times as long as the pedicel; catkin scales broad, obovate, apex rounded 1.5–2.8 mm long, reddish-brown, glabrous or sparsely pubescent with long marginal hairs.

A native of Arctic tundra in alpine Alaska and the Yukon to the Mackenzie Mountains and the North West Territories.

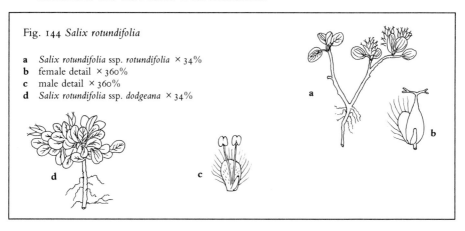

Fig. 144 *Salix rotundifolia*

a   *Salix rotundifolia* ssp. *rotundifolia* × 34%
b   female detail × 360%
c   male detail × 360%
d   *Salix rotundifolia* ssp. *dodgeana* × 34%

Salix rotundifolia Trautr. ssp. *dodgeana* (Rydb.) Argus; *S. dodgeana* Rydb. A low dwarf shrub differing from ssp. *rotundifolia* in the leaves, which are smaller and narrower, 4–6 mm long, 1.5–3.5 mm wide, up to two-and-a-half times as long as wide, apex acute, venation on the upper surface of the leaves less prominent, petioles shorter 0.8–1.6 mm long. The female catkins with only two to four flowers (occasionally up to nine).

Occurring in alpine Arctic tundra with a scattered distribution in North America; north-west Wyoming and adjacent Montana; Kluane Lake region of Yukon Territory; the Mackenzie Mountains, North West Territories and locally in Alaska.

Salix × semireticulata White (*S. herbacea* L. × *S. myrsinifolia* Salisb.) A creeping dwarf willow with sparsely hairy branchlets, later becoming glabrous; leaves broadly ovate, apex acute, base cordate or rounded, margins subentire and slightly revolute; lamina sparsely hairy on both sides with prominent venation; catkins coetaneous; ovaries narrow and densely pubescent; style distinct; stigmas narrow and divided into linear lobes. Catkin scales narrowly obovate, densely long-hairy.

Occurs locally on some mountain rock ledges in the Scottish Highlands. There is some doubt as to the parentage of this hybrid, believed by some to be *S. reticulata* × *S. herbacea*, or *S. lapponum* × *S. herbacea*.

Salix setchelliana Ball. (*S. aliena* Flod.) A prostrate or semi-prostrate shrub up to 30 cm (1 ft) high; branches greyish-brown or reddish, pubescent with flaking coriaceous bark; branchlets red-tinged, densely white-pubescent becoming grey-pubescent or glaucous; leaves coriaceous, narrowly obovate, 2.5–6 cm long, 1–2 cm wide, margins entire to glandular serrulate or glandular crenate; lamina yellowish-green with impressed venation above, glabrous pale green or glaucous beneath; petioles very short, up to 3 mm long, glabrous and merging into the branchlet below; stipules generally absent; catkins coetaneous on leafy branchlets; male catkins, two stamens – with filaments free and glabrous or with basal hairs; anthers slender, two nectaries, adaxial and abaxial; catkin scales 2–2.5 mm long, golden-tinted and glabrous; female catkins 1.5–2.5 cm long with 4–20 flowers; pistils up to 5 mm long, brick-red, glabrous; capsules 3.5–10 mm long, brown or brick-red; styles distinct and bifid to the base; stigmas 0.4–0.5 mm long; pedicels

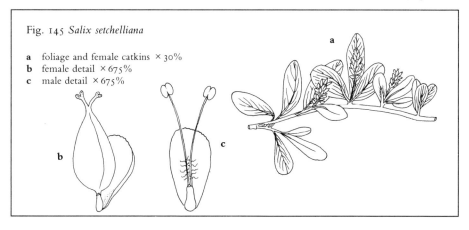

Fig. 145 *Salix setchelliana*

a   foliage and female catkins × 30%
b   female detail × 675%
c   male detail × 675%

glabrous; one adaxial nectary 1 mm long, approximately equal to the pedicel; catkin scales obovate, apex rounded, 2–3 mm long, golden-brown and glabrous.

A pioneer North American dwarf species growing on unstable glacial moraines and on the sandy margins of glacial rivers in mountainous regions of Alaska and the Yukon.

Salix × ***simulatrix*** **White (*S. arbuscula* L.** × **S. *herbacea* L.)** A dwarf, spreading shrub rising a few centimetres above ground level, with thick brown glabrous branches; branchlets sparsely pubescent at first, becoming glabrous, dark, shining reddish-brown; the leaves small, broadly ovate or suborbicular, finely pubescent becoming glabrous dark glossy green above, paler green or slightly glaucous beneath, with prominent venation and uniformly serrate margins; catkins coetaneous; the ovaries shortly flask shaped, densely pubescent, sessile or shortly-pedicellate; the styles distinct; the stigmas oblong and divided into four linear lobes; only female catkins have been recorded.

A small, dense dwarf hybrid occurring at high altitudes in the mountains of Scotland, Scandinavia and northern Russia.

A useful and ornamental, dense, slowly spreading ground cover well adapted to an exposed situation in the rock garden.

Salix × ***sobrina*** **White (*S. herbacea* L.** × **S. *lapponum* L.)** A dwarf, trailing, prostrate shrub with sparsely pubescent branchlets becoming glabrous, glossy dark brown; leaves ovate or obovate, dark green and sparsely and persistently greyish pubescent on both sides with prominent venation; catkins erect, coetaneous and cylindrical; the ovaries densely pubescent; the styles distinct; the stigmas narrow and divided into two linear lobes; two stamens – glabrous and free, anthers dark red or yellow; catkin scales obovate, pale brown or red-tinged, sparsely hairy.

A dwarf hybrid occurring on damp rock ledges on mountain sides in Scotland, Scandinavia and Russia.

Salix sphenophylla **Skv. *S. sphenophylla* ssp. *pseudotorulosa* Skv.** A dwarf shrub with brown, glaucous branches trailing and rooting; branchlets ascending, glabrous, greenish-brown, with a persistent bud scale at the base; leaves narrowly

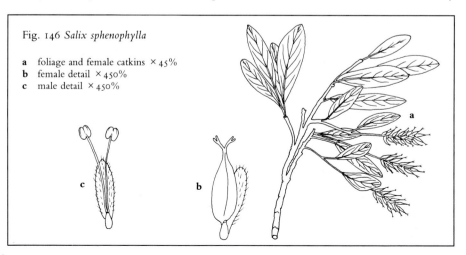

Fig. 146 *Salix sphenophylla*

a   foliage and female catkins × 45%
b   female detail × 450%
c   male detail × 450%

or broadly elliptic, 2–5 cm long, 1–2 cm wide; apex acute, obtuse or rounded; base cuneate to acute; leaf margins entire, sometimes ciliate; lamina pale green, glabrous and dull above, sparsely pubescent or glabrous and glaucous with prominent primary veins beneath; petioles 5–15 mm long; stipules very small or up to 5 mm long. Catkins coetaneous, borne on leafy branchlets; male catkins 2.5–3 cm long, two stamens with filaments 4.5 mm long, glabrous and free; female catkins 2–6 cm long; pistils 4 mm long, glabrous or sparsely pubescent and red-tinged; capsules 5–6 mm long; styles 0.6–1.8 mm long, entire or partly bifid; the stigmas 0.5 mm long, divided into four linear lobes; pedicels 0.5–1.5 mm long, glabrous or pubescent; one adaxial nectary 0.8–1.6 mm long, equal to or up to twice as long as the pedicel; catkin scales narrowly elliptic, 1.5–2 mm long, sparsely hairy and dark brown.

An Arctic alpine species occurring in Alaska, the Yukon and in Siberia. It closely resembles *S. arctica*, from which it can be distinguished only by its glabrous or subglabrous pistils and by its dull leaves.

Salix stolonifera Cov.   A dwarf prostrate shrub spreading from a thick caudex; branches short, reddish-brown, glabrous and glossy, sometimes glaucous, trailing above ground level, or developing underground rhizomes or stolons; branchlets glossy brown; leaves obovate, elliptic or orbicular, 1.5–4 cm long, 1–3.8 cm wide, apex round, obtuse or acute, sometimes unequal, margins entire or irregularly glandular serrate on the lower half; lamina glabrous or pubescent towards the margins, glossy with prominent venation above, sparsely pubescent to glabrous and glaucous beneath; petioles 5–20 mm long, red-tinged; stipules represented by small glandular lobes up to 1 mm long, occasionally narrowly elliptic. Catkins coetaneous arising from leafy, floriferous branchlets; male catkins 1–2 cm long, two stamens, up to 5 mm long, filaments glabrous and free; female catkins 1.5–4 cm long in fruit; pistils 4–6 mm long, yellowish, glabrous, sometimes glaucous; styles 1–1.6 mm long; stigmas two- or four-lobed, 0.2–0.6 mm long; pedicels 0.2–0.8 mm long, glabrous; one nectary adaxial 0.5–1.2 mm long, one-and-a-half to three times as long as the pedicel; catkin scales oblong, 2 mm long, brown, apex rounded, sparsely pubescent with long straight adaxial hairs twice as long as the scale.

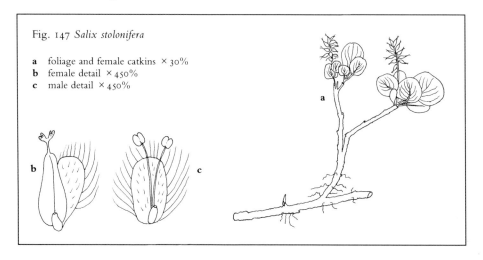

Fig. 147 *Salix stolonifera*

a   foliage and female catkins × 30%
b   female detail × 450%
c   male detail × 450%

S. *stolonifera* is closely related to S. *ovalifolia*, growing with it in coastal Alaska and Yukon. Hybridization occurs between S. *stolonifera*, S. *arctica* and S. *barclayii* when these species occur together on unstable glacial moraine.

S. *stolonifera* occurs in Arctic tundra, moraine and in the sandy margins of lakes, descending to sea-level along southern coastal Alaska, south-eastern Alaska and adjacent British Columbia.

Salix × straehleri Seem. (S. repens L. × S. cinerea L. × S. aurita L.)   A small, partly erect, low shrub; branchlets densely grey-pubescent becoming glabrous later; leaves oblong-lanceolate, dark green, sparsely pubescent above, more densely grey-pubescent beneath with prominent venation. Catkins coetaneous, cylindrical and subsessile; style short or indistinct; stigmas erect, entire or bifid; catkin scales rounded, blackish and densely hairy.

It is probable that this hybrid occurs more widely than is realized, considering the frequent occurrence of the parents together in the wild. It has been recorded from Sweden and Germany, with a scattered distribution in other European regions.

Salix subopposita Miq.   (see S. *repens* var. *subopposita*)

Salix uva-ursi Pursh. 'Bearberry Willow'   A prostrate, mat-forming shrub with branches up to 30 cm (1 ft) long, and short, slender, ascending glabrous and dark-brown branchlets; leaves elliptic, 5–20 mm long, 2–10 mm wide, apex acute to obtuse, base acute, leaf margins entire, rarely subentire or glandular-crenulate, glabrous and glossy above, brown-tinged and pubescent when young, whitish or glaucous beneath with prominent reticulate venation; petioles 2–4 mm long; catkins on leafy branchlets, coetaneous or serotinous; male catkins 1–3 cm long, female catkins 2–4 cm long in fruit; capsules ovoid, glabrous and shortly pedicellate; styles short; stigmas bifid; usually one stamen, rarely two; catkin scales obovate, sericeously pubescent, brown with blackish apex.

A North American dwarf alpine species occurring among calcareous rocks at high altitudes in Greenland and Baffin Island, south to the mountains of north-west Newfoundland, Gaspé Peninsula, Quebec, northern New Hampshire, north Vermont and north New York State.

An ornamental, very distinctive and hardy dwarf species requiring a well-drained rocky situation.

Salix vestita Pursh.   A decumbent or ascending shrub 20 cm (8 in.), rarely to 1 m (3 ft) high; branches stout, rough and gnarled with bud scars; branchlets stout,

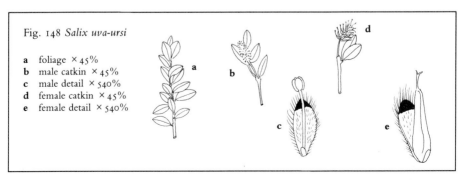

Fig. 148 *Salix uva-ursi*

a   foliage × 45%
b   male catkin × 45%
c   male detail × 540%
d   female catkin × 45%
e   female detail × 540%

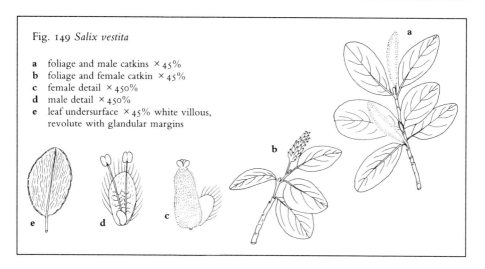

Fig. 149 *Salix vestita*

a foliage and male catkins × 45%
b foliage and female catkin × 45%
c female detail × 450%
d male detail × 450%
e leaf undersurface × 45% white villous,
       revolute with glandular margins

v c ely spreading, pale brown, pubescent; buds 5–10 mm long, pubescent; stipules absent; leaves broadly oblong, oval or suborbicular, 2–6 cm long, 1.5–5 cm wide, obtuse to retuse at both ends, margins crenate, slightly revolute and glandular; lamina thick, dark green, glabrous, rugose with deeply impressed venation above, glaucous and long-villous becoming glabrous, except on the veins, beneath; petioles stout, grooved above, pubescent, 2–10 mm long; catkins serotinous between June and August, 2–4 cm long, up to 1 cm diameter in fruit on peduncles 0.5–2 cm long; two stamens, filaments with basal hairs or glabrous and free; capsules ovoid, 4–5 mm long, sessile or subsessile, pubescent; styles indistinct, very short; stigmas short with cleft apex.

A dwarf mountain species occurring in north-eastern North America, from Newfoundland and Gaspé Peninsula, north through Labrador and Quebec, west to Keewatin, Alta, Montana and north-east in Oregon.

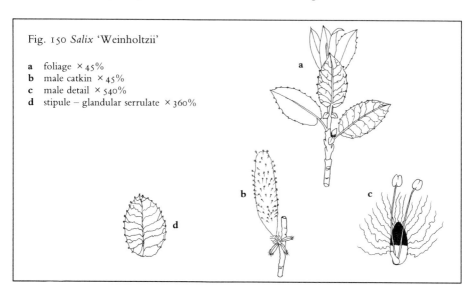

Fig. 150 *Salix* 'Weinholtzii'

a foliage × 45%
b male catkin × 45%
c male detail × 540%
d stipule – glandular serrulate × 360%

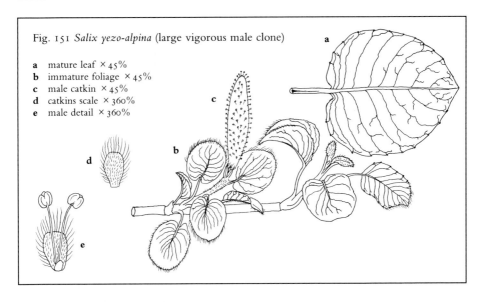

Fig. 151 *Salix yezo-alpina* (large vigorous male clone)

a   mature leaf × 45%
b   immature foliage × 45%
c   male catkin × 45%
d   catkins scale × 360%
e   male detail × 360%

A rugged dwarf species similar to *S. reticulata* L. slow-growing and suitable for planting in a rock garden or trough.

***Salix vestita* Pursh. var. *erecta* Anderss.**   A more erect form than the pure species, with narrower oblong to oblong-oval leaves and with the apical leaves broader. Occurs mainly in the western mountains of North America, rare in the east.

***Salix* 'Weinholtzii' Hort.**   A dwarf *S. hastata* male clone hybrid, rarely exceeding 60 cm (2 ft) high, typically with a single erect, thick, somewhat gnarled main stem. Branches short, stout, steeply ascending, glabrous, reddish-brown with numerous scars; branchlets short with very short internodes, glabrous, glossy, brownish-green; buds stout, reddish-brown, glabrous and glossy; young leaves translucent, pale green with long hairs beneath; mature leaves 3–4 cm long, 1.5–2.5 cm wide, broadly obovate, apex acute or shortly mucronate, base rounded or slightly cordate, margins glandular-serrate, lamina thick and coriaceous, glabrous dark green with impressed venation above, glaucous with a prominent midrib beneath, seven to ten pairs of lateral veins; petioles stout, glabrous 2–5 mm long, stipules 4–6 mm long persistent, suborbicular, glandular serrate, glabrous, glaucous beneath; catkins precocious in March or April with sometimes a second serotinous flowering in July; catkins 4–6 cm long, 1 cm diameter, erect, densely white-lanate borne on short peduncles 5–7 mm long with two or three basal leaf bracts; peduncles and rachis densely pubescent; two stamens, free and glabrous; anthers golden-yellow; catkin scales blackish, narrowly obovate, apex acute, densely covered with long curly hairs.

An ornamental erect male clone with attractive catkins.

***Salix yezoalpina* Koidz.:**   (see *S. nakamurana* var. *yezo-alpina*)

CHAPTER SEVEN

Tiny Willows for Sink Gardens

Permanent containers used for the smallest alpine shrubs can be diverse, varying from pots and ornate urns to troughs made of stone, concrete, terracotta, plastic or wood. All containers must be provided with large basal drainage holes. Disused porcelain sinks can be very effectively disguised with an external covering of a combination of peat, sand and cement, bonded by an adhesive.

Troughs or sinks should be not less than 15 cm (6 in.) deep inside or, better still, 20–25 cm (8–10 in.) deep. If there is only one drainage hole at the end, the trough should be slightly tilted towards it. They are best raised well above ground level, supported by rocks or blocks to obtain maximum drainage and exposure to the weather. They should never be overhung by trees or shrubs. The cracks between the supporting rocks may be planted with various small species of sedum including two British natives, *Sedum anglicum* (the pink stonecrop) and *Sedum acre* (the yellow wallpepper). *Sedum album* (the white stonecrop) is another attractive species.

Place a shallow layer of broken crock or coarse gravel in the bottom of the container, before filling it with a specially prepared mixture. The essential requirement of the small mountain species is a well-drained, moisture-retentive, slightly acid medium. The ideal growing medium is composed of equal parts of coarse grit, leaf-mould and light loam with a dressing of bonemeal. All ingredients should be very thoroughly mixed. Leaf-mould is preferable if available, otherwise you can substitute peat. After planting is completed, add a covering of 1–2 cm ($\frac{2}{5}$–$\frac{4}{5}$ in.) of finely crushed stone-chippings or fine pebbles to prevent the rotting of stems and assist moisture retention.

The trough culture of the tiny alpine *Salix* species does ensure their survival. If grown in large rockeries they tend to become overshadowed by larger species and eventually disappear.

Raised trough gardens on patios or other areas devoid of soil can be very attractive garden features.

It is not generally appreciated that many other species of willow, apart from the smallest, can be successfully grown in shallow troughs, becoming miniaturized up to 30 cm (1 ft) high without resorting to the intricacies of bonsai, and yet retaining all the attractive qualities of foliage, stem colour and catkins on a much smaller scale. Good subjects for this natural scaling down are *S. glaucosericea*, *S. lapponum*, *S. barclayii*, *S.* × *boydii* and *S. repens* 'Iona'. These willows readily adapt and will survive for many years with minimal interference.

Alpine troughs should not be forgotten during periods of drought and require watering once a week.

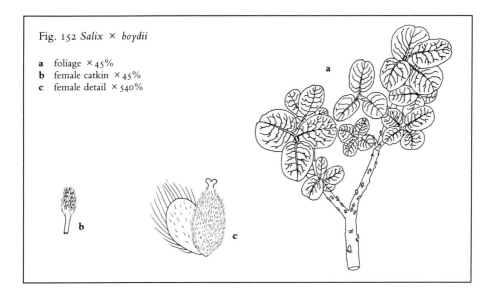

Fig. 152 *Salix × boydii*

a foliage × 45%
b female catkin × 45%
c female detail × 540%

The very small species are best grown in troughs to ensure their survival and to enable them to be displayed to the best advantage.

Salix × boydii E. F. Linton   Previously described in Chapter 6, this very slow-growing erect shrub, rarely exceeds 45 cm ($1\frac{1}{2}$ ft) high. Specimens up to 1 m (3 ft) high are rare and very old. With its thick, rigid, gnarled branches and rugose blue/grey leaves it is a sculpturally ornamental dwarf resembling a miniature tree. It is very effective when grown in a prominent position in the sink garden, surrounded by tiny rocks.

Salix cascadensis Cockerell, Muhl. (S. tenera Anderss.)   A slow growing mat-forming dwarf shrub on the surface of the ground with a slender, many-branched rhizomatous caudex arising from a central tap-root. Leaves thick, narrowly elliptic, 1–2 cm long, 3–6 mm wide, grey, hairy at first becoming glabrous with a few persistent marginal hairs, apex acute, margins entire, some leaves persisting for one or more years. Petioles short, 1–3 mm long; catkins smaller than in *S. arctica* Pall., coetaneous, shortly pedunculate, terminating short leafy lateral branchlets; male catkins, two stamens, with filaments connate below; female catkins up to 2.5 cm long in fruit; capsules 4–5 mm long, densely villous or occasionally glabrous; style distinct, longer than the bifid stigmas.
    A North American mat-forming dwarf shrub, cultivated forms often producing larger, broader grey leaves.

Salix × finnmarchica (S. myrtilloides L. × S. repens L.)   Previously described in Chapter 6; an extremely hardy ornamental dwarf shrub with a very conspicuous show of prolific golden male catkins along the leafless branchlets in early spring. It is best planted at the edge to allow the long slender branches to arch over the side of the sink garden.

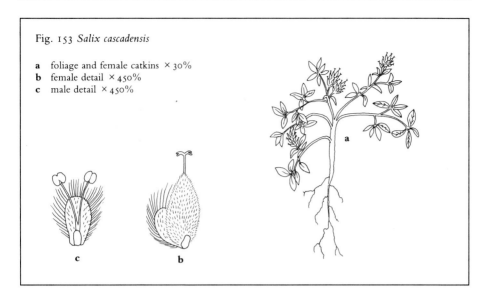

Fig. 153 *Salix cascadensis*

a   foliage and female catkins × 30%
b   female detail × 450%
c   male detail × 450%

Salix herbacea L. 'Dwarf Willow'   The smallest British willow, rarely exceeding 6 cm (2¼ in.) high, forming loose shallow mats, with many branching and rooting slender subterranean stems; the terminal aerial ascending branchlets sparsely hairy at first, becoming glabrous and glossy reddish or dark brown; buds red-tinged, broadly ovoid or globose, up to 3 mm long and 2 mm thick, sparsely hairy becoming glabrous; leaves suborbicular or broadly obovate, often broader than long, varying considerably in size, from 0.3–2 cm long and equally wide or wider, sparsely hairy above and below, soon becoming glabrous and glossy dark green with prominent reticulate venation, apex rounded or emarginate, rarely subacute, base broadly cuneate, rounded or cordate, margins crenulate-serrate or subentire; petiole short, up to 4 mm long; stipules minute or absent. Catkins coetaneous in June or July, or August at high altitudes, small, with a maximum of 12 flowers, subsessile or with hairy peduncles up to 1 cm long at the tip of small branchlets. Male catkins with two stamens, filaments glabrous and free, 2–3 mm long; anthers pale yellow or red-tinged; nectary cup-like and lobed, surrounding the base of the staminal filaments or comprising one or two lobed nectary scales; female catkins more conspicuous than the male, the ovaries narrow, glabrous, reddish, with a pedicel 2–3 mm long; style distinct; stigmas spreading and bifid; capsule dark red, up to 1 cm long; one or two nectaries, oblong, entire or variably lobed; catkin scales red-tinged, obovate, up to 2 mm long, apex obtuse with a sparse covering of hairs.

A mountain species, rarely found below 600 m (2,000 ft), with a wide circumpolar distribution in North America, Europe and Asia. It is also present in the mountains of central Europe and the Pyrenees. In Great Britain and Ireland it exists on moist rock ledges at high altitudes.

A very attractive tiny glossy-leafed species best displayed in the sink garden. (See Fig. 2.)

Salix herbacea L. × S. reticulata L.:   (see *S.* × *onychiophylla* Anderss).

Salix 'Lanata Repens' (S. lanata L. × S. repens L.)   See Chapter 6. A grey-leafed mound-forming dwarf shrub, neat and compact in habit. A good slow-growing subject for the sink garden.

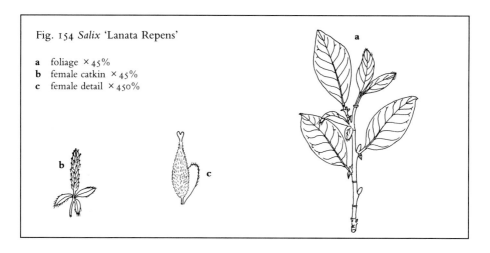

Fig. 154 *Salix* 'Lanata Repens'

a foliage × 45%
b female catkin × 45%
c female detail × 450%

***Salix lindleyana* Anderss.**   See Chapter 6. A very ornamental little shrub forming a very dense flat mat of tiny shining green leaves. A more suitable species for a sink garden than the more lax and spreading *S. hylemata* (*S. furcata*), with which it is often confused.

***Salix myrsinites* L. var. *jacquinii* (Willd.) Koch.**   A very miniature version of *S. myrsinites* L., a tiny shrublet approximatly 5 cm high and spreading to 23 cm with very small leaves, rich, shining green above and below. The catkins appearing with the leaves in late May and June are minute and ruby-red. An excellent non-invasive little shrub ideally adapted to sink gardens.

Salix nivalis* Hook. var. *nivalis   A tiny mat-forming shrub with slender rhizomatous stems at or just below ground level and foliage closely adpressed to the soil. Leaves small, 7–15 mm long, glabrous, thick-textured, dark green above, glaucous with prominent reticulate venation beneath, broadly elliptic to obovate, apex rounded or retuse, margins entire, sometimes with scattered marginal hairs. Catkins small, serotinous, borne at the tips of the main vegetative shoots of the season on slender peduncles; male catkins very small and slender with two stamens, filaments with long basal hairs; female catkins up to 1 cm long at maturity with up to 12 fruits; capsule tomentose, 3–5 mm long; style indistinct; stigmas bifid. Catkin scales pale yellowish, slightly puberulent within, glabrous on outer surface.

***Salix nivalis* Hook. var. *saximontana* (Rydb.) Schneid.**   A more robust form than *S. nivalis* var. *nivalis*. The leaves are larger, 15–30 mm long; female catkins up to 2 cm long at maturity, with up to 25 or more fruits.

   Both varities share a similar range in North America, although var. *saximontana* tends to have a more southerly distribution. Both occur on mountain slopes and rock ledges at high altitudes above the timberline in southern British Columbia and Alberta, extending to California, Nevada, Utah and New Mexico. Although not closely related to other dwarf species, it is similar to the more northerly *S. reticulata* L.

   S. nivalis is an attractive slow-growing little shrub, the leaves sometimes dying back prematurely during the summer. If left undisturbed, new leaves usually reappear during the following spring.

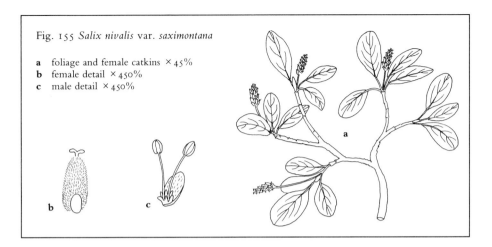

Fig. 155 *Salix nivalis* var. *saximontana*

a foliage and female catkins × 45%
b female detail × 450%
c male detail × 450%

Salix × onychiophylla Anderss. (S. herbacea L. × S. reticulata L.)   A small, entirely procumbent willow with dark-brown, glabrous, slender, tapering branches radiating from a woody central caudex surmounting a main tap root. Branches, unlike *S. herbacea* L., are not subterranean and do not take root. Branchlets glabrous, glossy, light green; young leaves glabrous, very glossy, tinged pale reddish-brown; mature leaves orbicular, reniform or broadly obovate 1–2.5 cm long, 1–3 cm wide, apex emarginate, rounded or broadly obtuse, base cordate, rounded or broadly cuneate, margins regularly crenate-serrate; lamina glabrous dark greyish-green, coriaceous and rugose with impressed reticulate venation above, the midrib and four to six pairs of primary veins prominent below; petioles 0.4–1 cm long, glabrous, channelled above; stipules absent; catkins coetaneous in June and July, female catkins 1–1.5 cm long, loose-flowered, comprised of six to ten flowers.

This hybrid has been recorded from Austria, Norway and Russia, occurring at high altitudes.

A very attractive slow-growing mat-forming little shrub, ideal for the sink garden.

Salix polaris Wahlenb.   A dwarf shrub with underground rooting stems; branches glaucous, reddish-brown; branchlets short, ascending, not trailing, glabrous purplish or brown; buds glabrous and glaucous, the bud scales often persisting at the base of the shoots. Leaves narrowly elliptic or obovate, the largest mature leaves 1–2.5 cm long, 0.8–1.5 cm wide and approximately one-and-a-half to two-and-a-half times as long as wide; apex round, retuse or obtuse, base cuneate or rounded and unequal; margins entire, flat, frequently red-tinged and occasionally hairy; lamina glabrous and glossy above, glabrous and non-glaucous below or rarely sparsely pubescent becoming glabrous, green and glossy later, with conspicuous raised primary veins. Petiole yellow or reddish, 3–10 mm long; stipules absent or represented by tiny glandular lobes. Catkins coetaneous on leafy branchlets; male catkins 1.5 cm long, two stamens, filaments 4–5 mm long, glabrous and sometimes slightly connate at the base; anthers 0.5 mm long. Female catkins 1.5–3.5 cm long; pistils 2.5 mm long, reddish, glossy, minutely and finely pubescent, capsules 4–7 mm long, pale reddish-brown and pubescent, styles 0.8–1.6 mm long, entire or bifid; stigmas dark reddish-brown up to 0.6 mm long

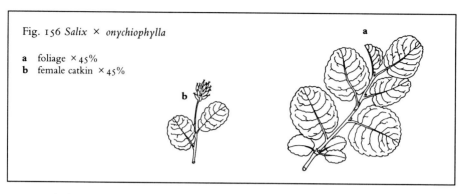

Fig. 156 *Salix × onychiophylla*

a foliage × 45%
b female catkin × 45%

with four distinct linear lobes; one adaxial nectary, two to five times as long as the stipe. Catkin scales very short, oblong to broadly obovate, brown, apex rounded, red-tipped, sparsely pubescent.

S. polaris is an Arctic alpine dwarf occurring with tundra vegetation on mountain scree slopes and areas recently occupied by melting snow. Its range extends from the Bering Sea, through central Alaska and the Yukon, eastwards to northern British Columbia and northern Eurasia. It is closely related to *S. arctica*, *S. stolonifera*, *S. rotundifolia*, *S. mummularia*, *S. ovalifolia* and *S. phlebophylla*. It can be distinguished by its pubescent pistils, long styles and the non-glaucous undersurface of the leaves which do not become skeletonized. Fig. 157 shows the typical form of *S. polaris*, contrasting with the cultivated specimen in colour plate 52.

Genuine specimens of *S. polaris* are rare in Great Britain but are included in a few collections. In addition to the closely related species several small montane forms of *S. retusa* have also been misidentified as *S. polaris*.

S. polaris is an ornamental little shrub, thriving in an exposed sink garden.

Salix repens 'Boyd's Pendulous' See also Chapter 6. A very effective weeping dwarf male clone, best placed near the edge with its branchlets trailing down the side of a raised sink garden.

Salix reticulata L. ssp. *reticulata* 'Net-Leaved Willow' A small, prostrate shrub rooting along its underground stems; branches light brown; branchlets pubescent becoming glabrous and green; leaves elliptic-circular to oblong, one-and-a-half times as long as wide, apex round, obtuse, sometimes retuse, base rounded or cordate; margins subentire, sharply recurved, minutely glandular to slightly crenate. Immature leaves densely villous above and below at first. The upper

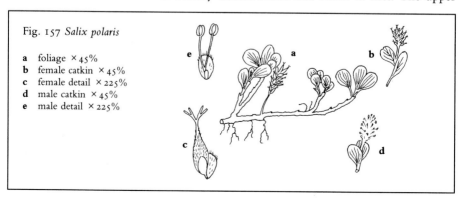

Fig. 157 *Salix polaris*

a foliage × 45%
b female catkin × 45%
c female detail × 225%
d male catkin × 45%
e male detail × 225%

surface of mature leaves dark glossy greyish-green and rugose with deeply impressed venation, pale greyish-green and sparsely pubescent beneath with markedly reticulate venation; petioles reddish and glabrous, long and slender, usually exceeding 1 cm; stipules tiny glandular lobes 0.2 mm long; catkins coetaneous or serotinous on leafy floriferous branchlets, in late June or July, narrowly cylindrical 2–3.5 cm long, 4–5 mm diameter, erect with a long glabrescent peduncle up to 5 cm long; male catkins, two stamens, filaments free, up to 3 mm long with basal hairs in the lower half, anthers suborbicular and purple before dehiscence; female catkins more robust than the male; ovaries broadly flask shaped, 2 mm long, densely white lanate; style short but distinct; stigmas spreading and bifid; male and female nectaries very variable, usually forming a cup around the base of the stamens or ovary; dehisced fruiting catkins often persist until June or July of the following year. Catkin scales suborbicular, about 1 mm long and almost as wide, brownish or purplish, densely pubescent.

It grows at high altitudes on moist, rocky ledges, with a circumpolar, boreal distribution across arctic and subarctic Europe, Asia and North America. In Europe it also occurs in the Pyrenees, Alps, Carpathians and Macedonian Mountains. In Britain it is relatively rare and generally restricted to altitudes above 600 m (2,000 ft) on some Scottish mountains.

A very distinctive little mountain willow, well suited to the sink garden. (See Fig. 1.)

Salix reticulata L. ssp. *glabellicarpa* Argus   Differs from ssp. *reticulata* in possessing glabrous, glaucous pistils, glabrous stipes and styles 0.2–0.4 mm long.

Occurs in alpine tundra on the slopes of Mount Gastineau; also on mountains of Queen Charlotte Islands, in British Columbia.

Salix reticulata L. var. *villosa* Argus   Densely long-villous on the undersurface of mature leaves, similar to *S. vestita*.

Occurs widely throughout Alaska and the Yukon.

Salix retusa L. 'Chamonii'   A tiny recumbent form of *S. retusa*, with leaves and catkins scaled down to approximately one-third of their usual size. This attractive miniature shrub occurs mainly among calcareous rock formations in the European Alps at altitudes of 3,000 m (10,000 ft) or more.

Salix retusa L. 'Pygmaea'   A misnamed small woody shrub 15–20 cm high, with a gnarled woody trunk surmounted by a many-branched compact crown up to 25 cm in diameter, presenting the appearance of a miniature tree. Branchlets dark brown, glabrous with very short internodes; leaves are unlike those of *S. retusa* L.; young leaves are bright green with a few scattered adpressed hairs above, pubescent beneath with long marginal hairs; mature leaves dark green 5–12 mm long, 2–5 mm wide, the largest leaves on new shoots are up to 2 cm long and 1 cm wide, narrowly ovate, apex acute, base rounded, margins entire with some persistent marginal hairs; lamina dark glabrous green above with impressed reticulate venation, glaucous and remaining minutely pubescent with prominent venation beneath; petioles 1–5 mm long, pink-tinged and channelled above; stipules absent; male catkins erect, globose with dark-red anthers.

A very ornamental willow adding character to a sink garden.

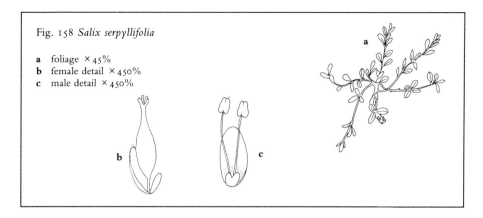

Fig. 158 *Salix serpyllifolia*

a foliage × 45%
b female detail × 450%
c male detail × 450%

***Salix serpyllifolia* Scop., (*S. retusa* var. *serpyllifolia* (Scop.) Ser.) 'Thyme-Leaved Willow'** A very small dwarf shrub closely related to *S. retusa*. Branches very slender and relatively short, forming a low, compact dense tuft. Leaves small, 4–8 mm long, 2–4 mm wide, spathulate or obovate, entire with a rounded apex, light glabrous green above and below, concentrated towards the tips of the shoots. In cultivation the shrub becomes more creeping with leaves 10–15 mm long. Catkins globose 5–8 mm long with few flowers (usually three to eight); style about one-quarter as long as the glabrous ovary; the pedicel is shorter than the ventral gland.

Present at high altitudes in the European Alps and the mountains of south-east Europe. Intergradation between *S. serpyllifolia* and *S. retusa* occurs locally in the southern Alps.

A tiny compact shrublet, rising a few centimetres above ground level. Liable to be overshadowed in a rockery. An ideal subject for a sink garden, providing attractive miniature ground cover.

***Salix tarraconensis* Pau.** A small shrub not generally exceeding 15 cm (6 in.) high in cultivation although taller specimens have been found in the wild. Branches glabrous, dark grey; branchlets short, slender, straight, dark reddish-brown, pubescent becoming glabrous in their second year. Leaves 0.5–3 cm long, orbicular, suborbicular or broadly elliptic, up to one-and-a-half times as long as wide, the apex obliquely deflected at the tip, the base rounded or cordate, margins irregularly undulate-crenate; lamina glabrous dark green above with a few hairs along the midrib, greyish or glaucescent and sparsely pubescent beneath; four to six pairs of lateral veins; petioles 0.5–5 mm; stipules small and confined to the most vigorous shoots; catkins 0.5–1 cm long, male catkins two stamens, connate for half their length, staminal filaments glabrous; ovaries grey-pubescent; pedicels about 2 mm long; styles 0.3–0.5 mm long; nectaries shorter than the catkin scales.

A hardy native of south-east Cataluna in Spain, living on calcareous rocks in the mountains at altitudes between 900 and 1,400 m (3,000–4,600 ft).

A beautiful little willow with unusual, almost circular leaves.

Attractive dwarf evergreen alpine shrubs can be used in the sink garden in addition to *Salix* species, maintaining added interest throughout the winter months. Good examples are: *Iberus sempervirens* 'Little Gem', forming a 10 cm mound of evergreen leaves with white flowers; *Gaultheria trichophylla* – a tiny

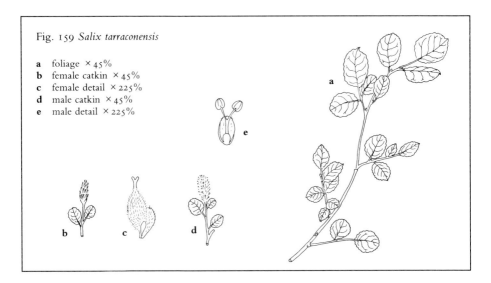

Fig. 159 *Salix tarraconensis*

a foliage × 45%
b female catkin × 45%
c female detail × 225%
d male catkin × 45%
e male detail × 225%

bushy little shrub with evergreen foliage and cream-coloured flowers in summer; *Hebe vernicosa*, with dark glossy evergreen leaves and white flower spikes tinged with violet.

Any small shrub which eventually exceeds its station can, of course, be removed and planted elsewhere.

I feel that I cannot conclude this book without emphasizing that for those who wish to indulge in an absorbing and therapeutic outdoor interest the establishment of a willow collection can prove to be most satisfying. The successful striking of cuttings is exciting and the speed of growth is often remarkable. There are so many *Salix* species, varieties and hybrids, large and small, and the international exchange possibilities are enormous. Considerable satisfaction is experienced in passing on to others willows to enhance a variety of landscapes, as well as in providing collectors with specimens that they do not already possess.

The full potential of the genus has yet to be realized. Undoubtedly it can play a major role in the rapid restoration of a 'green' environment.

GLOSSARY

Abaxial: facing away from a central axis.

Acumen: the tip of an organ.

Acuminate: tapering to a point.

Acute: shortly pointed.

Adaxial: facing towards a central axis.

Adpressed (or **appressed**): pressed closely against a surface.

Alternate: arising at different levels from a central axis.

Ament: catkin.

Androgynous: with mixed male and female flowers.

Anther: pollen bearing apex of stamen.

Aristate: abruptly acuminate and sharply pointed or bristle-tipped.

Ascending: curving upward.

Attenuate: tapered with a slender acumen.

Auricular: ear-shaped.

Axil: the angle formed above the junction of a leaf or bract with the stem.

Axillary: produced in the axil.

Bearded: tufted with long hairs.

Bifid: two-cleft.

Boreal: northern.

Bract: modified leaf at the base of a catkin or along the catkin-bearing shoot.

Branchlet: small branch of the current or preceding year.

Caducous: falling off prematurely.

Calcareous: containing limestone or calcium carbonate.

Cambial: derived from 'cambium', the growing layer in roots and stems.

Capsule: ripe pod, shedding seeds through valves.

Catkin: a compound spike inflorescence comprised of tiny, scaly-bracted flowers or fruits.

Catkin-scale: a small membranous bract subtending the flower in genus *Salix* and other catkin-bearing genera.

Caudate: with a long tail-like tip.

Ciliate: fringed with hairs.

Cinerea: ash grey.

Clonal: belonging to a clone.

Clone: a plant propagated vegetatively or asexually.

Coetaneous: catkins appear simultaneously with the leaves.

Compressed: flattened.

Connate: joined together.

Cordate: heart-shaped.

Coriaceous: leathery.

Crenate: scalloped, with blunt, rounded teeth.

Crenulate: minutely crenate.

Cultivar: a garden variety, or form found in the wild and maintained as a clone in cultivation.

Cuneate: wedge-shaped – narrowing towards the base (leaf).

Cuspidate: abruptly constricted at the apex with a short, narrow tip or cusp.

Deciduous: falling off, not persistent.

Decorticated: bark exfoliated.

Decumbent: lying along the ground, with an upturned apex.

Dehiscence: the bursting of a ripe capsule or anther.

Dentate: toothed.

Denticulate: with small teeth.
Depressed: flattened from above.
Diffuse: loosely or widely spreading.
Dioecious: with male and female flowers on separate plants.
Diploid: possessing two sets of chromosomes.
Divaricate: widely spreading.

Elliptic: widest at the middle, narrowing equally at both ends.
Elongate: lengthened.
Emarginate: indented at apex.
Entire: margin smooth, without teeth or lobes.
Erose: margin ragged.
Exfoliating: peeling off in strips.
Exstipulate: without stipules.

Falcate: sickle-shaped.
Fastigate: branches erect and close together.
Filament: stalk of stamen.
Floriferous: flower-bearing.
Foliaceous: resembling a leaf.
Free: not joined together.

Glabrescent: becoming glabrous.
Glabrous: hairless.
Glandular: bearing glands or secretory cells.
Glaucescent: becoming glaucous.
Glaucous: bluish/grey or whitish.

Hybrid: a plant arising from a cross between different species.

Imbricate: overlapping.
Impressed: sunken (leaf-veins).
Indigenous: native.
Indumentum: dense hairy covering.
Internode: the portion of stem between two nodes or joints.

Lamina: leaf-blade.
Lanate: woolly.
Lanceolate: lance-shaped, broadest below the middle and tapering to the apex.
Lax: loose.
Linear: long and narrow, with nearly parallel margins.
Lingulate: tongue-shaped.
Lustrous: shining.

Midrib: the central vein of a leaf.
Mucronate: terminating abruptly in a short point.

Nectary–scale: nectar-secreting gland or glands at the base of the stamens and pistils of *Salix*.
Nervation: system of primary nerves.
Node: the point of attachment of leaves on a stem.

Ob–: prefix meaning inversion.
Oblanceolate: inversely lanceolate.
Oblique: unequal-sided.
Oblong: of leaves, roughly rectangular, broadest at the middle with nearly parallel or slightly convex margins.
Obovate: inversely ovate, the broadest part above the middle.
Obtuse: blunt (as in apex of leaf).
Opposite: arising at the same level from opposite sides of an axis.
Orbicular: almost circular.
Oval: broadest at the middle.
Ovary: basal expanded section of the pistil, containing the ovules.
Ovate: egg-shaped in outline, broadest below the middle.
Ovoid: egg-shaped.
Ovule: immature seed.

Pectinate: like the teeth of a comb.
Pedicel: the stalk of an individual flower in an inflorescence.
Pedicellate: with a pedicel or flower-stalk.
Peduncle: stalk of an inflorescence.
Pedunculate: with a peduncle or inflorescence-stalk.
Pendulous: hanging or weeping.
Persistent: remaining attached.
Petiole: the leaf-stalk.
Pilose: hairy.
Pistil: female organ of a flower comprising stigma, style and ovary.
Polymorphic: represented by many forms or variants.
Polyploid: possessing more than two sets of chromosomes.
Precocious: catkins appear on bare stems before the leaves.
Procumbent: lying or creeping.
Prostrate: lying flat on the ground.

Pruinose: covered with a whitish bloom.

Puberulent: minutely pubescent.

Pubescent: downy, coated with short, soft hairs.

Pyramidal: broad-based, tapering to a point.

Rachis: an axis bearing flowers.

Recumbent: lying.

Recurved: curved backward or downward.

Reflexed: abruptly recurved.

Reniform: kidney-shaped.

Reticulate: netted (as in veins).

Retuse: apex slightly indented.

Revolute: rolled backwards (margins of leaves).

Rotund: nearly circular.

Rugose: wrinkled.

Scabrous: rough to the touch.

Sericeous: silky.

Serotinous: catkins appear after the leaves are formed.

Serrate: saw-toothed with forward-pointing teeth.

Serrulate: minutely serrate.

Sessile: without a stalk.

Setts: *Salix* (here) cuttings used in osier beds.

Sinuate: strongly waved (leaf margins).

Spathulate: broad at the apex, tapering narrowly at the base.

Stamen: male organ of a flower comprising filament and anther.

Stigma: summit of the pistil, often sticky, receiving the pollen.

Stipe: stalk.

Stipule: one of two appendages at the base of a petiole or leaf-stalk.

Stolon: a shoot at or below ground level, producing a new plant at its tip.

Striae: fine longitudinal ridges.

Striate: bearing striae.

Style: middle portion of pistil, between the ovary and stigma, of variable length.

Sub-: prefix meaning 'almost', e.g. subglabrous, subopposite, suborbicular etc.

Suckering: producing underground stems; also shoots from the stock of a grafted plant.

Tomentose: covered with dense, woolly hairs or pubescence.

Tomentum: a dense covering of matted-hairs.

Truncate: ending abruptly as if cut straight across.

Undulate: wavy.

Venation: the arrangement of the leaf veins.

Villous: with long, soft hairs.

Vitelline: coloured orange/yellow, like egg yolk.

BIBLIOGRAPHY

Anderson J. N. *A synopsis of North American Willows*, Cambridge, 1858.

Andersson N. J. *Monographia Salicum Pars 1.*, Stockholm, 1867.

Andersson N. J. *Salicaceae* in *De Candolle*, A. P. Prodromus Systematis Naturalis Regni Vegetabilis, vol. 16(2): pp. 190–331, Paris, Strasbourg, London, 1868.

Argus G. W. *The Genus Salix in Alaska and the Yukon*, pub. Botany, no. 2, Ottawa, 1973.

Argus G. W. 'The Genus Salix (Salicaceae) in the south eastern United States', American Society of Plant Taxonomists, Arnold Arboretum (Syst. Bot. Monogr. 9.), 1986.

Ball C. R. 'New or little known West American Willows', Univ. Calif., pub *Botany*, no. 17, pp. 399–434, 1934.

Blackburn B. *Trees and Shrubs in eastern North America. 'Salix'* pp. 257–262, 1952.

Camus A. and Camus, E.-G. *Classification des Saules d'Europe et monographie des Saules de France*, Paris, 1904–5.

Chmelar J. *Die Weiden Europas*, Wittenburg Lutherstadt, 1976.

Chmelar J. 'The Taxonomy of some European Willows', Int. Dendrol. soc. year book 1981, pp. 109–111, 1981 (pub. 1982).

Clarke D. 'Salix' in **Bean W. J.** *Trees and Shrubs hardy in the British Isles*, 8th edition, London, 1980.

Cronquist A. 'Salix' pp. 37–71 in **C. L. Hitchcock *et al.*,** 'Vascular plants of the Pacific North West', part 2, Univ. Wash., pub. *Biol.* 17, 1964.

Davy J. B. 'The distribution and origin of Salix in South Africa', *Journal Ecol.* no. 10, 1922.

Dorn R. E. 'A synopsis of American Salix', *Canadian Journal of Botany*, vol. 54, pp. 2769–89, 1976.

Floderus B. 'On the Salix flora of Kamtchatka', Kgl. Svenska Vetensk.-Akad. ark. *Bot.* 20A: pp. 1–68, 1926.

Floderus B. 'Salix' in **E. Hulton**, *Flora of the Aleutian Islands*, pp. 146–53, Stockholm, 1937.

Forbes J. *Salictum Woburnense*, London, 1829.

Gleeson H. A. *The New Britton and Brown Illustrated Flora of the N. E. United States*, vol 2, pp. 6–23, 1952.

Hao K,-sh. *Synopsis of Chinese Salix*, Berlin, 1936.

Hooker W. J. *Flora Boreali-Americana*, vol. 2, H. G. Bohn, London, 1838.

Hulten E. *Flora of Alaska and Yukon*, vol. 3, Lunds Univ. Arsskr. N. F., Avd 2, 39(1): pp. 415–567, 1943.

Hulten E. *Flora of Alaska and neighbouring territories*, Stanford, Calif., 1968.

Kimura A. 'Salix' in *Flora of Japan*, pp. 362–69, 1965.

Krussman G. *Manual of Cultivated Broad-leaved Trees and Shrubs,* vol. 3, 'Salix' pp. 273–300, London, 1986.

Linnaeus C. *Species plantarum,* 2nd edition, 1763, Stockholm, 1763.

Linton E. F. 'A monograph of the British Willows', *J. Bot. Lond.,* 51 (suppl.), 1913.

Meikle R. D. 'Salix' in **C. A. Stace** (ed.), *Hybridization and the Flora of the British Isles,* 1975.

Meikle R. D. *Willows and Poplars of Great Britain and Ireland,* B.S.B.I. Handbook no. 4, 1984.

Moss C. E. 'Salix', *Cambridge British Flora,* 2, pp. 13–68. Cambridge. FIG, 1914.

Polunin O. and **Stainton A.** 'Salix', *Flowers of the Himalayas,* pp. 380–3. Oxford, 1984.

Raup H. M. The Willows of Boreal Western America; in contrib. Gray Herb., Harvard Univ. 185: pp. 1–95, 1959.

Rechinger K. H. 'Salix', in **Hegi, G.** *Illustrierte Flora von Mittel – Europe,* 2nd edition, Munich, 1957.

Rechinger K. H. in **Tutin, T. G. et al.** *Flora Europea,* vol. 1, Cambridge, 1964.

Schneider C. 'A conspectus of Mexican, West Indian, Central and South American species and varieties of Salix', *Bot. Gaz.* 65. no. 1, 1918.

Schneider C. 'Notes on American Willows'; in *Bot. Gaz.* no. 66, pp. 117–42, 318–53, 1918; no. 67, pp. 27–64, 309–96, 1919; also in *Journal Arnold Arb.,* no. 1, pp. 1–32, 67–97, 147–71, 211–32, 1919; no. 2, pp. 1–25, 65–90, 185–204, 1920; no. 3, 61–125, 1921.

Seemen O. von 'Salicaceae', in **Ascherson, P.** and **Graebner, P.** *Synopsis der Mittel europaischen Flora,* no. 4, pp. 54–350, Leipzig, 1908–10.

Skvortsov A. K. *Willows of the U.S.S.R.,* Moscow, 1968.

Steadman K. 'Willows in their infinite variety', *Garden* no. 100, pp. 588–93, London, 1985.

Warren-Wren S. C. *Willows,* London, 1972.

White F. B. 'A revision of the British Willows', J. Linn. Soc., *Bot.,* no. 27: pp. 333–457, 1890.

Wimmer F. *Salices Europaeae,* Bratislava, 1986.

General Index

Figures in **bold** refer to line illustration figure numbers, those in *italics* to colour plates

Botanical Index

Figures in **bold** refer to line illustration figure numbers, those in *italics* to colour plates